A HISTORY OF
SOUTH AFRICA
SOCIAL & ECONOMIC

BY

C. W. DE KIEWIET

PROFESSOR OF HISTORY, CORNELL UNIVERSITY.
SOMETIME PROFESSOR OF HISTORY IN
THE STATE UNIVERSITY OF IOWA

OXFORD UNIVERSITY PRESS

Oxford University Press, Ely House, London W.1

GLASGOW NEW YORK TORONTO MELBOURNE WELLINGTON
CAPE TOWN SALISBURY IBADAN NAIROBI LUSAKA ADDIS ABABA
BOMBAY CALCUTTA MADRAS KARACHI LAHORE DACCA
KUALA LUMPUR HONG KONG

FIRST EDITION 1941
REPRINTED 1942, 1943, 1946, 1950,
1957, 1960, 1964, 1966

Reprinted photographically in Great Britain by
LOWE AND BRYDONE (PRINTERS) LTD., LONDON

PREFACE

THE writing of history is always a process of simplification. The temptation which any historian must learn to resist is the desire to write two volumes instead of one. The temptation is especially keen in a study which contains a large measure of the 'social stuff' at which Freeman scoffed in Green's *Short History of the British People*, for in social and economic history the infinitesimal events of the daily round of eating, working, and resting become significant happenings, and the total life of a community is seen to depend upon numberless men and women who lived obscure lives and lie in unremembered graves. This book has undertaken the task of setting down some of the essential facts in South African social and economic development.

The attentive reader will notice that I have devoted relatively little space to the Cape coloured people or to the Asiatic population. Dr. J. S. Marais's excellent study of the *Cape Coloured People* clearly establishes the important place of the Cape coloured people in the life of South Africa. The tendency which has become even more marked in recent years to extend special economic, social, and political privileges to this group calls to mind the deliberate policy of Spain to separate the *mestizo* from the full-blooded native Indian in the eighteenth century. The problem of South Africa's Indians is also an arresting one, for it is both local and Imperial. Yet, in spite of these differences, both coloured people and Asiatics continue to belong to the great mass of the non-European population from which the white population is socially divided, towards which it is economically competitive, and of which it stands politically in fear. Not a little of the language which I have used of European and native relations applies, therefore, to the rest of the non-European population as well.

The *leitmotiv* of all colonial history is growth. The essential unity of the history of the British dominions does not come from the mere fact of their association in the British Empire. It comes also from the similarity of their struggle to escape

from the isolation and the poverty and the helplessness of
their first tiny settlements. It comes from the same movement
from dependence to political maturity, from economic feeble-
ness to important positions in the economy of the world. Yet
there is a point at which similarity ends, and beyond which
distinctions and differences come into prominence. Canada's
common frontier with a powerful neighbour and Australia's
intimate concern with the politics of the Far East are but two
illustrations of the factors which create wide differences between the idiom of political life in Canada and Australia.
The distinctive place of South Africa amongst the dominions
of the Empire is established by the heterogeneous nature of
her population and by the problems of race and colour which
are the consequence.

This study is part of the history of the British Empire. By
its side will stand companion studies of the other dominions.
In a time of great crisis it will not be an unscholarly act to
point out that there is no end now, and there will be no end
in the future of interest in the British Empire. The Empire
is many things, even as it contains many races. Some things
may undergo change. Change has been the essence of the
Imperial process. But other things lie beyond the reach of
war. They are the imperishable and timeless things. In the
Empire's second war with Germany these timeless qualities
have already become evident, and a later generation of
Imperial historians will study them. The Empire is more
than a political system; it is more than an economic structure. It is a spiritual achievement, with the enduring qualities of spiritual achievements, whether in literature, art,
science, or in the relations of human beings on the face of
the earth.

It is becoming common for modern writers to use the
orthography established by students of native language. I
have not followed their example. To be linguistically accurate obviously has its virtues. But linguistic accuracy places
upon long-familiar names an unfamiliar garb which sometimes makes recognition difficult. For the purposes of the
ordinary reader names like Moselekatze or Moshete are
preferable to uMzilikazi or Mošwêtê. I have also not hesi-

tated to use a correct plural like Basuto side by side with an anglicized plural form like Zulus.

To write a book of this nature is to incur many obligations. My copies of the writings of Professor W. M. Macmillan, Professor E. A. Walker, and Professor S. Herbert Frankel are worn by much reading and consultation. My obligation is very great to scholars like Dr. H. M. Robertson, Dr. C. G. W. Schumann, Professor W. H. Hutt, Professor Grosskopf, and others. Professor E. A. Walker and Professor W. M. Macmillan kindly read the manuscript and made helpful suggestions. The keen eye of my student, Mr. Alfred Martin, caught several slips. My friend Mr. R. Windram helped me to overcome some of the handicaps of my absence from South Africa, and to benefit from the perspective of distance, by sending across the Atlantic Ocean a constant stream of cuttings, pamphlets, and his own shrewd comments. My secretary, Miss Mary Strong, was a tower of strength. To the cordial and generous attitude of Dean George Stoddard, of the University of Iowa Graduate School, this book owes much.

I wish to express my gratitude to the Social Science Research Council for a grant-in-aid of research of which this book is in part the result.

C. W. DE K.

IOWA CITY,
December, 1940.

CONTENTS

LIST OF MAPS

SELECT BIBLIOGRAPHY

Note: The following list of books is intended to serve as a guide for students and the general reader. It makes no pretence at completeness.

ARNDT, G. H. D., *Banking and Currency Development in South Africa 1652–1927*, Cape Town, 1928.

BROOKES, E. H., *The History of Native Policy in South Africa from 1830 to the Present Day*, Lovedale Press, 1924.

BUELL, R. L., *The Native Problem in Africa*, 2 vols., New York, 1928.

Cambridge History of the British Empire, vol. viii, *South Africa*, Cambridge, 1936.

Carnegie Commission, Report of: *The Poor White Problem in South Africa*, 5 vols., Stellenbosch, 1932.

DE KIEWIET, C. W., *The Imperial Factor in South Africa*, Cambridge, 1937.

DE KOCK, M. H., *Economic History of South Africa*, Cape Town, 1924.

EVANS, I. L., *Native Policy in Southern Africa*, Cambridge, 1934.

EVANS, M. S., *Black and White in South East Africa. A Study in Sociology*, second edition, London, 1916.

HOFMEYR, J. H., *South Africa*, London, 1931.

KNOWLES, L. C. A., *The Economic Development of the British Overseas Empire. The Union of South Africa*, vol. iii, London, 1932.

MACMILLAN, W. M., *The Cape Colour Question*, London, 1927.
—— *Bantu, Boer and Briton*, London, 1929.
—— *Complex South Africa*, London, 1930.
—— *Africa Emergent*, London, 1938.

MARAIS, J. S., *The Cape Coloured People*, London, 1939.

ROBERTSON, H. M., '150 Years of Economic Contact between Black and White', *South African Journal of Economics*, Dec. 1934, March 1935.

WALKER, E. A., *A History of South Africa*, reissue, London, 1934.
—— *The Great Trek*, London, 1934.

Official Publications

The following are some of the more useful publications:

Report of the Transvaal Indigency Commission, T.G. 13. 1908.
Final Report of the Low Grade Mines Commission, U.G. 34. 1920.
Report of the Drought Investigation Commission, U.G. 49. 1923.

Report of the Economic and Wage Commission, U.G. 14. 1926.
Report of the Native Economic Commission, U.G. 22. 1932.
Report of the Low Grade Ore Commission, U.G. 16. 1932.
Report of the Industrial Legislation Commission, U.G. 37. 1935.
Report of the Customs Tariff Commission, U.G. 5. 1936.

Both the *Round Table* and the *South African Journal of Economics* contain many excellent articles on South African economic history.

THE FOUNDATIONS OF A NEW SOCIETY

'The prodigious increase of the Netherlands in their domestic and foreign trade, riches and multitude of shipping, is the envy of the present, and may be the wonder of all future generations.' SIR JOSIAH CHILD.

THE southern end of Africa was first called the Cape of Storms. Then it was renamed the Cape of Good Hope. But its fame and importance grew till it was familiarly called the Cape, without any danger of confusion with the numberless other capes of the earth's surface. At the bottom of a great continent it was bound to become a memorable geographic point. Almost literally half-way between Europe and India, it was bound also to become a valuable strategic point. To the ships that rounded it on their way to the East or on their way back to Europe, it had the sentimental attraction of a half-way mark. The Portuguese discovered it; the Dutch realized its immense importance, and held it for a century and a half before the English acquired it as the most important single point on the way to their Indian Empire.

The Cape did not only occupy a commanding position on the route to India. It commanded the interior as well. It was the gateway through which settlers could best reach the healthy and temperate inland plateaux. The natural approach for European colonization was not from the east or the west, but from the south. There were better harbours than Table Bay on both the east and west coasts, but in the seventeenth century they all had defects which made them useless as bases for settlement and colonization. Though Saldanha Bay and Walfisch Bay on the west coast were excellent harbours, their hinterland lacked local water. The east coast, especially around the fine natural harbour of Delagoa Bay, was low-lying and malarial, afflicted by the tsetse-fly, dangerous to cattle and horses. Of all the locations on the coast from Cape Frio to the Zambesi River, the Cape was the best training-ground for South African colonization.

The fertile valleys immediately behind Table Mountain were like a nursery in which a handful of settlers could live and grow in numbers and in knowledge of their adopted land, before proceeding to conquer the vast hinterland. It was in that temperate region, free of fever and animal diseases, that men could raise the transport animals which were as essential to the opening up of Africa as ever they had been to the Spanish conquest of Mexico and Peru. The coastal natives were not numerous. Though sometimes troublesome and occasionally dangerous, they had not strength enough to resist European settlement.

It was the Dutch who first appreciated the importance of the Cape on the way to India. Ever since the great Viceroy D'Almeida had been killed on the beach of Table Bay by a band of Hottentots, the Portuguese had regarded the Cape with feelings of suspicion and superstition, preferring St. Helena as a port of call. To them it was the cape of Adamastor, the vengeful spirit of storms who in the *Lusiad* had appeared at dead of night to Vasco da Gama, predicting the woes that would befall those that sailed on to India. The Portuguese had paid comparatively little attention to the defence of the approaches to their East Indian Empire. It was chiefly on the east coast of Africa and in the Indian Ocean that they had organized the defence of their possessions. On the east coast, where there were gold and souls to be won, D'Almeida captured and fortified Mozambique, Sofala, and Mombasa. His successor Albuquerque, with an even more intense passion for empire, consolidated D'Almeida's achievements by conquering Goa on the Indian mainland, Ormuz, which controlled the Persian Gulf, and Malacca, which dominated the route to China and Japan. It was work well done. Less than twenty years after da Gama had first sighted India, the Arab domination of the Indian Ocean, unchallenged during hundreds of years, had been broken for ever. But in the seventeenth and eighteenth centuries the fate of empires was decided in the Atlantic. There, face to face across the North Sea, grew up two new commercial Powers, England and Holland, each committed to a struggle against His Most Catholic Majesty of Spain, whose ambition it was to win the Old World for the Church and keep the New World for Castile. Although England destroyed the Armada, it was the Dutch who first became the great sea-power. The herring-boats which had first brought them wealth, and the Beggars who had hurled the Spaniards bodily overboard at Bergen op Zoom, had become the first merchantmen and traders in Europe.

Had the famous foot-soldiers of Spain not followed Loyola and become the instruments of the Counter-Reformation in Europe, and had the treasures from Mexico and Peru not been squandered in Germany and the Netherlands, the annexation of Portugal by Spain in 1580 might have brought the crumbling Portuguese Empire under the protection of a mightier Power, and saved it from its rivals. Instead, Portugal's weaknesses became still greater because of her incorporation with Spain. To the corruption and mismanagement that was already sapping the strength of the Portuguese Empire was added the burden of an indifferent and greedy suzerain. Worst of all, Portugal inherited the enemies of Spain. The Dutch had already made themselves strong by capturing the lion's share of the profitable carrying trade from Lisbon to the rest of Europe. In 1595 the four ships under Cornelis Houtman that dared to sail round the Cape discovered that the Eastern Empire was as mortally weak as the metropolis itself.

Against the capital, the better ships, the greater energy of the Dutch, the Portuguese were helpless. The followers of Houtman brought to the East more than the daring of D'Almeida and Albuquerque. They brought the calculation and the foresight, the skill in organization and the adaptation of means to profitable ends that belong to the new mercantile age of which they were the first successful exponents. The formation in 1602 of the Dutch East India Company enabled the several Dutch trading companies to unite their pressure upon the Portuguese. Within five years the Portuguese monopoly of a century had collapsed. Within a dozen years the Dutch East Indian Empire was a fact. When they captured Malacca in 1641 and Ceylon in 1658, the Dutch surpassed the high point of Portuguese expansion. By expelling the English from Amboyna in 1623 they beat back the English challenge to a share in the trade of the island world. Now Holland's ships sailed the many seas; her barges ascended the German rivers, and her wagons rolled on the roads of Europe.

The paths of the English and Dutch crossed at the Cape as well. Since the vessels of the rival companies had the same need of a half-way house, both companies had had their attention drawn to the Cape early in the century. Two English captains, according to the habit of English captains in all seas and all ages, claimed the Cape for their sovereign in 1620. Like many similar claims to other points on the African coast, their claim was allowed to lie dormant. That the Dutch and not the British established themselves at the Cape was chiefly due to the discovery by the Dutch that the soil of the Cape peninsula was not infertile, and that the natives, because of their cattle, could be an asset instead of a menace.

In 1652, the year after Cromwell's Navigation Acts threw down the English challenge to the Dutch, Jan van Riebeeck landed in Table Bay with the first true European settlers ever to land on African soil south of the Sahara. He came to found a refreshment station, a half-way house to India. What began as a cabbage patch on the way to India became the most vital strategic point, with the possible exception of Malacca, in the entire Empire of the Dutch East India Company.

Jan van Riebeeck's instructions were precise. The Dutch East India Company had no desire to tame the wilderness, nor to find new homes for Dutchmen over the sea. Jan van Riebeeck's duty would be done if he provided the Company's vessels with fresh meat and vegetables, for the settlement at the Cape was not a separate venture. It was a cog in a great commercial system which every year yielded those dividends that were the envy of English merchants and the despair of Colbert and his French trading companies. In that system spices and profits came before souls and patriotism. The golden book of St. Francis Xavier and the obscure martyrs who died of African fevers are all but empty pages in the annals of Dutch colonial effort.

The climate of the Cape was well suited for the settlement of Europeans. Less bracing than the coolness of Holland, it was much less enervating than the steaming heat of Batavia. It was a Mediterranean climate without the winter frosts that sometimes nip the fingers of olive pickers in Greece and Spain. Yet for the first four or five years the little community lived wretchedly on the brink of failure. What they planted grew well enough, except the wheat which was flattened by the great summer gales. Although their purpose was to revictual the Company's vessels, they would have starved without the staples which passing vessels brought them. The trouble was not simply the natural struggle of an infant settlement to take root. The Company was trying to make a garrison under military control do the work of a farming community. It was not to live arduously on a desolate spot midway between the comforts of Europe and the opportunities of the Spice Islands that most of these men had joined the service of John Company. Quite naturally they were inefficient workers whose cost to the Company was out of proportion to the produce of their sulky labour.

In 1657 the Company decided to substitute self-interest for discipline. At the suggestion of van Riebeeck nine of the Company's servants became 'free burghers' and landholders. They were given small holdings of 13⅓ acres, free from taxation, on which they bound themselves to live for twenty years. It was a small freedom that the Company gave them, much smaller than the freedom given to the 200 labourers who helped to found the proprietary colony of Maryland in 1634. They retained some of their military duties. They were to supply the Company with its requirements at fixed prices. They were not free to grow tobacco, in which the Company had a monopoly, nor were they free to trade with their native neighbours. In this incompatibility between little freedom and much restraint was contained much of the Colony's subsequent history. The Company fought to save its monopoly against infringement; the colonists, slowly growing in numbers, struggled to be freed of the heavy hand of an almost feudal government. The Company set its face against the expansion of the Colony's limits; the colonists, because freedom proved hard to find in the shadow of the fort, sought it by turning their backs upon the sea.

The first free burghers suffered from want of capital and labour. In 1664 South African farming endured its first depression, and the burghers cried out aloud at the poverty of their lives and the smallness of their opportunities. For centuries this was destined to be the familiar cry of the land in South Africa. It had not taken long to discover that for those that till the soil South Africa was a poor land, capricious and unpredictable. The century came to an end with the Colony able neither to pay its own way nor to satisfy the needs of the forty-odd ships, Dutch and foreign, which stopped at the Cape each year. Most of the colonists were poor; many were in debt. Some even lived on charity. In the hopes that they might stumble upon wealth in gold and change the Colony's luck, van Riebeeck and his successors sent out a dozen poorly equipped expeditions before the turn of the century. But the fabulous Kingdom of Monomotapa which they sought remained a mirage. These romantic and unscientific Eldorado-seekers of the seventeenth century, who were so easily baffled by the desert, never knew that the solution which they sought for the country's poverty was the true one. But not in their generation nor in many generations to come would the key to South Africa's great stores of gold and diamonds be found.

The liabilities of the Cape in the ledgers in Batavia and Amsterdam were not the entire story of the settlement's career. The English war of 1665 and the French war of 1672 taught the lesson that the Cape held a valuable place in the strategy of the Empire. In 1666 was begun the construction of a fort, whose narrow and solid little bricks, so like the bricks of Vermeer, though bathed in a harsher light than Delft ever knew, were a symbol henceforth of the Cape's permanence. Because the fort needed defenders the Company encouraged immigrants. Though these came slowly, the nine free burghers of 1657 had become nearly 600 in 1688. In that year and the following year came the Huguenots. They were only 200 in number, yet in neither England nor Holland nor any of the territories of Germany was their influence in proportion greater. What they brought—their families, their industries, and their special skills—the settlement needed. Their coming gave the Cape more truly than before the contours and the substance of a colony. Had their numbers been greater they might have stood in the same relation to the Dutch in which their Catholic brethren stood to the English in Canada later in the century. They resisted the effort to make Dutchmen out of them and clung to their tongue. But their resistance was vain. Though their languages differed the two groups were brought close together by their piety and the habits of their lives. In two generations or less the two groups had grown together and become one.

That a self-conscious community had come into being in spite of poverty and depression was seen during the governorships of Simon van der Stel (1679–99) and his son Willem Adriaan (1699–1707). The van der Stels were reformers and innovators. They brought to the Cape some of the agricultural science that had already made the Dutch rural landscape famous in Europe long before the days of Jethro Tull or 'Turnip' Townshend in England. Simon planted oaks; his son planted modern vineyards and produced a more genial wine than the harsh and heady wine which ships' captains had taken reluctantly on board. Willem Adriaan also experimented with wool. The experiment, although it failed, made him the first governor to glimpse South Africa's possibilities as a pastoral country. Unfortunately Willem Adriaan turned his genius for reform and management to his own account. The mistake which he committed was not so much that he tried to enrich himself. In Holland and the East Indies many men made their fortunes by all the devices of smuggling, peculation, and corruption which the Company's economic system could not check. His mistake was that he tried to make his fortune at the expense of a poor, underpeopled colony, where dishonesty struck swiftly at the welfare of the struggling colonists. In defiance of the Company's instructions he became the biggest landowner, the biggest cattle and wheat farmer, the biggest wine grower and slave holder. With his father and his brother he created a

fantastic monopoly which engrossed a third of the Colony's
farming land and gave them a stranglehold on production
and sale. As a pure economic achievement it was admirable.
The van der Stels had found the secret of an efficient monopoly which had been the Company's original objective in
founding the settlement. Their discovery came too late. For
such a thorough monopoly, however efficient, the time was
past. A new period of colonization was opened by the outcry
of the colonists which finally led to Willem Adriaan's dis-
missal in 1707. What South Africa was to become was no
longer entirely in the hands of the Council of Seventeen.
From then on the efforts and aspirations of the men and
women for whom South Africa, and no longer Holland, was
their homeland, also influenced the course of the land's
development.

To protect its monopoly and to simplify its administration
the Company felt compelled to hold the settlement within
narrow limits. It insisted on the fewest possible contacts
between its colonists and the Hottentots, for it knew full well
the restlessness and quarrelsomeness of frontiers. Its ideal
settlement, not unnaturally, was an intimate neighbourliness
and an intensive agriculture that could be easily and profitably supervised from the castle. The Company wanted its
settlers to face the sea whence came the ships which carried
in their holds the wealth that made Amsterdam the commercial focus of the world. There ensued inevitably a
struggle between programme and performance, between
what the Company desired of the Colony, and what climate,
geography, and the population could provide.

The common accusation that the development of the
Colony was checked by the pressure of regulations and
restrictions is true, but it is not the only explanation of the
course of the Cape's development in the eighteenth century.
The picture, familiar to every South African schoolboy, of
the early burghers turning disconsolately away from the
coast, driven forth by a grasping commercial monopoly
which denied them the just profits of their labour, is much
overdrawn. When the days of the Company were over,
there was no legend amongst the Boers of oppression. While

the Boers of the nineteenth century never looked back upon the Company with regret, it is also true that they bore it no deep grudge. Economic restrictions, it is true, bore exasperatingly upon a population which was not stable but busily engaged in experimenting with its environment. Upon the consumption of bread and meat, brandy, wine, and tobacco, the sale of retail licences placed a virtual excise. The complaints never ceased against the Company's right to buy at fixed prices and against its control of the lion's share of the trade in wheat, wine, and meat with passing ships. It was a system that tempted officials to favouritism and chicanery, and the colonists to evasion. The eighteenth century smuggled on a grand scale. Smuggling had helped thwart the Seville monopoly and eased the weight of English mercantilism on the American colonists. At the Cape, too, men smuggled, and distilled, and trafficked clandestinely with the natives.

Yet had the Company been more liberal, it could not have overcome the Colony's natural handicaps. No great staple, like the timber of New England or the sugar of the West Indies, drew the Cape into the trade of the world. It could not compete with the rich soils and advanced agricultural technique of Europe, nor with the cheap labour and more abundant rainfall of the East Indies. The price of production was high and the quality often poor and unreliable. Cape wheat was usually too expensive for the European market and had no chance of making much headway against the natural monopoly of rice in the East. France and Portugal produced better wines, while ships' captains often complained of the poorness and dearness of Cape meat. Of the staples that brought prosperity to other parts of the colonial world none would flourish. Wool failed, though the wiry-haired fat-tailed sheep did well. In spite of the Mediterranean climate of the Cape neither olives nor silk would prosper. Coffee and sugar failed entirely, and so did tobacco. A colony so isolated, so poorly endowed, so dependent upon a tiny domestic market and the ships that anchored in its bay was unable to attract capital, and itself created new wealth with despairing slowness. In the seventeenth century it had

chronically produced too little; in the eighteenth century it
floundered between alternate crises of over-production and
lean years of drought and crop failure that made its efforts
seem like a task of Sisyphus. Immigrants were very few, and
Amsterdam made no effort to add to their number. While
tobacco, rice, lumber, and fish were drawing men to the
Atlantic seaboard, the Cape existed obscurely in the dol-
drums, breeding the increase of its population with the
strength of its own loins.

The real sinning of the Dutch East India Company was
not so much in its monopoly as in its effort to insist upon a
type of settlement more suited to the climate and conditions
of Europe than South Africa. The task of the eighteenth
century at the Cape accordingly was to find a level of
economic activity proper to the Colony's climate and its
geographical position in the world, and to produce a community adapted to its environment. In the American
colonies the quarrel with the economic system of the mother
country produced an involved political and constitutional
struggle. At the Cape political and constitutional matters
were, till almost the end of the century, relatively unimpor-
tant. Men's political energies are likely to be proportioned
to their hope for material betterment. Because trade lan-
guished and industry did not exist, men of wealth were
absent and public spirit was limited. Instead of fighting for
political liberties, the Cape's burghers began to turn their
backs upon the trouble of meeting the Company's regulations and to abandon the task of producing what could not
be easily sold at a profit. Theirs was the predicament of
Robinson Crusoe on his remote island. Like him they made
a virtue of necessity, producing in themselves the habits and
activities that were suited to the land they lived in. On the
slowly widening frontier of the Colony developed an economy in which self-sufficiency was more important than
profit. For men who gave up trying to raise cash crops and
used what they produced mainly for their own consumption,
the Company's monopoly had few terrors. Cattle bartering
with the Hottentots, hunting, and finally cattle grazing became the way of life of the frontier community. Twenty-five

years after the landing of van Riebeeck a cattle and hunting
frontier had already come into existence. The sons of the
first generation of free burghers became, some of them,
genuine frontiersmen. However much the government at
Cape Town might multiply and strengthen the penalties
against them and their way of life, their numbers grew.
Their guns gave them self-reliance, their wagons freedom of
movement, and their cattle economic independence. Though
there were amongst them vagabonds and the shiftless men of
all frontier regions, most of them were men with the best
qualities of their French and Dutch blood, who had embraced the poverty of the interior as a way of life and a source
of freedom. From the beginning of the eighteenth century
there was always a fringe of settlement that was not wholly
within the official limits of the Colony, and therefore beyond
the direct control of government. In 1702 a party had
wandered far enough afield to brush against some Ama-
Xosa tribesmen. It was the first clash between Boer and
Bantu. In 1760 Jacobus Coetsee, an elephant hunter, crossed
the Orange River.

Slowly settlement edged closer to the mountains that
separated the narrow coastal belt from the great interior
plateau. No great rivers or dense forest or fever stood between the Trekboers and the interior. South Africa has a
physiography much less formidable than that of Australia or
Canada. The hardships of hunger and thirst that dogged the
steps of every explorer who plunged into the Australian interior were all but unknown to the South African pioneer.
In the richest game country that the world had ever known
food was easily obtained. Ivory from the elephant, skins of
the wildebeest, like the buffalo robes of the American plains,
and thongs of rhinoceros hide were exchanged for the few
wants and fewer luxuries. Not till they reached the latitude
of Delagoa Bay generations later did the Trekboers suffer
from the tsetse-fly and the mosquito. The rigours and agues
of Canadian cold they never felt. Neither climate nor topo-
graphy seriously halted their progress. In what is the most
tropical of continents, South Africa contains the greatest
single area of temperate climate. The dryness of the air and

the elevation of the land tempers the heat of the sun. The climate has a bracing quality that gives men keenness in their youth and strength in their old age. Not even in the summer heat is physical effort an unbearable strain upon the constitution of white men. Although it lacks the coolness and the tempered light of England or Holland, the climate of South Africa, nevertheless, is well fitted to maintain a hardy and vigorous people.

As the Egyptian spoke of the nomads of Arabia, 'Their limbs are ever restless, nor can they find peace in one place', so did the Company feel about its subjects. It could never accustom itself to the preposterous areas which they so casually covered. Following them unwillingly, it followed them imperfectly, bombarding them uselessly with edicts which it could not execute and threats which it could not carry out. At no time was the Company able or willing to expend the resources and develop the administration necessary to bring European settlement firmly under its control. Expansion was therefore haphazard and largely independent of direction. Upon the frontier there developed a freedom far more advanced than existed in Cape Town. But it was a freedom often close to lawlessness, the freedom of a region where anomalies and irregularities throve in the absence of a competent law and efficient agents. The landdrosts and heemraden[1] tended to fall under the influence of their environment, so that their administration of unpopular laws, like those against cattle barter and shooting game without a licence, was lax and unavailing.

The transition from the small farming of the coast-belt to the pastoral pursuits of the interior was the proof that the burghers had left the groove of European habits and were living in a manner in keeping with their new native land. The nomadic habits of the Trekboers did not prove that they were bad farmers, unable and unwilling to apply themselves to the hard life of intensive agriculture. Too often and unfairly have the Trekboers been criticized for their inept and shiftless habits. The plain truth was that there was little purpose in being good farmers, since eighteenth-century

[1] Magistrates and burgher representatives.

South Africa rewarded industry and resourcefulness poorly. The evolution of the Trekboers was the story of a successful, not of an unsuccessful, adaptation to South African conditions, and their movement was in obedience to a simple law of economic life. Capital and labour were scarce, while land was cheap and plentiful. An extensive use of the land was really efficient, as intensive farming called for an expenditure of capital and effort for which the return was quite inadequate. Farming less and hunting more, bartering more and buying less, the standard of living of the Cape frontiersmen soon sank to the level of the thirsty land upon which they lived. Economic history once taught that man had developed by gradual steps from a life of hunting to pastoral pursuits, and finally to a settled and agricultural life. In South Africa the process was reversed (Map I). Coming from a land that had taken the lead in thrifty and intensive cultivation, the Company settler gradually became a herdsman and a hunter.

Upon the character of the Dutch farmer or Boer, as he came to be called, geography and climate left an indelible mark. The maps of the geographer, the geologist, and the climatologist are all more effective guides to South African history than the political map. A rainfall map shows how limited is the area of sufficient and reliable rainfall. Lying very much in the same latitudes, South Africa's climate is in many ways similar to that of Australia. Rain falls more plentifully on the east coast, diminishing in the interior, until almost desert conditions are reached in the west. The great land-mass of South Africa is not penetrated by any great body of water comparable with the Mediterranean or the Baltic Seas, nor does it contain any drainage basin like the Great Lakes to give it a régime of regular and well-distributed rainfall. Of the total area of the Cape Province, as shown on a modern map, fully half enjoys an average annual rainfall of only 10 inches or less. As this rain falls almost entirely in the summer months, the rate of evaporation under the strong African sun is high, far higher than in the narrow belt of winter rainfall immediately around Cape Town. In such an area arable farming was all but impossible. Even for domestic animals this arid region could provide only a spare subsistence.

A relief map shows that South Africa is for the most part a plateau of which the edges break down close to the coast, presenting a broken and mountainous aspect. The coast-land is somewhat like a hem following the base of the plateau and is uniformly narrow on both the east and west coasts. That South African rivers are not navigable and played no part in the settlement of the country is easily explained by their irregular water supply and the high elevation of all but the last miles of their course. The greatest South African river, the Orange, flows through the gorges of the broken, high country within a few miles of reaching the Atlantic Ocean. Of all the country's large rivers it is the least navigable. For the last part of its course it flows through country so dry that by the time it reaches the sea it contains less water than it does 800 miles nearer its source. In the dry winter months it breaks down, like most South African rivers, into a chain of pools and water-holes, so that it can be forded but a few miles from its mouth.

Since the interior is high, rarely lower than 1,000 and attaining as much as 6,000 feet above sea-level, South Africa is spared the climate of the Australian interior. Altitude and latitude balance each other. It may be said that in the summer the altitude tempers the heat, and in the winter the latitude mitigates the cold. In spite of latitude and its continental aspect, South Africa is spared the sweltering humidity of the American Middle West, or the burning temperatures of Australia's Marble Bar, 'the hottest place on earth'. Whereas the great majority of Australia's population came to live on the coast or near to it, the great majority of South Africa's white population ultimately came to live in the interior, away from the coast.

On a rainfall map Cape Town and the little peninsula on which it stands are all but imprisoned by a great arid area in which the average rainfall is less than 15 inches per year. This area extends along the coast in a north-westerly direction to the Orange River, inland almost as far as the present location of Kimberley, and eastwards to the present location of Bedford. Along the east coast there is a narrow belt with an average rainfall of between 15 and 25 inches. When this belt reaches the Great Fish River, it broadens and moves inland. A large area of what to-day is Natal, the northern Orange Free State, and the southern Transvaal enjoys a relatively generous and reliable rainfall.[1] In the eighteenth century, however, this area lay far beyond the reach of the Trekboers. It is clear that after leaving the winter-rainfall area of the coast the Trekboers entered a region, a quarter of a million square miles, in which they were destined to wander for far more than the Biblical forty years. It was a land where the wild flowers, the wheat, and the vinès of the Cape would not grow. A large part of it was called by the Hottentots the Karroo, or dry country. It is a region of flat-topped hills with slopes untidy with rubble and tussocks of wiry, dry grass. The numerous chains of hills were no obstacle to the Trekboers' flocks or their ox-wagons, for the terrain is flat, covered with dry grass and scrub whose thorns inflict an angry wound. Only the ant-hills, hard as kiln-fired brick, were an incessant menace to the wheels of carelessly driven ox-wagons. Underfoot the earth is brown, hard, and compact. In the distance it is purple, save when the dry west wind whirls the sun-baked ground into dust and fills the air with the haze which causes the breath-taking sunsets of winter. It is a treacherous wind that blows from the west, a wind that erodes the earth and that defeats the efforts of the north wind to bring its rain to the earth cracked by heat, the vegetation ashen with dryness, and animals weakened by thirst. Now and then a strong ravine cuts sharply through the land to show that when the rain falls it falls in sudden torrents that tear the earth, washing away its soil in tumbling tawny floods. It is a land eroded and treeless, not because man has used it wastefully, but because Nature herself uses it ill.

In the dry interior there was room neither for the agriculture nor the land system of the coast-land. The trekking herdsmen needed areas at least fifty times as great. In 1717 the Company decided to halt the issue of freehold land.

---

[1] Here are the true grasslands of South Africa.

Instead the farmer could obtain a 'loan farm' in return for an annual rent. As long as the rent was paid he had such security of tenure that he could even sell or bequeath the loan farm. Actually the loan-farm system was a form of leasehold, without any term of years, and for a nominal rent. It permitted the colonists to acquire land without capital and therefore enormously stimulated the rapid dispersal of colonists. After 1732 the pastoral farmer paid an annual sum of about £5 for the right to hold his loan farm of 6,000 acres and more. The fee which he paid was partly a grazing fee, partly a rental or leasehold payment, and partly a recognition of the Company's title to the land. It became a deeply ingrained habit of frontier society for each man to have such a farm of 6,000 and even 10,000 acres. When the youth left his father's farm, it was to take up his birthright, which was a farm of his own. The method of measuring their farms exceeded even the unprecision of medieval land measurement. To measure his 'hide' the Boer walked his horse from a central point for half an hour to each of the four cardinal points. A Boer 'hide' was thus about the size of a medieval 'hundred'. In this wise a relatively small population could push outwards the frontiers of the Colony with astonishing speed.

In theory the frontiersmen could not move on to fresh land without the sanction of the administration. In theory also the administration acquired sovereign title to all land upon which its colonists settled. But since allegiance and the authority of government came to rest ever more lightly upon the men of the frontier, there developed amongst them an attitude towards land not unlike that of the natives themselves. Though in strict legality the land tenure was not in freehold and was revocable at the will of the administration, actually the Trekboers availed themselves of the land with the utmost freedom. On the farthest frontier men did not always register their farms or pay their dues. The eighteenth century in South Africa did not develop the precise doctrine of Crown Lands which was of such importance in the history of land settlement in Australia, New Zealand, and Canada. At an early moment there was born the attitude that the right of public domain was qualified by the right of the individual to acquire land either at no cost or at a nominal rental. The claim of each man to a farm of not less than 6,000 acres became ultimately an inborn right. In subsequent South African history few factors are of greater importance than the uncontrolled and haphazard method of Boer land settlement and the habits which were bred by the Company's loss of control over Boer expansion.

In the long quietude of the eighteenth century the Boer race was formed. In the vast, unmysterious, thirsty landscape of the interior lay the true centre of South African settlement. When the Trekboers entered it with their flocks and tented wagons, they left the current of European life and lost the economic habits of the nations from which they had sprung. Though they never became true nomads, the mark of nomadism was upon them, and their dominant traits were those of a restless and narrow existence. They had the nomad's appetite for space and possessed the hardness and courage of men of the saddle who watch their flocks and hunt their meat. Their wealth was in their cattle and in their sons and grandsons, who were born numerously and who thrived amazingly. Their life gave them a tenacity of purpose, a power of silent endurance, and the keenest self-respect. But this isolation sank into their character causing their imagination to lie fallow and their intellects to become inert. Their virtues had their obverse qualities as well. Their tenacity could degenerate into obstinacy, their power of endurance into resistance to innovation, and their self-respect into suspicion of the foreigner and contempt for their inferiors. For want of formal education and sufficient pastors, they read their Bibles intensively, drawing from the Old Testament, which spoke the authentic language of their lives, a justification of themselves, of their beliefs and their habits. Continued immigration, even of such small groups as the French Huguenots, would have done much to keep them abreast of some of the thought of the new Europe of the Enlightenment. Instead the remotest corner of Europe was better informed.

Between 1803 and 1806, when the days of Holland's rule

were numbered, Lichtenstein travelled in South Africa. He shared the capacity of his fellow German, Humboldt, in Latin America to observe precisely and describe understandingly. Lichtenstein marvelled at the 'joyless existence' of those who had left the vicinity of Cape Town for a droughty land where the trees gave no shade, and wild animals were a constant menace. Gazing upon such a riverless land and observing the slow monotony of men's lives, he wondered 'how the first settlers could ever have thought of establishing themselves in so inhospitable a waste'. Men's wants and curiosity shrank as their distance from civilization grew greater. 'In an almost unconscious inactivity of mind', declared Lichtenstein, 'without action, without useful effect upon a wider circle of mankind, beyond the little circle which his own family formed around him, the South African colonist of these parts spends his solitary days, and by his mode of life is made such as we see him.'[1]

The very mildness of the climate dissuaded them from intensive effort. All they needed was protection against rain and wind. Theirs was certainly not the huge effort of the Canadian pioneer, who hacked his fields and his home out of a wilderness of forest. Out of green brick or reeds a habitation was easily made, so that a home cost as little in labour as the farm in money. Between wealth and poverty the distinction was not easy to find, for the chief values of their existence, land and cattle, were easily obtained. Yet there were always differences. Later they became more pronounced and much more important. The 'poor whites' of latter-day South African history already existed obscurely in eighteenth-century frontier society. The windowless hut of thatch in which some families dwelt, the bed of rough wood and raw thongs in which they slept, the poor variety of their diet, and the ambitionless round of their days, brought them closer to their native neighbours than, for example, to the industrious New Englander.

Men so widely scattered as they were lost the gregarious habit of their forefathers in Europe. They built few villages.

[1] H. Lichtenstein, *Travels in Southern Africa 1803 to 1806*, London, 1812. Reprinted by the van Riebeeck Society, Cape Town, 1928.

On the great farms each man fled the tyranny of his neighbour's smoke. It followed that their communal life was
loosely organized. They came together when compelled by
danger or crisis. In the face of the native population their
sense of race and fellowship was exceedingly keen. But their
co-operation was not continuous and sustained. The habits
of their social life were like the discipline of their commandos.
It was the sum of individual willingness; at its best it was
excellent, at its worst it destroyed the commando.

The Trekboers were not the whole of colonial society.
Their restlessness is likely to draw attention away from the
sedate communities near Cape Town. Here education went
beyond the Bible of the cattle farmers. Although the effects
of isolation were keenly felt here too, it was an environment
where conversation rose above cattle and rains. Cape Town
itself was proud of the liveliness which visiting Dutch,
English, and French merchantmen brought. As the healthi-
ness of its beautiful climate became known, officers from
India spent their furlough there. The citizens of Cape Town
and the wine and grain farmers were closer to the administration and suffered more from it. Yet because they were
closer to it, they could, when the time came, demand a more
responsible place within it, instead of escaping from it, as
had become the habit of the frontier. Their qualities, as
substantial as the sturdy furniture in their fine houses,
influenced the future no less profoundly than the more
spectacular traits of the frontier.

South African society was not formed by geography and
climate alone. From the beginning its physical environment
was complicated by the presence of other races and societies.
The development of white society was profoundly influenced
by its relations with slaves, Hottentots, Bushmen, and Bantu.
The true history of South African colonization describes the
growth, not of a settlement of Europeans, but of a totally
new and unique society of different races and colours and
cultural attainments, fashioned by conflicts of racial heredity
and the oppositions of unequal social groups.

The Hottentots looked upon the coast-belt as theirs. Behind them were marauding Bushmen and a less generous

climate. The settlement of white men upon their land was fatal to them. In the beginning the administration strove desperately to keep whites and Hottentots apart. It even thought at one moment fantastically of digging a canal or growing a hedge across the Cape peninsula. South Africa took the policy of racial segregation seriously from the very start. Bartering for cattle introduced the Hottentots to the white man's tobacco and firewater and diseases. As the Colony grew, quarrels over cattle stealing became quarrels over grazing rights, especially when the Company established its own system of cattle posts. The Hottentots broke down undramatically and simply. Their end had little of the tragedy which lies in the last struggles of a dying race. Before the pressure of the colonists upon them their institutions failed them, and their loose tribal structure collapsed entirely. Quarrelling amongst themselves for their shrunken lands, smitten by the white man's smallpox, they died out or drifted as labourers into the towns and on to the farms. 'It hath generally been observed', wrote Daniel Denton in 1670 of English settlement on Long Island, 'that where the English come to settle, a divine hand makes way for them by wars one with the other or by some raging mortal disease.' Even so did these colonists of the southern hemisphere regard the native population. According to their belief it was more than their arms that made them prevail over the natives, and their superiority depended upon more than their intelligence or their institutions. Their superiority was born of race and faith, a quality divinely given which could not be transmitted to other races or acquired by them. 'The black stinking dogs', as van Riebeeck already called them, suffered from an inferiority, predestined and irreparable, which fixed their place in a society of white men. Economically they had a place in the field and the kitchen; socially and politically they stood outside the circle of the rights and privileges of white men; even legally they existed in an ambiguous region between law and the arbitrary will of their masters. Hence it could be that they became in course of time a hybrid race, and yet did not dissolve the purity of the white race. Without reinforcement by immigration from Europe, South

African society in the eighteenth century seemed to have entered the same road as New Spain. The relations between whites and people of colour were often familiar. The number of mixed breeds grew. But whether it was the spirit of the Dutch women of the settlement, or a principle in the blood of the Huguenots which did not die with their language, the white community successfully contradicted the usual result of the intimate contact of different peoples, by giving freely of its blood to a different race without destroying its own ethnic purity. In other ways, however, white society was profoundly altered by the penetration of untutored and menial folk. All the more was this true because the influence of the Hottentots was increased by the presence at the Cape of slaves as well.

Slavery was developed at the Cape by circumstance rather than by necessity. For want of great staples and intensive use of the soil a true slave economy, like that of the sugar islands, could not develop. There were few compelling reasons and no climatic reasons why the Dutch and the Huguenots could not have remained a truly white society. But the Cape lay between the two great slave-trading coasts of the world. From its rapacious sister company in the West Indies the Dutch East India Company had learned to tolerate slavery. The conscience of French and English captains did not shrink from helping to pay for the Cape's expensive meat by trafficking in slaves. At the very beginning, therefore, there was woven the double strand of South African history: the servile worker and the free colonist. In 1708 there were 1,147 slaves, and in 1795 the number had risen to 18,000. Slaves and Hottentots together provoked remarkable changes in the thought and habits of the colonists, for climate and geography were not alone in forming the distinctive traits of the Boer race. Slaves and droughts, Hottentots and isolation, cheap labour and land, combined to create the institutions and habits of South African society. The sons and daughters born to sturdy Hollanders and Huguenots learned to look upon the labour of the field and upon all hard physical toil as the functions of a servile race. Three shrewd and eminent observers at the beginning, in the

middle, and at the end of the eighteenth century remarked
upon the devitalizing and unnerving consequences of the
Colony's reliance upon cheap and servile labour. It was the
distinguishing mark of the Cape's Europeans, declared one
of them, van Imhoff, Governor-General of the Dutch East
Indies, in 1743, that they preferred 'to be served rather than
to serve', considering it debasing 'to work with their own
hands'. In the West Indies such a large proportion of slaves
as were held at the Cape would have been a sign of wealth
and a source of prosperity. But observers had noted that at
the Cape slavery was the sign of an unenterprising economic
life. It was at the same time a cause and a consequence of
the Cape's poverty. As the entire community of Hottentots,
slaves, and Europeans grew more numerous without becoming appreciably richer, it began to create within itself a
privileged white caste, depending upon an excessive number
of slaves and servants, whose labour was wastefully and inefficiently used. Little effort was made to raise the standard
of living or increase the opportunities of the class of slaves
and servants. In this manner the limited wealth of the
Colony became the privilege of its white population, whose
higher standard of living was at the expense of the economic
and social welfare of a numerous servile population. Thus
early did South Africa learn that a self-conscious group may
escape the worst effects of life in a poor and unprosperous
land by turning distinctions of race and colour into devices
for social and economic discrimination.

The fierce Protestant zeal which had fought the Spaniards
was little concerned about the welfare of pagan souls.
Amongst them the familiar question of Spanish colonization,
whether God had created the natives 'free and not subject',
was hardly raised at all. Rather did they hold the belief
expressed by Canning in a later and more humanitarian age
that the Church 'was no more calculated for the negro than
for the brute animal that shares his toil'. When the faith of
Islam made headway amongst the Cape slaves, neither public
nor official opinion was alarmed. It was a pagan creed which
as good Calvinists they properly despised. But just on that
account it was fit for slaves and men of colour. Their faith,

like that of seventeenth-century Puritanism, drew much of its inspiration from the Old Testament. Their religion, setting them apart from the unelected pagans about them, bred in them a sense of special destiny as a people.

When slaves became builders and workers in wood, when slaves and Hottentots tended herds and washed clothes, there was no room for young men and women to become artisans, labourers, or domestic workers. As they came of age young people sought not work, but land. Because there were slaves in Cape Town and on the wine farms was one reason why more white men trekked into the interior. It was easier to carve out a farm than a career. In a mixed society of slaves, half-breeds, and their masters there was little room for active immigration, or for the introduction of the crofters, labourers, and hand-weavers who in Canada and later in New Zealand and Australia were the backbone of all schemes of closer settlement.

The Dutch were not the first trekkers in South Africa, nor was their famous trek of 1835–7 the first Great Trek. Trekking was the natural consequence of poor soil and unreliable climate from which suffered not South Africa alone but a very large part of the African continent. Before ever the whites penetrated the interior it had been a habit of native life not to abide continuously in one place. Like the herds of wild game the native peoples[1] had a slow rhythm of movement and change. Because they were not inseparably attached to any locality, they moved freely, especially as their primitive and wasteful agriculture exhausted the soil. Thus they developed the half-nomadic habits which were best suited to a land of low fertility and irregular rainfall. The Bantu whom the advancing huntsmen first met at an early moment in the eighteenth century were the country's original trekkers. Though their movement was far slower than that of the Europeans, whose greed for huge individual farms gave them seven-league boots, they were pushing southwards while the Dutch were advancing northwards.

Between the land and its Bantu inhabitants there was an

[1] The term 'natives' applies to the Bantu tribes of the interior and not to the coastal Hottentots.

equilibrium. But it was not a firm equilibrium. South Africa was not a land like the plains of India, of northern Italy, or western Europe that could give nourishment to invaders, absorbing them as the Lombards and Franks had been absorbed. In South Africa the impact of two competitive groups seriously disturbed the balance of soil and settlement. The effects of that disturbance were seen in friction and war between whites and blacks, in internecine struggles between the tribes themselves. It was seen also in the diseases which increasingly ravaged the native herds, in famine's 'sharp and meagre face' that appeared amongst the tribes more often, and in the transformation of both native and European society; for it is of the greatest importance to remember that the settlers in South Africa did not, as in North America, sweep the native population away from their path. Indeed every blow that struck at native life had its repercussion on the white community as well. This is the deepest truth in all South African history.

The natural road for European expansion to take was in the broad belt following the east coast where the rainfall was more dependable than it was along the west coast. Had there been no natives, the main stream of settlement would have swept in an easterly and north-easterly direction with the Indian Ocean on its right hand and the mountains on the left. Acquaintance with the rainfall map of South Africa throws the clearest light on the movements and conflicts of both its white and its black population. The search for water and grass was the first principle in the life of Boer and Bantu, for it was in their herds that both counted their wealth. When Boers and natives finally met in the last third of the eighteenth century, the natives had already penetrated beyond the area of comparatively high average rainfall. The frontier, commonly known as the Eastern Frontier, because of its position from Cape Town, lay in an area of uncertain rainfall and subject to drought. In one sense this area was a defile or pass through which the grassland beyond could be reached. The area of low rainfall lay behind the Boers, while the area of more bountiful rains lay behind the natives. This circumstance alone was enough to force the Boers to take the offensive. To secure sufficient grazing for their herds and especially in order to penetrate beyond the native frontier to the better-watered lands, the Boers were bound to press heavily upon the natives. Three things gave the Dutch frontiersmen an advantage. With the same three things Cortez and Pizarro had conquered Mexico and Peru. Their horses gave them swiftness of movement; their guns gave them an irresistible weapon; the wheels on their wagons enabled them swiftly to turn conquest into settlement by transporting their families and their goods.

Vainly the administration at Cape Town had tried to prevent the frontiers of white and black settlement from meeting. Each *placaat*, or edict, which fixed a boundary—there were *placaats* in 1727, 1739, and 1770—recognized past extension but failed to prevent further expansion. In 1774 Governor van Plettenberg issued an hysterical edict threatening to fine, thrash, and even condemn to death those who persisted in trafficking with the natives. Four years later he suffered all the rigours and discomforts of a journey to the far-off frontier to impress upon the Boers the prestige of his person and the authority of his government. It was wasted effort. In 1779 took place the first clash between colonists and natives serious enough to be called a war. From that time onwards the relations between the two groups were unbroken and intimate. Not van Plettenberg's beacon, nor any frontier or treaty line, nor any neutral belt availed in keeping white and black apart. In time the quarrels between Boers and natives became more complex in their causes. Men quarrelled over the stealing of cattle and their sale, over the possession of land, and over labour upon the land. The outbreaks of 1792 and 1799 were thus caused by grazing disputes, cattle thefts, trading prices, and conditions of labour. Each clash left a larger number of natives embedded in white society. In one sense frontier wars became civil wars between groups economically associated with one another. At the end of the century their association was still loose. The Dutch frontiersmen could not prevail so easily against the natives as they had against the Hottentots.

Nevertheless, the process of subjecting the natives to their service was well begun.

Since its founding the Cape had enjoyed very nearly 150 years of peace. That no enemy attacked it in this century of colonial wars was not due to its castle or its mercenaries. While England was fighting what Seeley called the Second Hundred Years War with France, Holland enjoyed about a hundred years of peace with her old colonial rival. Ever since William had sailed to England in 1688 to become its king, Holland and its Empire had remained under the lee of England's growing might. Thus was deferred the final reckoning between the two empires, which had seemed so inevitable in the days of both Cromwell and Charles II.

Throughout the century the Cape continued to suffer from what Arthur Young called a 'deficiency in consumption, activity, and animation'. The settlement built up its capital slowly. The Company was not a generous investor. Its monopoly checked the Colony's trade and prevented the creation of any industry whatsoever. All through the eighteenth century the Colony was drained of its currency to pay for the excess of imports over its poor and unreliable exports. A more liberal policy would have cleared the channels of trade, but it could not have removed the natural handicaps of climate and geography. There were years when hardly a cask of wine could be sold, and other years when cattle disease compelled a strict rationing of meat. Free trade could not have made Cape wine more popular or have enabled wheat to compete profitably with Surat or Baltic grains. After just one hundred years of existence all the Cape managed to export was 75,000 muids[1] of wheat per year. Upon an export so pitifully small the Cape nevertheless was dependent. Because of the dispersion of its population, the severity of the monopoly, and the improbity of officials, the Colony's internal market was underdeveloped and inefficient. Cape society was top-heavy with officials. In 1740 there were three Company servants to eight burghers. In 1778, when there were three Company servants to every

[1] A muid equals three bushels.

sixteen burghers, it was still true that the large size of the official population encouraged the characteristic malpractices of the Dutch East Indies. Prices that were naturally high were made even higher, until even the Company grumbled at the dearness of meat and other produce for its ships. Occasionally depression yielded suddenly to prosperity. South Africa in the eighteenth century had already learned to depend, as it depended so remarkably in the nineteenth and twentieth centuries, upon windfalls for its prosperity. Both the Seven Years War and the War of American Independence brought war booms to the Cape. The French troops spent freely, giving the Cape a few years of delirious prosperity, when the Cape became for a while 'little Paris' and built its lovely white gabled houses.

When prosperity departed with the French the Colony sank back into its normal depression. But it did so with an ominous sulkiness. The sweetness which it had tasted made the old order taste more sour. After the American war the signs became each year more clear that the Colony was approaching a crisis. At a time when the Thirteen Colonies had made themselves completely independent of the mother country the Cape at last began to stir against the Company's rigid and unenterprising rule. A petition sent to Amsterdam in 1779 showed that the Colony had outgrown a rule that had changed its spirit and methods but little in a hundred years. The petition protested against the rule of governors upon whose will there was no local restraint and demanded burgher representation upon the Council of Policy. It exposed in language that had not been heard at the Cape since the day of Willem Adriaan van der Stel the venality of officials, the confusion of laws that encouraged official lawlessness, and demanded not only that the Colony's laws be codified, but that half of the seats on the High Court be held by colonists.

The common picture of John Company—all purse and no conscience—is exaggerated. The Company was not without the spirit of compromise. When the war was over various reforms were introduced. If it is remembered that a purely trading company was granting constitutional liberties to a colony that had never shown any profit, the value of the reforms was real. Six seats on the High Court were yielded to the colonists, as well as a voice in the care of roads, taxation, and the fixing of prices. The concessions were, some of them, illusory. The right to export Cape produce on Cape ships, provided one-third of the crews were Cape colonists, was useless. Yet a beginning had been made. The Colony had obviously placed its feet on the bottom rungs of the ladder that led to constitutional liberty.

Colonial discontent took a sharper edge just when the Company began to experience dangerously the immediate effects of war and the cumulative effects of corrupt book-keeping and corrupter book-keepers. After Holland entered the war in 1780 the Company paid two more dividends. They were big dividends, but they were the last. The great commercial power which had provoked so much envy and admiration had come to its knees at last, weighed down by debts and stricken by English and French competition, against which neither its ships nor its organization could any longer prevail. Each year the number of English and French vessels that put into Table Bay grew larger. They were the outward and visible sign that the Company's monopoly was being rapidly broken. The Company tried to hold up prices by restricting production in the East Indies, by limiting supplies in Europe, and even by burning surplus stores. It was useless, for foreign enterprise had shattered its monopoly in the East and invaded its markets in Europe.

In the ten years following the end of the American war an avalanche of debts descended upon the Company. They doubled and then tripled, so that not even the States General could save the Company. Its last years were desperate with the effort to control expenses and check waste. Nowhere was the need for economy greater than at the Cape, for of its possessions none were as unprofitable as the Cape. In 1792 the Commissioners Nederburgh and Frykenius arrived at the Cape. Even before their arrival expenses had been slashed and troops withdrawn. It was a morose community that received the Commissioners. The colonists wanted their prosperity back. They wanted higher prices and the right to trade with vessels unhindered instead of smuggling with them. They wanted to be free of the perverse régime of too numerous and too dishonest officials. But it was not to please the colonists that the Commissioners had come. They could not carry water upon both shoulders. Economy was their first duty. Higher taxes, more revenue, and less expenditure were the paramount interest of the Company. Expenditures were cut and perquisites abolished. The wings of the Cape's official caste were severely clipped. But not even such wholesale reforms were enough to remedy the Cape's desperate plight. In a grim effort to force the Colony into solvency the Commissioners announced taxes on slaves and wine, new customs, wagon duties, and auction fees. Port fees were imposed on foreign vessels. Still it was not enough. The Company's life-blood was ebbing away at too many points. To stanch the flow at the Cape could avail little when in Holland the Company had lost its credit and was ten millions in debt. As the Company drifted closer to the bankruptcy which came in 1794, contradictory experiments in inflation and economy at the Cape failed to halt a loss of confidence, a disappearance of credit, and finally an economic collapse.

In Europe the princes had challenged the French Revolution at Pilnitz; France was defiant; the tumbrils began to roll. Goethe announced the birth of a new Europe after Valmy and Jemappes. The century ended.

II

NEW IDEAS FOR OLD

'Du droit de tuer dans la conquête, les politiques ont tiré le droit de réduire en servitude.' MONTESQUIEU: *L'Esprit des Lois,* x. 3.

THE Cape Colony which an English force took over in 1795 was economically more underdeveloped, politically more inexperienced, and culturally more backward than any of the greater colonies of settlement. After one and a half centuries the Colony contained one town worthy of the name, and five or six little villages. The rest of the population was scattered over an immense area. In the more compact western districts the population was about 13,500. Throughout the rest of the Colony was dispersed a population of seven or eight thousand, one individual to approximately ten square miles.

To General Craig and his troops his Colony seemed at first a bountiful place. In 1795 there was a bumper crop of wheat. But in the very next year the Colony showed its other and equally familiar face. Crop failures and ill-advised exports of wheat brought the Colony perilously close to famine. Poor years in 1798, 1799, and 1800 gave the first British Government an ample demonstration of the uncertainties of South African seasons, which during the preceding century had plunged the Colony into alternate and unsettling crises of surpluses and famine.

The English brought the beginning of a revolution to the Cape. It was not the revolution of Robespierre or Danton, for Jacobinism stank in the nostrils of His Majesty's right-minded officers. Yet the coming of the English brought a break with the past. Many of the perquisites and fees which the reforming Commissioners had left untouched gave way to regular salaries. Nor was it Jacobinism to cancel monopolies or to throw open the trade with passing vessels to all alike. The régime of monopolies and official privileges was mortally stricken, and the economic life of the Colony became more healthily connected with the channels of world trade. Above all did the British administration begin to see that the Cape was not simply a port and a refreshment station. It was a colony, a very extensive colony, and in its problems aston- ishingly complex. The short-lived British administration gave signs that it recognized, as no trading company could recog- nize, that there was need for a greater resoluteness of govern- ment and for the submission to the authority of law of all the Colony's inhabitants and of all relations between them. Hot- tentots and slaves and frontier Kafirs—sooner or later their condition was bound to undergo the scrutiny, not so much of the new British régime, as of the new age which it had inaugurated. It was the new age of the Somersett case, of Clarkson and Wilberforce, of humanitarianism and Evangeli- canism, and of the discovery, which the Spaniards had already made in the sixteenth century, that savages had souls and were fit, through God's Word, to be civilized. Therein were the seeds of the revolution which the Cape was destined to undergo. It was not a revolution, therefore, bred within the Colony, rising from a sense of grievance and frustration. How- ever strong had come to be the resentment against economic restraints, and however great the impatience with a narrow and selfish government, Cape society was deeply conservative. Nothing stood higher than its desire to preserve the differences and distinctions which had grown up within it. It was ready for the economic, the legal, and the constitutional reforms of which the Company had been so sparing, yet its displeasure was certain to be quick and strong against whatever changed or challenged the relations of master and servant, of white and black. It was upon the Eastern Frontier that this truth was first made manifest.

There was rebellion on the frontier in 1795 before the British came. Attempts have been made to see a close con- nexion between the French Revolution and the rebellion of the burghers of the eastern districts of Graaff-Reinet and Swellendam. The connexion was very slight and cannot obscure the truth that the uprising was the result of what the burghers considered an unwarranted invasion upon their freedom to deal with their Kafir neighbours as they saw fit. Each year after van Plettenberg's bootless journey to the frontier the quarrels over cattle and land had grown more chronic and intractable. In 1793 the Company again issued one of its perpetual edicts *de coercendo intra fines imperio*. This time, however, it happened that the frontier possessed in Honoratus Maynier an official who was determined that the frontier should both hear the voice of the Government and obey the command of the law. That at this time the frontiersmen were far more sinned against than sinning did not make them more tolerant to a government that stood between them and revenge for the lives, the cattle, and the land that had been lost to the raiding Kafirs. In February 1795 South Africa saw its first rebellion and in June its first independent republics at Graaff-Reinet and Swellendam. Rebellion and secession, those constant spectres of the nineteenth century, had made their appearance.

When General Craig turned his attention to the frontier, he held a language that jarred upon the ears of the burghers even more than the pro-native sentiments of Maynier. Let no hand be raised against the Kafirs, and let no man seek to deprive them of their land. In Craig's words there was unconcealed an accusation that it was the burghers who had brought violence to the frontier. Craig, like so many of his successors, misunderstood what a tangled web had already been woven. To sound an appeal to quiet was to ignore dangerously the tension and resentment that years of conflict had bred. To such a frontier it was not enough to bring order. Knowledge and tact were necessary as well. In the years to come the law, which the frontier indubitably needed, was often applied ignorantly and tactlessly. Between 1795 and February 1803, when the Cape was restored to the Batavian Republic, there was no rest upon the frontier. Quelled by a show of military force, the rebellious burghers rose again in the first days of 1799. The uprising was not serious and subsided when a military force appeared upon the frontier. But it precipitated a Hottentot rebellion and brought the Kafirs into the Colony to draw for the first time the blood of British regulars. Now in this smoking triangle of insurgent burghers, Hottentots, and Kafirs it was clear why the Company's edicts and General Craig's admonitions had been without effect. There were Hottentots without land, unhappy in their relations with their employers; there were Kafirs, skilful cattle thieves and cunning enemies, yet bewildered by the turmoil in their rear, the unrest in their midst, and their inability to make any lasting impression on the forward line of European settlers; there were the Boers, angrily immersed in the irritations of fractious Hottentots and reiving Kafirs, baffled by the false doctrines of native rights declared by Maynier and Craig, and above all offended by the refusal of the administration to respect the self-rule which the neglect of the Company had enabled them to develop. For any government to impose its will upon such a frontier, whether the government were Dutch or English, was a task too arduous to be easily successful. Upon such a frontier vacillation, false economy, and ignorance were faults certain to be punished. And these faults were doomed to be characteristic of frontier policy.

In 1803 the Cape was returned to the Batavian Republic according to the terms of the Peace of Amiens. The brief rule of Governor Janssens and the Commissioner de Mist, both enlightened men, was not remarkable for its achievements. It could not be. After three short years the English were back again, for it was now clear to them that in their struggle with the French the Cape was of the very first importance. Yet the rule of Janssens and de Mist was noteworthy for what it attempted. To read Janssens and de Mist is to read the text of the next generation of South African history. Even more than their English predecessors did they recognize the narrow and fickle foundations of economic life, and how little they could be strengthened by even the most liberal edicts or pronouncements. The plain truth was that the Colony produced neither the quantity nor the quality to enable it to respond swiftly to a more liberal commercial policy. Indeed, just before the English left the Colony another wheat famine, the consequence of three wretched harvests, stared them in the face. The Colony had yet to find the products which would enable it to take a higher and more efficient place in the colonial world of the nineteenth century.

Janssens and de Mist recognized the inadequacy of institutions at Cape Town. Their reforms of the High Court were of capital importance. By making it independent of the executive and making a seat on the bench dependent upon thorough legal training they laid the basis for the especially brilliant role which the judiciary has played in South African history. But it was more important that their vision extended away from the sea to the hinterland. Their gaze revealed more clearly than before the greater colony that sprawled outside the settlement of wheat and wine farmers round Cape Town. Their reforms were embarrassed by their want of officials, of money, and of time. Implicit in the innovations which they undertook, however, was the understanding that the deepest need of the Colony was organization. To its sprawling character must be given compactness, to its dispersed people more coherence, and to its ramshackle social organizations greater discipline. Before he yielded to the English in 1806, Governor Janssens knew that it was hunger for land that had driven the Hottentots on the Eastern Frontier into rebellion, and that in their treatment of servants the farmers were much inclined to ignore the law and its magistrates, applying their own justice and inflicting their own punishment. On the frontier his conduct was both courageous and far-sighted. He gave locations to the Hottentots and sought to bring masters and labourers under the rule of the same law by requiring farmers to record their labour contracts. Aware that regulations avail nothing without agents to apply them, Governor Janssens turned his attention to the lax and infirm officialdom of the frontier. He had the wit to accept the framework of officials which he found on the frontier. Since the landdrosts and heemraden were frontiersmen themselves Governor Janssens strengthened the control of the central government over them, without weakening the bond that joined them to their fellows, and gave them a truly representative character. It was an admirable policy. Like so much that was undertaken at this time it suffered exceedingly from a lack of men and money. Like so many promising innovations it was never subjected to the test of time.

In Europe the Treaty of Amiens proved to be no more than a truce. When hostilities were resumed England understood more clearly than she had ten years before how to organize the defence of her interests. Of the vital need of controlling the Cape there was little serious question. In January 1806 the British fleet entered Table Bay. Within a fortnight the faint-hearted resistance of Governor Janssens's forces ended. The Cape became British again, and this time, as events proved, it remained British.

The history of the first thirty years of British rule has sometimes been described as a period of unimaginative and stumbling autocracy that bequeathed a legacy of grievance and misunderstanding to the future. Yet the history of the Cape before 1836 can also be told as the effort of a new and more conscientious government to give coherence to the vague and inchoate structure of the Colony, so that it might more adequately be fitted for the place which it was finding in the new Empire. For all its age the Cape Colony had the political immaturity and formlessness of colonies of very recent settlement. Although the Cape Colony had almost the age of Canada, it did not possess nearly as rich and well-founded a political structure. It was a period in which vital problems of greater immediate import than constitutional liberty were to the fore. The tide of political liberty which rose slowly enough in the Empire after 1815 rose still more slowly at the Cape, because there was a greater need to know what was to be the destiny of the slaves, who outnumbered the whites. What place were the Hottentots to have in the social order? In what manner were whites and blacks to live beside each other on the frontiers which European expansion had created? British rule was often arrogant and occasionally cruel. But a massive and sustained discipline it never was. It was always too poor, or, more accurately, too pennywise to be that. However confused the intentions of secretaries of state, however inadequate the resources of governors, it was nevertheless true that the British Government recognized that slaves without freedom, Hottentots without rights, and a Kafir frontier without peace were issues that had precedence over representative assemblies. It is a narrow view of the nineteenth century that only sees the white colonist, oppressed and misunderstood, fleeing into the wilderness to escape a tyrannous Imperial power. At the Cape the economic and social revolution of necessity preceded the political revolution.

The second British occupation actively stimulated the economic life of the Colony. Cape Town especially enjoyed the boom caused by expenditures for the maintenance of ships and troops. The new capital which was thus introduced, the sale of the cargoes of captured ships, and the removal of restraints upon trade created at once a brisker demand for the produce of the Colony and a swifter movement of trade. Between 1806 and 1820 there was a sixfold increase in imports and exports. Even the abolition of the slave trade in 1807 proved for a while to be a source of gain, for the value of slaves increased, and slave owners obtained much profit from the hire of their labour in busy times. Even the far-off frontier felt the influence of prosperity. Between 1806 and 1824 the number of cattle in the Colony more than trebled. To no section of the community, however, did the British connexion bring greater benefit than to the wine farmers. From 1806 to 1831 were the piping times of the Cape wine trade. French and Rhenish wines paid 4s. 7¼d. more per gallon in duty than Cape wines. In 1813 the difference in favour of Cape wine was increased to 6s. 8d. In 1825-6 the preference on Cape wine was sharply reduced to 4s. 10d. per gallon in the case of French wines, and 2s. 5d. in the case of Spanish and Portuguese wines. Till then, however, wine exports were greater than all other exports put together. In 1817 1,621 tuns of wine left the Cape, whereas in the eighteenth century the years had not been infrequent when not a single tun was exported.

The currency of the Cape Colony, like that of most other colonies at the beginning of the nineteenth century, gave the impression of a numismatical collection. There were gold mohurs and rupees from India, pagodas from Madras, johannas, doubloons, and dollars from Spain and her Empire, sequins from Venice, and guineas and shillings from England. Most of the currency was in paper Rix dollars, wretchedly printed on poor paper, which was easily defaced and outrageously counterfeited. Since the end of the War of American Independence the Cape Rix dollar had been unstable. In

1806 the British administration inherited an inflated and poorly secured currency. Because the plight of the Cape was the plight of many other British possessions as well, it was found impossible to halt the decline of the Cape's currency. The crisis of war, the chronically unfavourable balance of trade, the inevitable speculation in exchange—all these were causes for still further inflation. In 1808 the Loan Bank, founded in 1784 and now a bank of discount and deposit as well, was authorized to increase its capital by printing half a million Rix dollars. A further half-million was authorized for public works. Not all the effects of inflation were harmful. Cape Town received waterworks and several essential public buildings; its citizens built new houses. Upon their old houses they put new flat roofs with a plaster course and got rid of the picturesque thatched roofs which had caused so many disastrous fires in the eighteenth century. A plentiful supply of money stimulated business activity and helped the wine growers to put in nine million new vines between 1811 and 1819.

Fully as marked as these benefits were the pernicious effects of an unsecured debt and an inflated currency. From 1806 to 1825 the Rix dollar slowly collapsed. The Commissariat disposed of its bills in England to the highest bidders and paid its bills at the highest average rate of exchange. The pay of the garrison rose as the Rix dollar fell. The Governor's salary also rose from 60,000 Rix dollars to 136,250 Rix dollars. Upon the failing financial strength of the Colony was accordingly placed an increasing burden. Not all of the Colony's products responded as readily as wine to the stimulus of cheap money and the opening of the English market. Ten years after the British occupation all the exports of wool, hides, ostrich feathers, and grain were only half the value of wine exports. In 1826 the value of wool exports was only £545.

A colony that could sell little could buy little and was forced to depend upon adventitious aids to its prosperity. It remained subject to sudden fluctuations. British imports, for example, fell from 3 million Rix dollars in 1817 to 1½ million Rix dollars in 1820 and rose as sharply again to 3 million Rix dollars in 1824. From an early moment the Cape formed the habit of depending on British military expenditures. The reduction of the garrison from 4,000 to 2,500 men in 1821 was immediately and severely felt. Only slowly and painfully did the Cape find a more assured place in the economic system of the British Empire. It was a sign of the slow movement of Cape life that the old weights and measures of the eighteenth century were not assimilated to the English standard till 1848.[1] As late as 1849 the Cape of Good Hope was still listed in Treasury accounts not as a Settlement or Plantation, but as a Military and Maritime Station.

The Cape was fully exposed to the post-war depression by which England and the Continent were stricken. Hard times came in 1820 and stubbornly stayed. The wine trade had passed its peak, although it was not till 1831 that a drastic reduction in the preference against foreign wine began its real collapse. A series of crop failures bore witness to the exhaustion of the wheat lands. While government expenditure increased, revenues were depressed by the now chronic weakness of the Rix dollar, which had fallen from 4s. to 1s. 6d. In 1825 the British Government decided to put the Rix dollar out of its misery. The exchange of new money for old was part of a comprehensive reform of currency throughout the Empire, a reform as valuable and important in New South Wales, therefore, as at the Cape. The wiping out of the paper dollar at 1s. 6d. in British silver imposed much hardship upon many colonists. To others it was a boon, and in the main the elimination of the Rix dollar brought an end to unsettling speculation in exchange rates, wiped out debts which hard times had made onerous, and gave the Colony a sound system of coinage which was as valid in England as it was at the Cape. The reform of 1825 was an essential step in the assimilation of the Cape to the economic system of the Empire.

In 1820 the Cape Colony was a British possession, but with a population almost entirely Dutch. In that year came a group of 5,000 colonists, known as the 1820 settlers. The British Parliament had voted £50,000 to pay their passages in the hopes that their going might relieve the acute unem-

---

[1] Certain measures like the *morgen*, two and one-ninth acres, continued to be used.

ployment in Great Britain. The 1820 settlers were important because they were the first considerable body of men and women of British stock to arrive in South Africa. Their arrival raised the question whether they were the advance guard of still further large additions of British population who would profoundly modify the Dutch character of the Cape Colony. Implicit in their arrival was also the question whether Dutch blood and language might ultimately be absorbed by the British race and tongue. They were questions which were later explicitly raised in Lord Durham's famous report on Canada which considered the possibility of a similar fusion of French and English in Canada. Upon the answer to these questions depended much of South Africa's future, in which relations between English and Dutch played an impressive and sometimes a tragic role. Since the great majority of the Dutch population was rural, it was of much consequence that the British tried to settle the men of 1820 on the soil, in the district of Albany, confronting the Eastern Frontier Kafirs, and with an outlet to the sea at Algoa Bay.

The 1820 settlers said good-bye to depression in England and found depression to greet them at the Cape. From the beginning they had to struggle against all the adversities of the Eastern Frontier. Unfamiliar conditions made them poor farmers, and blight destroyed their wheat. In the middle of 1823 less than a third of the original 5,000 settlers remained on the land. Most of the rest had drifted to the towns. Thus was founded the significant distinction between the English in South Africa as mainly urban and the Dutch as mainly rural in character. The relative failure of the Albany settlement illustrated the especially great handicaps to settlement in South Africa. The Cape Colony was itself too poor to finance immigration on a large scale, and after 1820 the Home Government was reluctant to undertake further expensive ventures of the same kind. The great stream of immigration, therefore, that went to Canada and Australia passed South Africa by. Upon Dutch and not English pioneers fell the responsibility of opening the interior of South Africa and determining its character. However great the influence of English customs and institutions, the history of the Albany settlement and of subsequent British immigration made it clear that 150 years of Company rule had set upon the Cape Colony and ultimately upon all South Africa an indelibly Dutch stamp.

As great as the confusion which the British administration found in the Cape's currency was the disorder in its land system. The loan-farm system of the eighteenth century had given the farmer a maximum of freedom and the Government a minimum of authority. So limited had become the power of government that many of the frontiersmen had settled upon land without ever troubling to register their farms or pay the annual quit-rent of 24 Rix dollars. It was a system which the British administration found objectionable on administrative grounds, because it largely ignored the authority of government to regulate the conditions of settlement. It was objectionable on legal grounds because the farmer had no unchallengeable right to sell, subdivide, or bequeath the land. All he owned was the 'opstal' or buildings upon the land. The Government was entitled to resume possession of a loan farm at a year's notice. It was objectionable on economic grounds because the farmer, having no security of tenure, had no inducement to undertake expensive improvements on his land. The loan system encouraged poor farming and restless improvident habits. It was objectionable on financial grounds. All loan farms, regardless of size, location, or quality paid a uniform rental which the collapse of the Rix dollar had caused to fall from £3 to £1. 16s. per year. It was clear that the land was contributing an exceptionally small fraction to the revenue.

In 1813 Governor Sir John Cradock issued a proclamation permitting loan places to be converted to permanent quit-rent tenure. What was regarded in Canada at the time as an archaic device which dragged upon the progress of the community was an important reform in South Africa. The proclamation was an effort to apply to the Cape Colony something of the orderliness of land-holding which was normal in England and its other colonies of settlement. It was also, however, an effort to compel land, the Colony's chief resource, to make a larger contribution to the Colony's revenues. Com-

pared with the land system in New South Wales or Canada
Sir John Cradock's reforms were mild. The administration
was aware that nothing was so likely to defeat its purposes as
a régime of high taxation. The quit-rent was to vary with the
quality and the situation of the land and was not to exceed
250 Rix dollars per year. Conversions were not compulsory
but optional. That not a single conversion was made during
the first year was some indication of the distaste with which
the population regarded the new land system. Thereafter
conversions proceeded slowly in the agricultural and richer
western districts; in the rest of the Colony they proceeded
with exceeding slowness. It was clear that the pastoral farmers were offended by this effort to alter a land system which
had pleased them very well. They were unimpressed by the
privileges and benefits promised in the preamble to the proclamation. The legal weaknesses of the loan-farm system or
the uncertainty of boundaries had never bothered them. Indeed, the very flaws which the British Government sought to
correct were the source of the astonishing freedom with which
they had moved on to the land. Resistance to direct taxation,
especially upon the land, and hostility to any restraints upon
their freedom to appropriate a farm for each man had become deeply ingrained traits of the Boer character. Much of
the land was poor. Over a large part of the interior it was
rich land that could keep an ox on 5 acres; 12 acres for an
ox was more usual. The land reforms pressed upon a population that was poor in all but its herds. Because land and cattle
were of the very stuff of their being, the Boers grew ever more
sullen at the efforts of the administration to subject them and
their land to a stricter control. Thus early was the British
Government faced with the ever present dilemma of making
the land bear its due share of taxation. Two concepts of
government clashed. The one was brisk and enterprising;
the other was diffuse and unambitious. In a way that was
vague even in their own minds, for they were altogether lacking in apologists, the farmers conceived of a State that should
intervene very little in the affairs of their lives and that should
be especially reluctant to influence the manner in which they
acquired their property or the manner in which they used it.

Their ideal State was a racial fellowship of large pastoral land-holders with laws that aided them to acquire property easily when they did not have it and to retain it easily when they had acquired it. With such a concept Ireton or Locke in the seventeenth century were more familiar than British colonial governors in the generation of Gibbon Wakefield.

Gone was the Company's neglect of the frontier. The rule of law and the orderliness of a modern government invaded the isolation of the frontier. The establishment in 1811 of a Circuit Court, and the erection in 1819 of eight new magistracies brought the law and its agents even more emphatically into the midst of the frontier. In 1827 the famous Charter of Justice took still further the process of modernizing the Cape's institutions. It put an end to judges who knew no law and could be made the tools of a self-willed governor. The governor himself was no longer the final court of appeal. Instead a competent bench and an independent judiciary were a guarantee that the military and autocratic nature of the Cape Government would also be tempered by the rule of law. In the judicial system of the inland regions the charter also made telling changes. It abolished the old courts of landdrosts and heemraden, substituting for them civil commissioners and magistrates. Had the new officials been well paid, and had their numbers been great enough for the duties of administering such a wide land, it is conceivable that the history of the Cape frontier might have been different. But now in 1827, as so often afterwards, the British Government tried to reconcile a sincere desire for excellent reforms with a great unwillingness to pay the price in money and well-chosen men. The Colony itself was far too poor to bear the burden of a sufficiently paid and sufficiently numerous magistracy. To the familiar and popular court of landdrosts and heemraden the new magistracy was not in every way clearly superior. It had the great defect that it was not representative of the burghers at a moment when a rising tide of grievance would have made a link between the Government and the frontier of the greatest value.

It was more than the law and its agents that came into the lives of the burghers. The spirit of a new age came to perplex the conservative mind of the Colony as well. Even had the English not taken the Cape the new forces of European intellectual and religious life, of humanitarianism and missionary enterprise, would still have come to South Africa. The coming of the English, however, opened the door peculiarly wide to the ideas and the men of the Emancipation movement, the London Missionary Society, and all the others whose purpose it was to improve the lot of slaves, Hottentots, and Kafirs. Their coming coincided with long-deferred changes. In the baggage of English army officers and in the libraries of missionaries came views to which Enlightenment and Romanticism, Wesleyanism and the Evangelical Revival, each contributed its share. The pressure of these views was so great, and the ardour of their exponents so intense, that Cape society had to endure, in the short space of about twenty-five years, sweeping changes in its relations with slaves, Hottentot servants, and Kafir neighbours. To a slow-moving and Tory society they were radical changes, shocking to men's minds and disturbing to the habits of their life. To emancipate the slaves, to establish political equality between the Hottentot and his master, and to compel the frontier to submit to the control of government was to compress much change into little time. All the problems which had been neglected during the life of the Company were now incontinently thrust forward for settlement.

The impact of European city-bred liberalism upon Cape rural conservatism was severe. It was made the more severe because it entered South Africa through religion. The chief exponents of the liberal ideas which opposed privileges based on tradition or creed or race were missionaries. They had a sense of urgency and the exhilaration which came to men who work for the Gospel's sake. They were too eager to reach their ends to await the slower change which time would have operated in the mental climate of the colonists, and hurried to impose from without changes for which the Colony was not altogether prepared within. On that account they were quick to demand that the powers of government be peremptorily used to shape society as they wished to see it. A government that was already engaged in extending its authority over the Colony bore still more heavily upon the lives of the people because of the influence and prestige of the missionaries. The success of liberal missionary enterprise was therefore seriously prejudiced by the lasting resentment which was provoked in the minds of the population, for the Boers took with them wherever they went a memory of wrongs roughly done. The triumphs of liberalism were not, therefore, without their real failures.

The spear-head of the missionary and philanthropic attack upon the debased status of the Cape's servile population was Dr. John Philip of the London Missionary Society. In the history of South Africa his name is still the stuff of contention. Coming to the Cape in 1819 he quickly made its problems his own concern. He had the Scot's quality of quickly apprehending a new country. He was a traveller before Livingstone, and some of his thought on Imperial matters was repeated fifty years later by Cecil Rhodes. Men in high places in England soon came to know his name and listen to his views. Wilberforce, Lushington, and Thomas Fowell Buxton were amongst his correspondents. Although these men and their circle were engaged in the last stages of their great battle against slavery, they were sensitive to his appeal on behalf of the Cape's Hottentots.

The philanthropic challenge to the Colony's social habits synchronized with a serious crisis in the labour market. A general improvement in the productive capacity of the Colony caused a demand for more labour. Millions of new vines were planted in the western districts, and greater herds of cattle were acquired in the eastern districts just when the abolition of the slave trade ended the flow of new labour. Between the abolition of the slave trade in 1807 and of slavery itself in 1834 a growing number of restrictions in favour of the slaves impeded the efficient use of the existing supply of labour. Quite naturally the colonists turned to the Hottentot population for help. By this time the term Hottentot was a misnomer, for their tribal cohesion had long since dissolved with the purity of their race. In the veins of the Cape coloured folk, not less than 30,000 in number, ran the blood of Hottentots, Malays, negro slaves, and white men. In strict law they were not slaves, and yet because of their rightless and inferior place in society the two groups of slaves and coloured folk were very close to one another. After slavery was abolished in 1834 the two groups grew together easily and rapidly. The destiny of slaves and Hottentots was therefore the same. The evidence is also clear that a very large proportion of the non-slave population was already in the service of the white population. As early as the first British occupation their plight had been noticed. They were outside the protection of the law and the conditions of their service were at the mercy of their employers. Since the landdrosts were themselves farmers and employers of labour their authority was normally used in favour of the farmers. Until 1809 very little was done to submit the relations between master and servant to a stricter supervision. Governor Caledon's Code of 1809 was the first serious effort to bring the coloured population within the rule of law. This code has been oppositely interpreted as the Magna Charta of the coloured population, and as an instrument that thrust them still farther under the dominion of the labour-hungry farmers. It is true that very little was done in 1809 to relieve their immediate condition. Indeed the code went far to meet the demand of the colonists that vagrancy be checked and that all Hottentots be compelled to take service. It is certain that the hold of the farmers over the coloured population was actually strengthened. But it meant much that the Hottentots were brought inside the law, however heartless that law might still be. By providing for the registration of labour contracts and the regular payment of wages, by limiting contracts to a year and forbidding colonists to force their labourers to work for additional periods because of debt, the Caledon Code brought the relations between master and servant within the ordinary processes of law. The law, however, did not immediately bestir itself in their behalf. Until the days of Dr. Philip and the Charter of Justice of 1827 the law was applied by landdrosts. They were naturally inclined to arrest the Hottentot as a vagabond and compel him to take service or achieve the same result by refusing him the pass or certificate without which he could not move from one district to another. That a law which seriously depressed the condition of the coloured population none the less contained the promise of better things was seen in the notorious episode in 1812 known as the Black Circuit.

The Circuit Court, freshly created in 1811, announced a new era by making itself accessible to the Hottentot as well as the European population. Of the cases promptly brought against European masters many were malicious, collusive, and false. Certain missionaries undoubtedly overreached themselves in trying to strike a blow for their protégés. But other accusations were proven. The sentences which the court pronounced against white masters shook the Colony with indignation. The action of the court was a declaration that the protection of the law extended to the servant as well as the master. The social revolution had begun. It was the achievement of Dr. John Philip and the philanthropic movement to carry it significantly farther.

After he had been only two years in the Colony, Philip boldly resolved to demand the amendment of the entire legal and civil status of the coloured population, instead of seeking to correct individual acts of oppression or injustice. When Philip secured the interest of James Stephen, the Permanent Under-Secretary in the Colonial Office, of William Huskisson and Sir George Murray, successively Secretaries of State for the Colonies, his case was won.

Ordinance 50 of 1828 is a landmark in South African social history. Under its provisions vagrancy was no more an offence, and coloured folk were free to move without passes. Gone at a blow were therefore the two instruments which had been used to drive the Hottentots into the service of the Europeans. Gone, too, was any restriction upon the purchase of land by the Cape's men of colour. Above all they were free to offer or withhold their labour and therefore to improve their condition through their right to abandon bad masters and cling to good ones. The immoral elements amongst them were also free, naturally, to steal and cheat and trespass. Of the conduct of these latter men the Colony was immediately loud with complaints.

The great resentment of the colonists was the natural response of a community which saw itself stricken in its economic privileges and its social prestige. Robespierre's utterance: 'Perish the colonies rather than a principle', seemed to have been cynically applied to them. The philanthropic opponents of their institutions did not appreciate the extent to which slavery and the bondage of the coloured population were the pillars upon which white society had held itself aloft. They did not understand that in a land that was as poor as the Cape Colony economic and social distinctions were more important and sharply drawn than in a land that was richer and more thriving. Their egalitarian sentiment certainly made them blind, if not indifferent, to the effects of their success upon the mind of a people in whom social habits and religious convictions were so fused that to attack the one was to offend the other. The shock of Ordinance 50 was the greater because it was passed on the eve of slave emancipation. Posterity rightly acclaimed Ordinance 50 as a liberal and constructive measure, destined to secure for an important group of the population a place of dignity and worth. Its passage was, nevertheless, a rude disturbance of an already unsettled labour market. For that reason it was a measure which, for a while at least, impeded closer settlement and the more intensive economic life at which British land policy aimed. It very clearly stimulated the old *trekgeest*, the spirit of the open veld, of greener grass beyond the horizon, of a land where only those should be free who were free by God's design.

A determined effort was made to undo Ordinance 50. Public opinion clamoured for a Vagrant Ordinance that would make the coloured population once again amenable to the labour needs of the farmers. In 1834, the year of slave emancipation, the Legislative Council passed a Draft Vagrancy Law, designed to surrender the Hottentots to their former disabilities. But Philip and his following defended their victory. Downing Street had not yet grown weary of South African native problems, and the ordinance was disallowed.

In no other British colony of settlement were the difficulties of racial contact so bewildering. The problems of Indians in Canada, of aborigines in Australia and Maoris in New Zealand, together could not match the complexities of slaves, Hottentots, and Kafirs. And of South Africa's racial problems the greatest by far was over 800 miles from Cape Town on the Eastern Frontier. Instead of 30,000 Hottentots, who already spoke the language of their Dutch masters, there was a great native population on the frontier and beyond, which numbered millions. The contact between these and the Europeans is the dominant theme of all South African history.

In the writing of South African history it was long customary to believe that the chronic conflict of the Kafir frontier was the result of the spontaneous hostility of a savage and treacherous people to the presence of a superior race. Actually the conflict of black and white was fed more by their similarities than by their differences. The opposing lines of settlement struggled for the control of the same natural resources of water, grass, and soil. It was not a romantic frontier like the American West or heroic like the North-West Frontier of India. Legend has denied the Pondos, for example, a place beside the Pawnees or the Pathans. The stuff of legend is not easily found in a process which turned Ama-Xosa, Zulus, or Basuto into farm labourers, kitchen servants, or messengers.

The frontier to which the British administration turned its attention suffered from too little government and too poor officials. The Company had never even dreamed of directly governing the frontier Kafirs. Upon the colonists themselves had fallen much of the responsibility of managing their relations with their Kafir neighbours. For want of regular troops the frontier had developed in the burgher commando its own mounted field force—the famous sharpshooters of South African history. A commando, it had already been observed in the latter days of the Company, had the same marauding habits as a Celtic clan in the days of William III, and its usages of war were much the same as had aroused Dundee to wrath in 1689. Now, however, the frontier saw red coats and pipe-clay. It saw more officials, too, and a more energetic administration. But the chief agents of British policy were British regiments. It was a policy that presupposed that the chief need of the frontier was peace and that peace could be maintained by force of arms. In 1812, after the chronic tension had flared up into an outbreak, Governor Cradock made the first of a series of attempts to keep whites and blacks apart by driving the Kafirs across the Fish River and building block-houses to check their return. In 1819, after the blockhouses had failed to keep white and black apart, a neutral belt was created between the Fish and the Keiskama Rivers. A neutral belt sounded well enough in dispatches to England. It was a tantalizing device, however, which increased the tension of the colonists and the tribesmen. Empty land was too great a temptation for the land-hungry frontier, and no interdict could save it from encroachment. Once encroachment began, it resulted in a confused and overlapping settlement that made all the frontier clamorous with charges and countercharges of trespass and cattle lifting.

To a few far-sighted men it had become clear that the troubles upon the frontier were not the cattle stealing, of which the farmers complained so bitterly, nor even the periodic out-breaks which went by the name of Kafir Wars. The frontier was the stage where, more spectacularly than elsewhere, was taking place the great revolution of South African history. Its military annals hide the story of trade and labour, of measles and typhus, of Sheffield hoes and greasy cotton clothes, of crop shortages and unbalanced diets, of cattle disease and the collapse of tribal discipline, which were the signs that these men of opposite race were doing more than quarrelling with each other. Even though they did not know it, they were engaged in the formation of a new society and the establish-ment of new economic and social bonds. Had miscegenation taken place as readily as it had in the older western districts, the nature of these changes would have been more obvious. As the Europeans advanced, they did not succeed in driving the Kafirs back into their hinterland. The Kafirs were crowded into areas which steadily grew less able to maintain them, or lived as squatters and labourers upon the land that had fallen to the Europeans. This was the pattern of every subsequent frontier of contact between Europeans and natives.

Colonists and even officials spoke of great unpeopled spaces behind the frontier tribes into which the natives could easily withdraw. The evidence which is available indicates that the Eastern Frontier suffered severe pressure from both front and rear. In the twenties a prolonged crisis shook the entire Bantu world. From the interior waves of unrest tossed up against the foremost tribes. The causes of these events can never be adequately investigated. The history of savage tribes, like the history of the *Völkerwanderung*, must always suffer from a lack of records. A common explanation of the confusion of Bantu life at this time was the sudden emergence of highly disciplined warrior tribes—Zulus, Matabele, and Mantatees—who carried death and destruction far and wide. A knowledge of the structure and habits of Bantu life suggests that these fighting tribes were an effect and not a cause. It is clear that throughout a large part of South Africa there had developed an intense competition between the tribes for grazing and sowing land and, in the vast arid regions, for the 'eyes' of land where springs provided an adequate supply of water. A universal competition for land, grass, and water was a fact of South African Bantu life before ever the colonists had passed beyond its fringes. Tribes like the Zulus under Chaka, and their offspring the Matabele under Moselekatze, found refuge in military organization. As is the way of military powers born in times of depression and unrest, they used their discipline to tyrannize and plunder their neighbours. Amongst the causes of this singular crisis that smashed tribes, scattered others, and dashed the fragments into new combinations, the halting of the Bantu vanguard on the Eastern Frontier probably had much influence. Into the midst of the embattled and packed frontier tribes hurtled splintered groups of Tembus, Bacas, and Fingos, who lodged themselves in the mass of the population, increasing their discomfort and the sum total of their quarrelsomeness.

By 1834 the Colonial Office had begun to realize the ineffectiveness of muskets and pipeclay and the need for an active and competent civil administration to govern the frontier. Governor Sir Benjamin D'Urban, who was charged with devising a new frontier system, was sympathetic to the demand of philanthropic sentiment for a better administration. But before he could apply a single reform disaster descended upon the frontier. The restlessness of the tribes and the disgruntlement of the colonists were tortured by a severe drought which set the Kafirs to pillaging and the colonists to reprisals in

December 1834. When the Governor arrived the sight of charred houses and ruined farmers turned his anger against the Kafirs. He concluded that they were savages who only understood force and punishment. Troops and commandos struck shrewdly at the economic resources of the Kafirs. Though official reports told of deeds of soldierly daring, the real warfare was directed against the cattle and food supply of the Kafirs. Their fields were burned, their corn destroyed, and their cattle driven off. Most Kafir wars throughout the century were very much like a Smithfield cattle driving. Nothing was more calculated to bring them to their senses and, when the war was over, to leave them impoverished.

The peace which Sir Benjamin D'Urban made was after the heart of the colonists. All land between the Keiskama and the Kei Rivers was annexed. In this new Province of Queen Adelaide the colonists and their sons would at long last find the farms which in recent years had been growing uncomfortably scarce. Because the Governor found that it was humanly impossible to expel all the natives, his plan meant that black and white settlement would be even more interspersed than before. Sir Benjamin D'Urban did speak of bringing law, industry, and civilization to the new subjects of the Crown. He appointed Resident Agents to the principal tribes. It was a valuable first step towards bringing the tribes under the tutelage of competent officials. But before the Governor could give effect to his peace settlement it was destroyed by the displeasure of the Colonial Office. Upon the Colonial Secretary, Lord Glenelg, the protestation of Dr. Philip against the causes and the conduct of the war had a strong influence. He saw the harsh régime of land hunger and reprisals. He failed to see the great losses which the colonists had endured. His command that the Province of Queen Adelaide be restored to the independent tribes was a gesture of the sympathy of His Majesty's Government towards the native, and a reprimand to the Governor and the men of the frontier. As an act of practical policy it had the value of leaving the natives in entire possession of their land. Yet by affecting to treat the tribes as sovereign and independent societies outside the pale of British rule it maintained a dangerous fiction and staved off the inevitable day when the pretence of a dividing line between black and white would have to yield to the truth that the natives were as much a direct responsibility of government as the colonists themselves.

By the pretence of recognizing the independence of the tribes Glenelg tried to avoid the expense of administering the frontier. The British Government shrank before the expense and labour of establishing an elaborate frontier system in a colony so poor as the Cape. With a revenue no more in 1830 than it had been in 1815 the Cape was incapable, without Imperial aid, of maintaining the officials necessary to administer effectively a frontier so anxious, an area so extensive, and a population so scattered. In spite of severe economies the expenditure after 1823 had been constantly in excess of revenue. Glenelg, like so many secretaries of state after him, engaged in the vain and dangerous search of the British Government for policies that should in the first place be economical. The generation between Waterloo and the Indian Mutiny had not yet learned that in the end magistrates were cheaper than soldiers and that the secret of ruling inferior peoples was not found in pipeclay and bayonets, but by the more prosaic means of paying officials to supervise, not their periodic outbursts of anger, but the daily acts of their lives. British policy in South Africa was doomed to advance through disasters. Glenelg's decision in 1836 was a decision to allow the sores of the frontier to fester for another season till another outbreak.

The year of the abandonment of the Province of Queen Adelaide saw the beginning of the famous movement of population known as the Great Trek. Though tradition has placed the two events in an immediate relationship of cause and effect, the forces behind the spectacular expansion of the Cape's population were more diverse. In South African history the Great Trek has been given epic proportions, and a hundred years after its occurrence it had become the focus of a powerful patriotic sentiment. Like the Fathers of the American Constitution, the Voortrekker leaders came to be considered the founders of modern South Africa. Every South

African schoolboy knows their many grievances. As the Voor-trekkers were given high places in South Africa's Hall of Fame, the Great Trek, as befitted a great occurrence, became rich in grievances. Even so did Martin Luther in his later years become ever more resourceful in discovering causes of the Protestant defection from Rome. The wise student will remember this and know that, however genuine were some of the grievances of the Trekkers, the Great Trek is not simply the story of a people, oppressed and misunderstood, fleeing into the wilderness to escape from a tyrannous imperial power.

In one sense the Great Trek was but the acceleration on a large scale of the movement of expansion that had been going on for a century. Since the end of the eighteenth century an important section of the population had been checked in its freedom of movement by the opposing native tribes. Had the natives not been there, European settlement would have fol-lowed the belt of greater rainfall (Map I). But since the natives were there, European settlement had two alternatives. The first alternative was to carry out a frontal attack upon the tribes in an effort to thrust through the broad coastal belt in the direction of Natal. Between the sea on the one side and the mountains on the other the native tribes had a compact-ness that made their extrusion a difficult task. It would also have been a most hazardous task. Further advance through this region of relatively dense native settlement would have left the flank of the colonists exposed to the great bastion of Basutoland's tumbled mountains. The second alternative was to cut inland past the edge of native settlement. On the inland side away from the sea were the rich arable lands which nourished the powerful Basuto tribes. Here they were more vulnerable. When the British Government helped the natives resist the frontal advance of the colonists by disallowing the annexation of land won in the war of 1835, the colonists adopted their second alternative. Tactically the Great Trek represented a decision to give up the frontal attack and under-take an outflanking movement. When fully carried out it was a manœuvre that carried the colonists beyond the range of British influence and enabled them to strike at the vital resources of the natives at numerous points.

The trek movement was therefore a natural movement with an instinctive strategy of its own. It was stimulated by the knowledge that plenty of good land lay beyond the official boundary. But it was pricked also by a deep sense of grievance. In ways both great and small very many of the innovations of the British Government had been offensive to the Dutch population. The western districts had suffered most from the depreciation of the Rix dollar and the emancipation of slaves. Both eastern and western districts had resented the influence of Ordinance 50 upon Hottentot labour. There were few sections that did not feel that the effort of the British Government to apply the same law to all classes of the population cruelly upset the proper relationship between white and black, between master and servant. In the mouths of the Trekkers no grievance was more bitter than the refusal of the British Government to maintain 'proper relations between master and servant'. That was why the Trekkers and their descendants could never forget the Black Circuit of 1812, and why the name of Dr. John Philip stank for ever more in their nostrils. It followed from the habits of their lives that land, or rather their great hunger for land, provided their acutest grievance. Hitherto land had been a natural benefit, rather like the rain which fell upon it. It was open to all with very little restriction. The endeavours of the British Government to regulate land settlement and to define its economic responsibilities made it harder to obtain land and more expensive to hold it. When Governor Cradock introduced his land reforms in 1813 there were already 3,000 applications for land grants. In the same year that the British Government forbade all settlement outside the Nineteen Counties in New South Wales, an ordinance commanded the Boers not to pass beyond the official limits of the Colony. In 1832 the predicament of the farmers was made still worse by the announcement that grants of free land could be made no more. Henceforth new land was to be sold at auction. The announcement was not carried into effect, yet the shadow of Gibbon Wakefield, systematic colonization, and the sufficient price, fell across an aggrieved frontier. The true Voortrekker hated a boundary. When the British Government insisted on fixed boundaries for the Colony and for the farms within it, something was taken from him. It was a sense of spaciousness that was an intimate ingredient of his sentiment of freedom. When the frontiersmen heard Lord Glenelg's decision that, despite their real sufferings, they could carve no farms out of Kafirland, their cup ran over. The drought that burned on the frontier made their grievances seem more unbearable. So many precious beasts they had lost to theft and thirst. Like the congregation of the children of Israel they thirsted for water and murmured against those that governed them. It was best surely to betake themselves across the border where there were water and free land and no British Government to disallow Vagrancy Laws, and where white men could not be haled to court to answer the complaints of their servants.

The implicit aim of British policy had not been to drive the farmers from their land, but to attach them more firmly to it. The tendency of this policy had been to make land scarcer and more valuable; economically this was an essential preliminary to a more productive use of the land. The signs before 1836 were very clear that the frontier was being drawn into brisker commercial relations with the outer world. Before the Kafir War of 1835 the number of cattle, and especially of wool-bearing sheep, had steeply increased. At long last the Cape was discovering that its true wealth was its pastoral wealth.

III

NEW FRONTIERS FOR OLD

'Behold, how great a matter a little fire kindleth!' *James* iii. 5.

IT is in its effects that the essential causes of the Great Trek may be discovered. It burst the bonds which the Dutch and British Governments had endeavoured to place on territorial expansion and gave the Trekkers access to the immense acreages of the interior for which frustration had whetted their appetites. It was the defeat of the policy of more intensive settlement. The practice which required the area of an entire Canadian township for the settlement of ten families was extended throughout all of South Africa. It made for ever impossible the segregation of the white and black races in separate areas of settlement. It immensely complicated the problems of controlling their relationships. By taking the Boers beyond the reach of British law, the Great Trek enabled them to establish 'proper' relations with the native population.

The Great Trek indissolubly linked the future of all South Africa with the Boer race. Within fourteen years a thin layer of Dutch settlement had spread over the most desirable parts of the interior, leaving no considerable areas vacant which might, like Ontario, have become a region of almost exclusive British settlement. The Trekkers did not merely escape from the ordinances and laws of the Cape Colony. A large and determined part of the population moved beyond range of the modifying influences of the thought and swiftly changing mental climate of the mother colony. For two generations more the children and grandchildren of the Voortrekkers continued to receive the education of the farm, the veld, and the Boer home. Deep into the nineteenth century they took the non-literary and non-industrial habits of the eighteenth century. Thus were fixed those attitudes and habits of mind which later returned from exile profoundly to influence all South Africa.

The individual trek was usually a company of neighbours, from the same district in the old Colony, under leaders like Piet Retief or Andries Pretorius, who had their confidence.

Each trek was an organized group of land-seekers, and the whole trek movement was like a great land association designed to give its members the freest access to the land resources of the interior. The first rudimentary forms of government set up by the Trekkers were instruments which put a seal of legality upon the acquisitions of their subjects. Even the better organized and more orderly republics which finally emerged from the confusion of the early years were land-owning States which had few obligations higher than the encouragement and protection of their burghers in their rights to land. Thought and life and land were inseparably involved in the Boer mind. From the beginning, therefore, systematic settlement of the interior was out of the question. The story of republican land policy is a record of arbitrary selection and haphazard settlement. From the beginning, too, the power of government was limited by the refusal of the burghers to accept any but the lightest restrictions or burdens upon their property. The inability, for example, of the republican governments to tax significantly the land of their subjects was not the only explanation of their chronic financial weakness. Yet few explanations are more important. Not till 1876 did the Free State impose a land tax of 2s. per 100 morgen.

Between the exodus of the Boers and other colonizing movements in the nineteenth century similarities are easily discerned. The thrust of Australian sheepmen into the interior grasslands, the land rushes of the American West, the Old Testament character of the Mormon treks—these are full of reminders of the Great Trek. In all unsettled regions there was the same eagerness for cheap or free land, the same impatience of the demands and delays of government, whether in Washington or Downing Street, Sydney or Cape Town. Between the Boer and the Australian squatter certain resemblances are very marked. Both left the region of settled government in search of the wide ranges they loved, and both flouted the authority of their government in doing so. Both made wool the greatest staple of the country, making commerce brisker, creating new opportunities, and increasing the income of government. In the figures of wool exports from the Cape ports there is a meaningful record of economic growth. 144,000 lb. of wool were exported in 1834; 491,000 lb. in 1838; 1,060,000 lb. in 1841; and 5,447,000 lb. in 1851.[1] But more pronounced than these similarities were the striking contrasts which make the Great Trek a movement unique in the history of colonization. The Australian sheep-farmers emigrated from the England of the Industrial Revolution; their attention and that of their sons remained focused on England. In their new land they strove to relate their activities to the great industrial and commercial metropolis to which their essential loyalty never wavered. The roar of shuttling looms was never out of their ears, nor were the needs of great industrial towns for food and raw materials out of their minds. The forces that built the great factories of the Midlands impelled them, too. Macarthur, the first breeder of fine sheep, belonged to the same tradition as Jethro Tull and even James Watt and Stephenson. It was the same ingenuity and enterprise which later invented the Australian stump-jumping plough and the binder, and all the other innovations by which an active and profit-minded society fights and overcomes the obstacles in its path. Even more clearly can these impulses be discerned in the careers of the pioneer communities of Canada and the United States. New means of conveying men and goods, new techniques of exploiting the land, new markets provided the incentive to fell forests and turn the prairie sod.

In South Africa the early movement of population did not try consciously and purposefully to adapt itself to the new age and to derive profit from the new populations that needed food and the machines that craved raw materials. The Boers moved inland not to found a new society and to win new wealth. Their society was rebellious, but it was not revolutionary. Fundamental innovations in the use of land or in social practices were not easily made in their minds. They trekked in spite of the Industrial Revolution, moving away before it reached them. In one sense the Great Trek was the eighteenth century fleeing before its more material, more active, and better organized successor. Although the emi-

[1] Of this amount the great bulk still came from the old settled colony.

grant farmers opened the hinterland and made a great contribution to the development and enrichment of later South
Africa, theirs was not the aggressive movement of a people
braving the wilderness for the profit that it would bring their
purses, or the education that it would give their children.
The energy and determination of the early settlers were not
conspicuously used in wresting from the soil all the fruits that
it would yield. Against the diseases that ravaged their flocks,
the drought that withered their crops, they opposed the habits
and outlook of an earlier and more ignorant generation.
Though they were skilled in the ways of the veld, good horsemen and superb marksmen, expert at breaking in an ox or a
horse, able to tan leather, make bricks, and work in wood and
stone, they developed in a far lesser degree than their Australian or Canadian contemporaries the inventive faculty to
overcome the physical and material obstacles of their environment. Even in the area which became the Orange Free State,
where sheep-farming was a success, the methods employed
were crude. In the Transvaal wool was for a long time an in-
cidental product, grown under conditions that placed Transvaal wool amongst the lowest grades on the wool markets of
England.

In understanding the genesis of modern South African
society it is of the greatest importance to know that the land
beyond the Cape's borders was not the open land which lay
before the Australian squatter. It was already an area of
settlement, of settlement by a great Bantu population. Much
of the energy and determination of the Boers was used more
against the natives than against Nature. It is here that lies
the true story of South African settlement in this period. Out
of those raw materials of sun and grass, of earth and the riches
beneath it, of black man and white man, what new environment and what new community would be built?

To the settlement of the open grassland of the interior there
were few great natural obstacles. On the other hand, the
military power of the Matabele under Moselekatze, and the
Zulus under Dingaan, held the key to the interior, the one to
the High Veld, the other to the fertile valleys of Natal. In
this environment the Boers were as much at home as the

natives themselves. Their days on the Cape frontier and their experiences as hunters of wild game had made them shrewd Kafir fighters. When drawn in a circle or laager, their ox-wagons were a fort against the onset of the fiercest impis. Their guns gave them a range and their horses a mobility against which the tribesmen could only prevail in a surprise attack. Their ox-wagons and their commandos were, in the phrase of Cromwell, 'the chariots and horsemen of Israel'., The Trek endured its disasters and proved its heroism by shedding its blood. Stabbing suddenly by night, the assagai spared woman nor child. The name of the village of Weenen or Weeping in Natal bears witness to one of several grievous massacres. But not even the power of Matabele and Zulu impis, the scourge of all the High Veld and Natal, could prevail against the Boers. A commando attacked the kraal of Moselekatze at Mosega in January 1837, and in December of the same year a small Boer force, less than a squadron of dragoons, routed the Matabele so thoroughly that they withdrew to the present land of Southern Rhodesia and troubled the Trekkers no more. The High Veld was henceforth theirs, and they could speak, as the Puritans had spoken, of 'the fatness of God's mercies'. In the beginning of 1838 a thousand wagons were drawn together on the upper Tugela River, gazing upon a land richer in water and grass than the Trekkers had hitherto known. Before the year was out, this land of Natal was theirs too. To make it theirs they paid a heavy price. Their leader, Piet Retief, and a hundred men were treacherously slain while trying to negotiate a cession of land from Dingaan. Altogether nearly 400 lives were lost before a Boer commando, at the expense of three men wounded, slew 3,000 Zulus at the battle of Blood River on 16 December 1838. 'God made them as stubble to our sword.'

In the space of two years the Trekkers had flowed round the edge of the great body of native tribes and, by their seizure of Natal, had split in two the long coastal line of native settlement. Strategically it was a position of great effectiveness. The Boers were in the rear of the Eastern Frontier. Their flank curved back in the direction of the old Colony, hemming the rich Basuto lands at the base of the Maluti

Mountains. They held the Bantu and the tribes of Kafirland as in a pair of pincers. They had enormously extended the frontier between European and natives, and of this frontier the greater part was beyond British control.

In Canada and in Australia it was assumed that British settlement on the coast established an implicit British right to the hinterland. The 'untrodden wilderness' into which the sheepmen pressed, in defiance of scowling secretaries of state, was as much the Queen's territory as the 'demesne of Hampton Court'. To the South African interior the British Government did not apply the doctrine of the systematic colonizers like Gibbon Wakefield that all colonial land was held by the Crown in trusteeship for present and future inhabitants of the Empire. The British Government assumed that all territory beyond the official limits of the Cape Colony was as independent of the Crown as were the tribes themselves. It was therefore unable to follow the expansive movement of the farmers, automatically extending the Crown's jurisdiction to each addition of territory. For seven years the British attitude towards the Trekkers was a record of vacillation. Governor Sir Benjamin D'Urban tried to bribe them to return by kindness. He spoke of them as a 'brave, patient, industrious, orderly, and religious people; the cultivators, defenders, and tax contributors of the country'. His kindness was as unavailing as the menaces of the governors who succeeded him. Even the British Parliament called upon them to halt by passing the Cape of Good Hope Punishment Act in 1836 and was unheeded. Under the Act magistrates had the power to try offences committed by British subjects up to the twenty-fifth degree of southern latitude. It was an Act that needed a regiment to give it effect, and in the first years of Victoria's reign the British Government had little mind to chase Boer miscreants in the wilderness. Already the question was asked: Where in this great continent was British expansion to cease? At that very moment New Zealand's fate was hanging upon an answer to a very similar question. Because the Boers were a restless people, did it follow that wherever they went the British flag was sure to go? What would England gain from its pursuit of the Boers into a land which a Colonial Office weak in geography thought of as an inhospitable wilderness?

To these questions the Trekkers themselves gave the answer. With the instinct of men of seafaring ancestry they had found their way to the sea at Port Natal. It was a master-stroke fraught with promise for the future of their independence. If they could control a good port their position would be greatly strengthened. The struggle of these pastoral and inland people for a window upon the sea is a fascinating episode in the nineteenth century. But a Power that had captured the Cape because it commanded the vital route to India could not complacently watch the establishment in Natal of a body of men who denied their British allegiance. Greatly more disconcerting than Natal's maritime position was, however, its position in the native world, and its effect especially upon the Eastern Frontier. Upon that frontier the settlement imposed by Lord Glenelg had been followed by the irritations and alarums that were inevitable in a region where government was insufficient in its organization and timid in its conduct. True to its belief that native chiefs could be treated as foreign princes the British Government had persuaded the chiefs to accept the responsibility, affirmed by solemn treaty in 1836, to prevent trespass and theft by their followers. Native chiefs were, in other words, asked to impose upon tribesmen the orderliness which the British Government had hardly succeeded in imposing upon its own subjects on the other side of the frontier. It was an impossible expectation. Many of these British subjects were the men who had taken the place of the emigrant Boers. They were active men, impatient of the ways of Cape Town and Downing Street, eager to obtain even more land for the sheep-farming which, thanks to their efforts, was beginning to boom. From about 1840 the frontier system drifted towards collapse. The heat of another drought would set it to burning again.

The annexation of Natal, which was sanctioned by Lord Russell in 1843, was a humanitarian gesture and a strategic move. The humanitarianism of the Colonial Office shivered at the frightening name of the battle of Blood River, and was uneasy over reports that Boers were capturing and apprenticing native children. The annexation also relieved the pressure from the direction of Natal upon the Cape Eastern Frontier. By thrusting the Trekkers back from the coast-line the British Government turned whatever States the Trekkers might erect into landlocked States, economically dependent on British ports. South Africa's exceptional poverty in good harbours greatly simplified the British control of the coast-line. North of Port Natal there was no other useful harbour till Delagoa Bay, protected for another generation to come by its swamps and fever.

Rome had already shown how distant frontiers expand ever further in search of peace and order. The annexation of Natal brought close the annexation of the territory beyond the Orange River. Here the storm centres were the lands of the Griquas and the Basuto border. The Griquas were a tatterdemalion group of half-castes who had drifted across the border very much in the manner of the Trekkers themselves. Their offence in the eyes of the Trekkers was that they had settled upon the most desirable land on all the parched southern border. The shales and jaspers, lying in crumbled layers beneath the soil, held the scanty moisture and gave much of Griqualand the power of resisting drought. Rainfall that elsewhere was insufficient was conserved, and enabled a permanent pasture to thrive. On the Basuto border in the valley of the Caledon River was one of the 'eyes' of rich soil for which competition was inevitable.

In 1846 the Eastern Frontier took fire at last. Behind the incident which 'caused' the war were the realities of drought, land-hungry colonists, and sulky, apprehensive Kafirs. It was a war fought more by British regiments than colonist commandos, and the bill presented to the British Treasury shocked men like Cobden and Bright, apostles of free trade, of a balanced budget and a diminished Empire. Soon their indignation would make itself felt in the affairs of South Africa. In the meantime a new star shone in South Africa. It was Governor Sir Harry Smith, Peninsular veteran, Kafir fighter, and Indian soldier. He brought charm, a capacity for lightning decisions, and the conviction that the best way to deal with the troublesome people was to take over their land and

rule them. Out of defeated Kafirland he carved a new Cape
district called Victoria East and a fresh Crown Colony called
British Kaffraria. To the tribes thus made British subjects he
assigned reserves under the supervision of magistrates; for the
farmers there was new land. The frontier was gone, and so
was the policy of keeping whites and blacks apart. Henceforth the two races lived together cheek by jowl, in a manner
that multiplied the causes of conflict, but also, far more significantly, increased their dependence upon one another. Kafirs
and colonists belonged to the same society. For a moment
there was an end to the timidity of British frontier policy.
There was an end also to the belief that Kafir tribes could be
treated as sovereign States. Sir Harry Smith saw that such
a belief prevented the extension of the rule of law to the inter-
locked elements on the frontier. What the frontier needed
was government, and the authority of able administrators.

Then Sir Harry Smith annexed the Orange River Territory. He was apparently convinced that because he liked the
Boers and they liked him, his action would find favour with
them. All of the Kafir frontier from Natal down to the Eastern Frontier by way of Basutoland was now British. The
strategy of Smith's annexation was, therefore, excellent. But
Downing Street beheld this addition of a new province to the
Empire with uneasiness. British colonial policy was on the
eve of great changes. Dr. Philip was dead and so was Wilberforce. The humanitarian conscience of Downing Street was
now less ardent and less sensitive than it had been in the
crusading days of slave emancipation. Its action was more
intermittent, and it harkened more often to the protest of the
Chancellor of the Exchequer that it was always expensive and
often inexpedient to yield to the importunities of missionaries
and philanthropists. The struggle between ethics and politics,
between right and expediency had begun. By annexing Natal
and by assuming control over the entire native frontier from
the mouth of the Bashee to Port Natal the British Government
had actually captured the trek movement. If British policy
were to control the destiny of all the sub-continent then Sir
Harry Smith's move had been excellently devised. But to
those who subjected Sir Harry Smith's daring settlement to

the severest scrutiny economy meant more than strategy. If there could be an end to native disturbances and Boer unrest, then his settlement might be upheld. Yet let British regiments be forced to march again and Treasury funds be poured forth again, then there would be little mercy in the Cabinet or Parliament.

The shape of things to come in South Africa was determined by forces that affected the entire Empire. Since 1840 the attitude in England to colonial questions had undergone striking changes. The prevailing mood was opposed to any increase of Imperial responsibilities. The feeling grew that the dependence of the great colonies of settlement upon the mother country could be lessened. There was an unspoken alliance between the liberal desire of the Durham Report to give the colonists a greater liberty in governing themselves and the timidity of those who believed that it was better to separate from the colonies in friendship before it was too late; between the conviction of the disciples of free trade that it was unprofitable to govern colonies that could govern and pay for themselves and the assurance that the proper place for British regiments was not on colonial frontiers where they too readily became the instrument of local ambitions. Out of such a variety of motives was born the self-government which Canada, the Australian colonies, and New Zealand achieved during those years. When these colonies were taking the tide of their own self-development, it was not likely that the British Government would willingly encourage South Africa to take an opposite course. Indeed, taken by itself, the Cape Colony in 1848 was ripe for a more advanced form of government. Wool, a bigger population, and improved revenues had made the Cape more like New South Wales and the other colonies of the Empire. As early as 1846 opinion in the Cape and sentiment in the Colonial Office were in agreement that the time for popular institutions had come. The draft constitution for the Cape Colony which was sent to England in 1848, therefore, confirmed the hope that in the fullness of time all South Africa would share in the blessings of self-direction under the same flag.

In 1850 all questions of territories and constitutions were

incontinently thrown into the melting-pot. Almost simultaneously war raised its head again on the Eastern Frontier of the Cape and the Basuto border of the Orange River Sovereignty. The two occurrences were closely connected. They afforded the clearest proof that all European and native settlement was now so interdependent that a Basuto could not steal a Boer ox or a soldier set fire to a Xosa hut without the effects being felt far and wide. On the Eastern Frontier the chiefs resented the loss of their land and the inroads which magistrates and colonial law were making upon their authority and the familiar customs of the tribes. What they resented was, in reality, a process that was dissolving the allegiance and sanction of the tribes, making a new society out of them, dependent upon the Europeans for land, labour, and justice. On the Basuto border the contest was more clearly for land. Boer and Basuto each claimed the fine corn land of the Caledon Valley. The two groups had sifted on to the land with little supervision, so that their intermingled settlement inevitably bred conflict. On neither frontier did the colonists or burghers rally eagerly to help British troops. Their conduct seemed to prove the familiar accusation in Parliament that British South African settlers would feel no responsibility as long as the consequences of their conduct could be shifted on to the shoulders of British regiments and the British taxpayer. In the counsels of Whitehall economy prevailed over strategy. It was decided to curtail the area of British responsibility in South Africa. In 1852 the Sand River Convention recognized the independence of the Boers living north of the Vaal River; two years later the Bloemfontein Convention withdrew British sovereignty from beyond the Orange River. The two conventions meant that the Trekkers were free after all to establish independent republics. They meant that the Trekkers were free to manage their own relations with their native neighbours. They meant that the representative government which the Cape received in 1854 would not be the foundation on which all South Africa would build its political future. The Great Trek had conquered. South Africa was a land divided.

As the gold seekers of forty-nine converged on California in their covered wagons, and the Victorian gold-fields attracted shiploads of new emigrants to Australia, South Africa seemed the least endowed of colonial regions. Its poverty was enhanced by political subdivision and the abiding menace of native wars. Capital followed the settlers into the interior timidly and was exasperatingly ready to take to flight when there was any danger. Interest rates of 12 per cent. were customary in the Transvaal till as late as 1877. Even in the Cape the same rate was frequently charged in the sixties on well-secured mortgages. Neither the Natal nor the Cape governments found it easy to borrow money in London at less than 6 per cent. Six per cent. was the rate of interest which Natal had to pay in 1861 on a loan of £165,000 for harbour improvements. It was not simply that the country was starved for capital. There was too little to attract capital. Domestic capital was accumulated very slowly. Cattle diseases and locusts, Kafir wars and drought, caused periodic setbacks.

Like most young and struggling countries the Cape and Natal depended upon import dues for a large proportion of their revenues. As a result there developed a cut-throat and demoralizing rivalry between the Cape ports and Durban for the trade of the Republics. Neither colony could be induced to yield a penny of their import dues to the poverty-stricken interior communities. Each effort by the Republics to escape from their landlocked position was baulked, and they had no means of retaliation. Poor as the Cape and Natal were, the Republics were poorer. In 1858 the Cape Colony had fifty times the revenue of the Orange Free State. By 1860 Gladstone and phylloxera between them had all but killed the once flourishing wine industry of the Cape. There was little money in grain. Wool alone gained. Average exports of £30,000 in the five years following the Trek had soared to over £200,000 in the five years ending in 1850. In 1869 wool exports had risen to £1,700,000. By the side of the vast Australian exports of wool it was not much. Although the Great Trek did not exploit its huge acreages like the Australian squatter, it had made South Africa a pastoral and sheep country and wool the chief source of South African wealth.

But wool was not enough to subsidize all the needs of a

colonial community in the middle of the nineteenth century. An economy of wool and hides could not pay for the immigration, the bridges, the roads, the railways, the harbour facilities, the improved instruments of government with which colonies in other parts of the world were equipping themselves. Until 1860 the Cape could not afford the breakwater and docking facilities without which Table Bay, although an excellent natural anchorage, was an inefficient and dangerous harbour. The day of the sailing-vessel was practically over before a beginning was made to render Table Bay safe for shipping. For just two hundred years the vessels plying on the Eastern route had anchored in Table Bay, where they were served by rowing-boats and a single primitive wooden jetty. Against the great gales that soared over the bay they had no protection.

In the sixties the Cape Colony, followed at a distance by Natal, made a gallant effort not to fall too far behind the other colonies of the Empire. The founding of the London and South Africa Bank in 1861 with a capital of £400,000 and of the Standard Bank with a capital of £500,000 expanded the capital revenues of the Colony. The government itself borrowed boldly at 6 per cent. In a brief burst of activity jails were built for won't-work Kafirs and roads for wool-laden ox-wagons. Natal worked hard on roads and bridges so as to tighten her hold on the trade with the Republics. Private enterprise finished two miles of railway in Natal between the Point and Durban, and by 1864 sixty-three miles between Cape Town and Wellington. Then suddenly confidence collapsed. The forces of war and depression coming from America that made the looms of Lancashire cease their shuttling reached South Africa too. From 1862 to 1870 depression gripped the land. Unprecedented droughts and the ravages of insect pests made the crisis harder to bear. Sheep died for want of water in the summer, and of cold in the winter. During the short boom there had been a surfeit of capital and, in such a poor country, too few opportunities of sound investment. The result had been speculation in land and bubble commercial schemes. Now land prices fell, and commercial credit collapsed. For a whole decade not another sleeper was added to South Africa's railways. The truth was plain to see. Neither the wool of the Cape and the Orange Free State, nor the sugar which Natal found that it could grow, were enough to pay for the imports and public works needed to keep South Africa abreast of an industrial and commercial age. Some other source of wealth was needed. South Africa found that source of wealth in diamonds and gold.

Before the story can be told of the revolution brought by diamonds and gold, there is another story to be told, no less important, of how South Africa developed and organized its resources of land and population, for, together with minerals, land and labour are the keys to South African economic development. The land system of the eighteenth century and the occurrence of the Great Trek together defeated all efforts at systematic colonization, or of using the land, as in the other colonies, as an important means of financing immigration. It is generally agreed amongst colonial economic historians that the principles of systematic colonization were nowhere entirely successful. Yet nowhere were they so completely lacking in the conditions of success as in South Africa. One after another the Emigration Commission, appointed by Viscount Goderich in 1831, the Select Committee of the House of Commons in 1836, which was appointed to report on the disposal of colonial lands, and the Board of Colonial Land and Emigration Commissioners, appointed in 1839, shook their heads over the land system of the Cape Colony. Between 1812 and 1840 31,500,000 acres were disposed of for less than £46,000 paid at the time of alienation, in addition to quit-rents amounting to £13,818 a year, which gave an annual rent of about one penny for every 10 acres. In 1842 Governor Napier gave it as his considered opinion that not more than 5,000,000 acres fit for grants remained in the Crown's possession. These acres were, however, scattered between land already granted or so interspersed in patches amongst 64,000 square miles of 'utterly useless country' that the labour of finding them out and bringing them to sale would be expensive and troublesome. In the surveyor-general's department the greatest inaccuracy ruled. Most of the land of the Colony had been granted without any previous general survey upon which grants could be laid down accurately and planfully. Such surveys as existed had, for the most part, been conducted by inefficient and ignorant men who substituted confusion for ignorance. It is clear that well before the Kafir War of 1846 the Cape Colony had exhausted the better part of its patrimony of land. From that land it did not obtain revenue enough to spend on immigration on an important scale in the manner of the Australian colonies. In the distant districts farmers complained of quit-rents of 6*d.* per hundred acres as ruinously high. Large acreages were held at as little as 1*d.* for a hundred acres. Land revenue was never more than a small fraction of the total revenue. From 1850 to 1870 it was never more than one-tenth of the total revenue. In 1860 New South Wales had twelve times the land revenue of the Cape Colony.

To encourage an active flow of immigrants the Cape also offered few opportunities of employment. The lack of intensive cultivation and the exceedingly low rates of pay for agricultural labour discouraged the crofters and labourers who went so numerously to Canada, Australia, and New Zealand in the middle of the century. The average rate of farm wages in the forties and fifties was from 10*s.* to 20*s.* a month with keep. It was a rate set by the use of cheap Hottentot and Kafir labour. Of those who sought homes in Canada, Australia, and the United States the great majority were men and women who earned their living with the skill that was in their hands and the strength that was in their backs. Of these South Africa could absorb only very few. Thus the great movement of emigration in the first seven decades of the nineteenth century passed South Africa by, even though Cape Town was six thousand miles closer to London than Sydney. For most years the volume of emigration to South Africa was so small that the Emigration Commissioners in London did not even bother to mention it in their reports. Between 1820 and 1860 the average number of immigrants into the Cape Colony was perhaps no more than 750 a year. Even in the years from 1847 to 1850 when hundreds of thousands of desperate Irish, English, and Scots poured across the seas, South Africa received only a few thousand. The highlights of immigration into the Cape Colony were the 5,000 settlers of 1820, 4,300 labourers between 1844 and 1847, and 12,000 German and British settlers between 1857 and 1862. Thus the energy and the enterprise that new immigrants bring were not given to South Africa in the same abundance as to the other great British colonies. It missed the healthy unsettlement of the established population by new-comers. The greatest increase of population came from within, from the powerful birth-rate of the colonists, and not from without. The Great Trek, for all the vast area of new territory which it occupied, was not followed by a second wave of pioneers, challenging its economic attitudes, dissolving its homogeneity, breaking down its separation and aloofness. The habits of mind of the Trekkers fixed themselves firmly in the interior, and even, in the course of time, flowed back into the Colony whence they had come, setting the stamp of their thought upon the whole of South Africa.

Although Natal had its share of 'baboon rock' and barren soil, the proportion of good land was higher than in the Cape Colony. Yet Natal disposed of its land in a manner no more rational or systematic than the Cape. Before ever the British annexed Natal the emigrant Boers had introduced the régime of the 6,000-acre farm. When British rule was established there was an immediate exodus of Boers. In order to hold them the British Government assigned to each man a farm of 6,000 acres provided he occupied it himself and did not sell it during a period of seven years. Because the Boers continued to desert the Colony even these restrictions were removed. Some Boers stayed; others accepted their grants, sold them to speculators, and moved off after all into the Republics. From the beginning absentee and speculative land-holding was the bane of the Colony's land system. Twelve years after the British annexation between three and four million acres had thus passed into the hands of speculators. It was, as one governor remarked, as if the land had been suddenly stricken with barrenness. Neither in British Natal nor anywhere else in South Africa was the warning of Isaiah heeded against those 'that lay field to field, till there be no

place, that they may be placed alone in the midst of the earth'
(Isa. v. 8). Every vast estate thus withdrawn from the public
domain was removed from the reach of the small settler with
little capital and interposed its bulk between the settler and
other available land. As early as 1851, when the Colony was
not even ten years old, there was very little Crown land situated
at a convenient distance from the port. An attempt by Lieutenant-Governor Scott in 1857 to encourage immigration by
a system of assisted passages brought less than 300 immigrants
into Natal and alienated 1,360,000 acres of land, of which the
greatest proportion fell once more into speculative hands. In
1864 the Immigration Board, as a result, explained ruefully
that it could not encourage immigration because land was so
scarce. A population of a third-rate English town suffered
from a shortage of land in the midst of 12,000,000 acres! Land
distributed in this manner could not be rationally taxed and
was a serious restraint on the growth and enterprise of the
population.

In the Republics, also, the immigrants gulped up the land.
The practice of granting a farm of not less than 6,000 acres
to every burgher of age made swift inroads upon the land
resources of the Republics. If the land surveyors of the Cape
had proved themselves incapable and dishonest, the Republics
apportioned their land, for the most part, without any survey
at all. Details of the landscape, a tall tree, a flat-topped hill,
or a gully served to indicate the boundaries of farms. It was
not surprising that there were many farms of 10,000 acres and
more, instead of the conventional 6,000 acres. Nor was it surprising that the land speculator descended upon the Republics
even as he had descended upon the British colonies. The Republican administration insisted very imperfectly on occupation or beneficial cultivation. It happened, even in the very
early years of the Trek movement, that building plots began
to change hands as soon as they had been allocated. Blocks of
privately owned land, especially in the Transvaal, of 200,000
and 300,000 acres were not unknown. From Winburg to
Harrismith in 1854 there stretched an almost unbroken line
of 200 farms held by absentee owners. The burghers themselves came to complain bitterly of absentee ownership, for

in the Republics there came the inevitable day when there was no longer a farm for every man and his son. That day had arrived before the British annexation of the Transvaal in 1877.

The great acreages of South Africa were not unsettled spaces open to the unhindered occupation of Europeans. That European settlement took place in a land settled by a relatively numerous native population is a fact of first-rate importance. Great areas, especially of the Cape, were very lightly peopled or even entirely uninhabited. These were the rainless parts of little value to man or beast. But from the Eastern Frontier onwards native settlement was relatively dense. It was densest in Kafirland, where dwelt the Ama-Xosa, the Tembu, the Pondo, the Xesibe, and the Ama-Baca; in Basutoland; in Natal and Zululand, where dwelt the Zulus; in Swaziland; in the Northern Transvaal, where dwelt the Bapedi, the Maguambe, and the Baramapulana; on the western border of the Transvaal, where dwelt the Bamangwato, the Bakwena, the Bangwaketse, the Baralong, and the Batlapin. This line curved like a horseshoe round the Orange Free State and the Transvaal. By the Boers it was claimed that they had found the land within this curve empty of population, laid waste by the hordes of the Mantatees and by the impis of the Matabele and Zulu. Native wars, even the fiercest, are not very destructive of life. It is certain that many tribes were harried and dispersed. That the land taken over by the Great Trek, including Natal, was empty of population is much less certain. In Natal and parts of the Transvaal the evidence is very clear that scattered and broken tribes succeeded, as did the Boers themselves during the Boer War, in finding refuge in broken and hilly country, whence they emerged when the Boers had broken the power of their enemies. From the beginning Boers and natives were therefore intermingled. Many farms were established over the heads of native kraals. To many other farms returned straggling fragments of tribes. These natives became squatters, owning no land in their own right, more or less tolerated by the European landowners for the rent they would pay or in the labour they could render.

In Natal this commingled settlement of black and white can

be most clearly discerned. When British rule was established in 1843, there were not less than 100,000 natives in Natal, and their number was daily increasing by immigrants from Zululand. This immigration strengthened the white settlers in the belief that they were the first settlers. Hence all native settlement was looked upon as strictly encroachment. Even so able an authority on the natives as Theophilus Shepstone toyed for a while with the idea of clearing Natal of its natives by leading a Great Trek of the entire native population into Pondoland, south of Natal. In 1846 a Commission was appointed to assign lands to the natives. Not at any time was an opportunity so clearly presented for the formulation of the fundamental principles which should govern the place of natives within Natal. But the Commission worked in the midst of a popular belief that Natal's natives should be expelled northwards into Zululand or southwards into Pondoland, leaving behind only enough to satisfy the need for labour. Consequently, it was an important achievement for the Commission to establish eight locations with a total area of 1,168,000 acres. Compared with the Transvaal or the Cape's Eastern Frontier, Natal's natives were well off. Yet more than half of its native population continued to squat rightlessly on private and Crown lands.

Of greater importance in social and economic history was the meeting of white settlement with the compact and organized masses of natives like the Ama-Xosa and the Basuto. The native wars, from major campaigns to unheralded skirmishes, were spectacular phases in a lengthy process of encroachment, invasion, extrusion, and dispossession. For the most part the wars were not caused by the inborn quarrelsomeness of savage and warlike tribes, but by the keen competition of two groups, with very similar agricultural and pastoral habits, for the possession of the most fertile and best-watered stretches of land. In the arid regions the struggle was for the 'eyes' of good land, near the invaluable springs or fountains. It is a bootless effort to ascertain the responsibility for each war. Ama-Xosa tribesmen were skilled and daring cattle thieves; Zulu impis thundered their knees against their war shields; the black nodding plumes of Swazi warriors were feared in the Transvaal; Natal lived for a generation in terror of a great native uprising; upon every frontier the story of burning houses was familiar. Yet the general causes of these wars were seen most clearly in their effects. They can be seen in the loss of native land, in the growing inability of the natives to maintain themselves in more restricted and less fertile areas, and in the diminishing means of independent livelihood of the tribes. Fielding's comment that 'the sufferings of the poor are less observed than their misdeeds' has much meaning in frontier history. It was no chance that the great majority of wars came in seasons of drought. The relationship between the tortured barrenness of a South African drought and native uprisings is too obvious to be missed. Burned under a cruel sky, as empty of moisture as the soil was of nourishment, the cracked and cropless land was often the trigger of revolt. Yet not all the frontier lands passed into European hands by violent means. There were cessions made by chiefs who put their marks on pieces of paper which they did not always understand, or afterwards always respect. Land was bought with harness, guns, and cases of brandy. It was acquired by the process of turning a permission to graze into the right to occupy. In the background of frontier land settlement was many a sordid story of land speculation. Many a missionary, not always innocently, was the tool of land-sharks. These locked up great blocks of land and almost literally compelled the Boers in the Republics to wrest the land they wanted from the natives.

The complex process of dispossession was made more difficult to regulate by the differing attitudes of whites and blacks towards the ownership of land. In the European mind ownership was more important than use; in the Bantu mind use was more important than ownership. Native borders were open, vague, and imprecise. They encouraged trespass. The notion that a signature or the gift of a spavined horse gave a white man the right to hold land to the exclusion of all others was foreign to the native mind. Even more foreign was the notion that land where all men's beasts had grazed without let could be reserved for the herds of a single individual.

Between the native policies of the British colonies and the Dutch Republics no very significant distinction can be drawn. In all of them the process which allotted the privilege of land to the Europeans and the duty of labour to the natives was similar. In the new society which was being created the possession of land was a badge, and dispossession was a stigma. The endowment of the whites and the disendowment of blacks obeyed the social and moral rules to which the ruling group was attached. Similarly, the abstention of one group from hard physical labour, and the subjection of the other were more than economic differences. They were social differences as well. At the end of the Kafir War of 1846–7 the lands of which the tribes were shorn turned an already crowded condition into a critical shortage of land. After the war of 1851 the Gaika tribe lost another 600 square miles of land. The territory that remained to them was less fertile. Henceforth there was less fuel for their fires, less herbage for their animals, and a leached and less generous soil for their crops.

In 1857 the Eastern Frontier was stricken by a disaster which must be told for its tragedy and its meaning. The deep unrest of the Kafirs turned for help to magic instead of the assagai. Prophets amongst them proclaimed that they must kill their cattle and consume their corn even to their seed. Then a day would come when the spirits would write their power in the heavens, unleash the tempest to blow the white men into the sea, and make their land to be fat with corn and cattle. It is men who are in want that are most given to dream of plenty. The fat acres and lubberlands of joy of Ama-Xosa and Tembu superstition point to the intimate causes of their unrest. The proud white cattle that were to rise from the earth would take the place of the thin and diseased beasts that were really in their herds; the grain that would shoot to sudden ripeness would yield the abundance they did not have. Most desired miracle of all, the white man would be driven into the sea. The Kafirs appealed to their spirits to do what they had been unable to do in half a dozen wars. But the spirits of the tribe failed them too. How many cattle were killed, what tons of grain were destroyed cannot be told. It is enough to know that the tribes that took this fantastic gamble against fate were broken beyond repair. Besides the thousands, some say 25,000, that perished of hunger, many thousands more tramped into the colony begging for work that they might not die. Yet it was more than famine that drove them. It was the admission that they could no longer defend or maintain their own way of life. It was a movement of economic submission. Henceforth Kafirland was a reservoir of labour. For their folly the Kafirs were punished by the loss of even more land. The old chief Kreli, proud and incorrigible, was expelled from his land. It was like blood-letting for an anaemic condition. In the Gaika country were settled German legionnaires. There was no doubt now, if there had been any doubt before, that Kafirland and the reserves within the Colony were crowded to suffocation. When the Imperial Government permitted Kreli to return to most of his land in 1864 it eased the bursting beyond the Bashee but could not relieve the hunger of all the frontier for land.

On the Basuto border the Dutch had come with their cattle and the Basuto had come down from their hills at about the same time. From the beginning settlement filtered so irregularly into the rich cornlands that no line could succeed in separating white farmers from black herdsmen. For four years after its creation the Orange Free State jockeyed for position. The Basuto were strong in numbers; the Free State was weak and penniless. In a struggle in 1858 the Free State Boers found that they did not have the strength to defeat, much less to repel, the Basuto. It was at this moment that the Free State addressed its famous request to Sir George Grey, Governor of the Cape Colony, for federation with the Cape Colony. Sir George Grey saw an opportunity of bringing the Europeans back under the British flag, and especially of bringing under a single control policy on the common native frontier. Enthusiastically and brilliantly he recommended federation to the Colonial Office. But the Colonial Office remembered that the Kafir War of 1857 had cost nearly a million pounds. It had no desire to enlarge the Queen's territories, especially when they were inhabited by such as Boers and Basuto.

In 1865 when war came again the Boers were stronger. Flying patrols rounded up Basuto cattle and loaded their grain on to wagons. No surer means of breaking Basuto resistance could be found. In 1866 the Boer commando destroyed the harvest again and forced the Basuto to submit. The land war was won. The Basuto yielded well over half of their arable land, so rich that nothing in the Free State could compare with it in fertility. The conquered territory was 'cleaned' of its Basuto. What was left of Basutoland was for the most part rock and mountains, with narrow eroded valleys and shreds and patches of good land. Basutoland, which was annexed in 1869 by the British Government to preserve it against further dispossession, was henceforth a land like the Eastern Frontier, heavily peopled and limited in its resources of land, grain, and wood.

The story of land and settlement on the long native borders of the Transvaal is a record of treaties and cessions, of forays and encroachment. There was much encroachment at the Zulu border, although the Transvaal escaped a Zulu war. Farther north in the direction of the Swazis, the Bapedi, and the tribes of the Zoutpansberg Mountains, Boer settlement made more difficult progress. Fever and broken country aided the natives in opposing European settlement. On the western border, where was Livingstone's Kuruman, the land was thirsty. The struggle was less for land than for the springs and watercourses without which land was useless. By possessing themselves of these the Boers were able to control large areas. Because their access to water was severely limited, the area of land in which the natives could live was very much lessened, for the loss of even a single spring could destroy the value of thousands of acres.

Thus everywhere did white settlement press upon black settlement. Everywhere the conditions of native life were changed, but were not destroyed. Not measles or diphtheria or alcohol could make their numbers shrink. They belied the truism that the lesser vitality of primitive races must yield before the energy of a superior race. They answered military defeat by enrolling in the ranks of their conquerors, for the native wars were merely spectacular phases in a social and economic revolution. How the native became a member of white society is one of the most vital passages of South African economic history.

The purely naive and uncritical philanthropists will see in

the changes which the tribes underwent an indictment of white civilization. The historian knows that when two people, different in their history and the manner of their living, come to live in the same land, adjustments, often accompanied by violence, are inevitable. He also knows that the weaker society does not simply yield to the stronger. They yield to one another, each undergoing profound modifications in its habits and attitudes. A dominant race does not signify a race untouched by those whom it dominates. As the century reached closer to its end it became less true to speak of two societies living their separate lives. Now that the agony of the Boer War has abated, and time has done much to compose the quarrel of Boer and Briton, it is clear that the leading theme of South African history is the growth of a new society in which white and black are bound together in the closest dependence upon each other.

The common picture of the tribal life before the coming of the white settler as stable, carefree, and spacious is not quite true. Tribes waxed in numbers and strength or shrank into weakness according to the skill of their chiefs, the power of their neighbours, and the vicissitudes of climate and season. In their ebb and flow they moved on to fresh lands or were expelled from the old. Long before the European musket was heard in Kafirland, land and cattle wars between the natives themselves were not unknown. Yet between population and land there was a reasonable balance. As the tribes exhausted the soil or grass they could move on to fresh soil and find new pastures. The freedom to exploit new resources of land, even though it was sometimes challenged, was the balance-wheel of tribal economic life. Within the tribe there were differences in wealth and social position. That one member could be richer in land or cattle than another was not incompatible with tribal custom. The tendency of the tribe, however, was to guard against extremes of poverty or of wealth. Truly wide differences between too much land and too little, between conspicuous wealth and grinding poverty, were unknown. Tribal land was a resource from which all drew, not with mathematical equality, but with a high degree of fairness. The wealth of the family or clan in food and cattle nourished all its members, the young and the old, the halt and the lame. As an economic system it was simple; its mechanism was not intricate, and its standards were modest. In the close dependence of men upon each other and in their common adherence to the customs of the tribe Bantu society was strong. It was a system strong in endurance and amazing in its power of recuperation, else it could not have borne the impact of white colonization so long, nor lived so long within the ruins of its institutions.

To lose land was to lose the most important foundation upon which tribal life was built. And everywhere, it has been seen, the natives lost their land entirely or were thrust into ever narrower areas. Some of the land that was left to them was fertile and well watered. Much was poor of soil, deficient in water and wood. In Natal, for example, parts of the native locations were a vast cluster of crumpled hills that lifted their rugged and scarped sides in fantastic shapes, intersected by deep ravines from which the summer torrents had torn away all useful soil. In the Impofana location for every 225 acres there was 1 acre that was arable. Upon the Eastern Frontier of the Cape there were parts where the scraps and patches of arable soil were too small for a plough. Though there were tribes and portions of tribes that were well off, the majority lived upon too little land to maintain them as in days of old. Even the Fingo tribes, traditional allies and favourites of the Government, choked upon their land. Such a crowding of men and beasts placed a severe strain upon the land that was left. By their primitive and wasteful husbandry they ruined poor land beyond repair; the rich land became steadily poorer. The breakdown of soil into sand, the replacement of nutritious grass by weeds, the disappearance of trees and shrubs, the scarring of the land by dongas and ditches—these were the signs that the land could not withstand the pressure upon it of too many men and too many beasts. Tribal life set great store upon cattle. It was with cattle that the young man paid the bride-price for his wife. As in many primitive societies, cattle were more than wealth; to them was attached a religious meaning which made them and their increase a guarantee and a symbol of the welfare of the tribe. To preserve the herds, even though they contributed to their undoing, the natives made the greatest efforts.

It is well known that, when there is pressure upon the food supply of a people, meat and fresh foods are the first to disappear from their diet. In the days before the white man the diet of the natives was more varied than it later became. Kafir corn, pumpkins, sweet reeds, beans, and wild fruits of bush and field afforded a diet which, with occasional meat, was healthful. But weeds, erosion, and overcropping diminished the supply of fresh foods. From the time of the Eastern Frontier War of 1850–1 may be said to date the monotonous and insufficient diet of maize or Kafir corn porridge with too little meat or fresh vegetables. Many Europeans came sincerely to believe that the natural diet of the natives was a stodgy porridge. Actually such a diet was lacking in many qualities necessary to health. An unbalanced diet of cereal foods lowered resistance to disease and deprived men of their energy. Natives in their original state set great store by leisure. Warm subtropical days empty of toil, spent on the shadow side of a hut, are one of the delights of tribal life. Yet it is reasonable to suggest that the laziness of which colonists seeking labour complained was frequently the lethargy of malnutrition.

Upon the life of the natives rested also the weight of the benefits and burdens of civilization. Each greasy blanket and torn pair of trousers they wore, each hoe or length of copper wire they bought, each bottle of Cape 'smoke' they drank, was a charge upon their frail economic resources. Poor though they were, the consumption of salt and sugar, tea and coffee, soap and candles, the use of buckets and spades ultimately became habits. Amongst the agencies which transformed the life of the natives the trader was most influential; for it may freely be said that by 1870 there was scarcely a man or woman who was not in some degree a consumer of manufactured goods. In the same measure did the natives become taxpayers of the Republics and colonies. In Natal above all, but in the other communities as well, heavy contributions were levied upon the natives. In 1862, when the customs revenue of Natal amounted to £40,672, native taxes amounted to £17,925. A very important means of native taxation was by import duties on articles of native consumption. The increased tariffs of 1860 and 1863 in Natal were imposed chiefly on articles consumed by the native population in order to cover the expenses of the introduction of coolies from India to work in the Natal sugar plantations. Upon the very numerous population on European land there dwelt the obligation of rents. Many a landowner, especially in the British colonies, obtained an important income from 'Kafir farming'. The great landholding companies were able by this means to lock up blocks of land without loss to themselves by levying rentals upon the native squatters.

The subsistence economy of the tribes could not meet these charges. Against selling their cattle in order to pay taxes, or buy hoes and blankets, the resistance was very strong. In good years they sold or bartered their grain. But too often they were compelled to buy back their grain at famine prices. The economy of the tribe, in short, could not consistently show the profit needed to meet new wants and new taxes. Tribal economy had to be supplemented by other sources of income. The tribes had one thing to sell which was in steady demand. It was their labour. In the land in which they lived the free resources of soil, water, and grass had been expropriated or diminished. These resources represented the capital upon which tribal life had been based. Without these resources of soil, water, and grass the natives were obliged to do labour for those who now controlled them. Acquisition of land by Europeans was quite frequently a method of annexing labour as well. Since the earliest days it was a frequent practice for farmers to buy land, not for the land's own sake, but in order to command the labour of the natives upon it. It was a process that deliberately extinguished native property in the land and their security of tenure upon it, so that they were helpless before the power that private ownership conferred on the whites. A surplus of land in the hands of the white community and an insufficiency in the hands of the natives made possible an exploitation of the natives' need. In such action one may read implicitly the language of the eighteenth-century inclosure movement.

'The use of common land by labourers operates upon the mind as a sort of independence', whereas inclosure would make labourers work every day in the year, and induce that 'subordination of the lower ranks of society which in the present times is so much wanted. . . '. Native agricultural industry was undermined. The efforts which it might have made, given land and encouragement, to bear the burden of taxes and needs were obstructed, and the native agricultural population was diverted into the subsidiary industry of serving the European community with its labour.

It can be proved beyond any doubt that from the middle of the century onwards the proportion of those who did labour for some period during each year grew ever larger. From complaints in the press, in Parliament and Volksraad, however, it seemed that the most serious shortage of labour prevailed, which not even increased taxes or other forms of deliberate pressure could correct. It is a well-established fact of economics that in an undeveloped society, where wealth is held in common and freely shared, the incentive to earn a living by individual effort is not paramount; in the same manner the incentive is not strong for the individual to grow in wealth and economic importance. The conviction of the whites that the natives were indolent individuals whose habitual shyness of work made them a sort of naked leisure class had some foundation. But the most important explanation of the labour shortage, which caused Natal to complicate the problems of race and colour by importing a large number of Indian coolies in 1860, was that native labour was wastefully and inefficiently used. Much labour was tied up on individual farms. The efforts of republican and colonial legislation to make this labour more mobile by limiting the number of native squatters on a farm were defeated by the desire of each landowner to monopolize the services of the natives on his land. Service was given intermittently, for cash and for kind, and without plan. Behind the demand for labour was no systematic effort to improve farming and increase production. Upon acreages uneconomically held and in an unprogressive agricultural industry, there was room for only a casual and unbusinesslike labour system. Between master and servant there was ofttimes a medieval relationship in which the native held land of the white man and in return performed duties and made payments quite similar to those in a feudal manor. Had there been a keen industrial demand for native labour, due to the intensive production of a marketable surplus, native labour would have been more efficiently distributed and more skilfully used. Above all, native labour could have found advantage in the competition for its services by securing improvements in its economic status. Labour which is paid in kind rather than in cash, and which has little freedom to offer itself where it wishes, cannot benefit from the law of supply and demand. It is certain to render inefficient service and receive an insufficient reward. Depressed rewards for labour and a shortage of labour existed incongruously side by side in the latter half of the nineteenth century in apparent defiance of all economic principles. Not a genuine dearth of labour, but chronic under-employment was the fault which neither Republics nor colonies could correct. Driven by destitution from their own land to seek a livelihood, the natives entered a European society that was itself economically backward and too poor and unproductive to turn their labour to profitable account. It is easy to see that such economic conditions caused a disproportionate pressure upon the native population.

The entrance of natives into European society as the universal hewers of wood and drawers of water was not essentially a violent process. It was because their economic habits were similar that whites and blacks had fought. But when they had fought and the natives had suffered defeat, the same similarity led to co-operation. The natives, herdsmen and tillers of the soil, were absorbed as servants whose duties were still to herd cattle and till the soil. The inducements to toil were the right to occupy land to earn cattle, and these were after all the highest values of their own economic life. The close economic bonds which tied natives and Europeans ever more closely were the outcome of a very great measure of compatibility between them. This compatibility, far more than their conflict, was the secret of their intimate economic relationship. It is important to understand that the modification of native life was only partly the result of deliberate exploitation on the part of the European population. Altruistic motives were not confined to missionaries alone. Sir George Grey settled white men in the very midst of natives on the Eastern Frontier after 1857 so that the natives might learn habits of industry from their neighbours, and become 'a source of strength and wealth for the Colony'. To labour was to learn. How could savages better acquaint themselves with white civilization than by becoming its apprentices? Within the tribe they could only remain the prisoner of their own primitive habits. The more completely they were withdrawn by 'holy ennobling labour' from the influence of chiefs and witchdoctors, the swifter would be their emancipation. Arguments such as these were not always speciously put forward to excuse the white man's greed of native labour. There was a genuine belief that service with Europeans was a means of escape from barbarism. Only the exceedingly few, and these mostly unheard, discerned that the real movement of the natives was from barbarism to pauperism. The nineteenth century in South Africa did not easily recognize poverty even when confronted by it. Rags upon a native's body, instead of nakedness, were a badge of progress rather than of degradation. The distinction between poverty and riches in white rural society itself was hardly drawn at all. Furthermore, the average republican or colonial community accepted no responsibility for poverty amongst the natives. To the sight of destitution their answer was that there was work for every man. Confiscation of land, discriminatory taxation, and all the means used to drive the natives into the labour market could thus be justified on moral grounds because they struck at superstition and sloth.

European settlement expanded for the most part in advance of ordered government. Relations with the natives were conducted with only little help from officials whose duty it was to understand the nature of tribal institutions. The struggle for land and water and labour was aggravated by ignorance and misinterpretation. Even when government sought to control settlement it remained for a long time poorly informed of native thought, land tenure, or laws. Only in the

twentieth century after a full century of contact did the
natives become the object of sober scientific investigation.
At least two generations of settlers grew up in ignorance of
the ingenuity and appropriateness with which the natives in
their tribal state met the many problems of their lives, in
ignorance of the validity of many of the social and moral
rules which held them together. European society most easily
saw the unattractive aspect of tribal life. It saw the superstition and witchcraft and cruelty. But it failed to see, or saw
only imperfectly, the rational structure of tribal life, the protection which it gave the individual, the comfort which it
gave his mind, the surveillance which it kept over the distribution of food and land. European society condemned as
stagnant and unenlightened a way of life in which happiness
and contentment were, for the native, not difficult to find.
Between soldier and settler, missionary and magistrate there
was an unvoiced conspiracy against the institutions of the
tribe. 'The process of Europeanizing the native', declared a
modern Government Commission, 'by destroying all his institutions as a preliminary, deprives him of the sheet-anchor of
self-confidence, and substitutes for it an inferiority complex,
engendered by the acquired belief that everything which is
peculiarly his own is worthless and a hindrance in the path
of progress.'

Within tribal life there ran a corrosion that forced the
natives to depart from the ways of their parents and embrace
alien ways which their parents had not known. No gentle
process of education nor the slow suasion of a friendly contact
led them to accept the inevitable changes in their lives. The
promise of early missionary effort and of British humanitarianism was poorly kept. Instead of a continuous and ex-
panding sense of trusteeship, native policy was in the main
the sport of ignorance and the victim of neglect. A collapsing
form of society dies from the top. The authority of the chief,
because he was so narrowly identified with the law and the
custom of the tribe, broke down even before the tribe lost its
apparent unity. Without a head and focus it decayed in-
wardly, till, in the worst cases, it was no more than a shell.

These changes were uneven. In some tribes they were deferred. Many tribes even revealed the amazing endurance of native life by clinging to the ways of old. None the less, the history of the tribes is one of collapse and change. By the time diamonds were picked up and the first gold was discovered, black and white were far on the way to a new society in which both elements were joined indissolubly to one another in the closest of economic relationships. Here finally may be seen the explanation of the failure of South Africa to attract as many immigrants as Canada or Australia. The truth is that she did receive a very considerable immigration. It was an immigration from within. Her immigrants were black.

IV

NEW INDUSTRIES FOR OLD

'. . . but I must tell you, that their liberty and their freedom consist
in having of Government, those laws by which their life and their
Goods may be most their own.' CHARLES I, on the scaffold.

UNTIL the eighteenth century the diamond, like most of
the other 'stones of fire', came from the East. Golconda
was the Indian market-place for miners of precious stones.
In the legend and story of gems it had a place like that which
Ophir or Eldorado had in the legend and story of gold. The
famous stones of antiquity almost certainly came from the
sands and gravels of the Indian mines. For a hundred years
after the middle of the eighteenth century Bahia and other
mines in Brazil took the lead in producing the diamonds of
the world, and great Brazilian stones were added to famous
Indian collections. Then after 1867 such great quantities of
diamonds were produced in South Africa that all other
known deposits in other parts of the world shrank into
insignificance.

In chemistry the diamond, being pure carbon, is one of
the most common of elements. Yet it is fashioned by nature
into a magnificent crystal with the most dramatic history of
all the gems. It takes pride of place in the tales of Schehera-
zade, of Aladdin, and of Sheba's 'great store of precious
stones'. None of the chosen jewels of the Bible, 'the sardius,
topaz, the beryl, the onyx, and the jasper, the sapphire, the
emerald, and the carbuncle', can equal in truth or legend
the multifaceted Great Mogul, the blood-stained Orloff, and
the fabulous Koh-i-noor. Harder than any other gem, it is
also more brilliant and more varied in form and colour. Its
natural colour can be black or pink, blue or yellow, or as
pure as a drop of distilled water. It sparkles with both the
brilliance of reflected light and the red, blue, and violet
flashes of refracted light.

In the history of South Africa its importance is very great.
When the superb 'Star of South Africa', the rival to Brazil's
recently discovered 'Star of the South', was found in 1869,

South Africa was lagging far behind Australia, Canada, and even New Zealand in the search for the staples that could be sold in the markets of the world. It was wool, for example, that gave New South Wales and Victoria the power to buy and to borrow, and tc equip themselves with the instruments and institutions of modern communities. In South Africa wool production had, it is true, responded to the swift growth of England's textile industry. The Great Trek had not run its course before wool had already outstripped wine as the most important single export. In 1862 25,000,000 lb. of wool were exported. Since 1840 most of the growth which South Africa made was due to wool. But wool in South Africa did not nearly approach the commanding position of wool in Australia, and could not produce the purchasing power and the credit needed to obtain the benefits of nineteenth-century science, industry, and education.

South Africa has advanced politically by disasters and economically by windfalls. Diamonds, much helped by wool, were the windfall which undertook for South Africa what wool was doing for Australia, wool and a little later mutton for New Zealand, and fish, furs, lumber, and finally wheat for Canada.

The diamond fields were South Africa's first industrial community. There South Africa really faced for the first time the modern problems of capital and labour. There South Africa confronted a new competition between its white and black inhabitants, not for land and cattle, but for a place in industry. In a year after the rush began, Kimberley was the most populous settlement in South Africa outside Cape Town, with two churches, a hospital, a theatre, and probably as many grogshops as the rest of South Africa put together. In 1871 the number of whites and blacks was reckoned at 50,000. The whites were more than had taken part in the entire Greak Trek. They were naturally a floating population, drifting from field to field in search of the fortune that eluded the grasp of the great majority. The confusion of the early days—the cracking whips and bawling oxen, the hot dust that hung in a red haze over the landscape at nightfall, so fine that the slightest wind blew it into hair and eyes and watches, the deafening roar of hail on galvanized iron roofs, men digging up the gravel, and hurrying it in buckets, barrows, and carts to the water's edge to sort it—was likened to 'an insane asylum turned loose on a beach'. Much of it was the familiar story of rushes the world over, of the Pike's Peak gold rushes, or the Californian and Australian rushes. There were some who were poor in June and rich in December. But soon enough the glow of impending success which enveloped each digger in a warm atmosphere of anticipation grew less ardent. Phenomenal though the finds continued to be, they could not, had they been evenly distributed, give each digger more than a pittance for reward. Thus after a year or two only the fortunate and the dogged ones remained. And even upon these pressed new and intricate problems. As the cluster of tents and shanties became a town and the separate burrowing of each claim-holder became a great warren, there arose the need for order in government and order in the now considerable industrial enterprise of mining. Fortunately the demoralized and violent frontier mining societies of America were not duplicated on the African veld. True, the fields were born in a wrangle for their control between the British Government, the Orange Free State, and the Transvaal. There were ugly moments when factions confronted one another; once British troops marched up to fight. But they drank beer with their opponents instead of fighting them, for the essential problem of the diamond fields was not whether they belonged to the Orange Free State or the Crown. Of far more importance was the answer to the question how mining enterprise, with which the entire public of South Africa was destined to be bound up, was to be organized and controlled. What was to be the effect upon the white and black race of the emergence in their midst of a great industry? By what means could diamond mining abandon its disorderly and wasteful methods, and become as it must an efficient industry? Kimberley was the cradle and testing ground of social and economic policy.

It is customary to point to the soaring imports and exports of the Cape Colony and Natal as a measure of the great changes caused by diamond mining. Another measure may be found in the thousands of sleepers and the miles of steel rails that raced inland from Cape Town, Port Elizabeth, East London, and Durban. But neither tons of goods nor miles of steel can tell adequately how the lives of men were affected, how the exploits of mining industry were registered, not alone on the stock exchanges of the world, but in the fate of thousands of families and thousands of native kraals. To the fields came two streams, one white and one black. For every little clerk, deserting sailor, drought-stricken farmer, or turn-collar parson who came to the fields, there came two, three, and four Zulus, Basuto, Bechuana, and Xosas. To say that between 1871 and 1895 there were employed 100,000 natives, with some 400,000 women and children dependent upon them, can scarcely be an exaggeration. From the beginning diamond mining became vitally and irremediably dependent upon native labour. Of the 10,000 natives who worked on the mines each year, some came to earn enough money to buy guns; some fell victims to the Cape 'smoke' and Hamburg firewater which white scallywags sold them. But the great bulk came out of a stronger compulsion than guns or drink. They were evidence of the disruption of tribal life and economy. Henceforth the native problem was urban and industrial as well and no longer simply rural. The first step was taken towards the later detribalized and landless urban proletariat of South African industrial towns.

Sir Richard Southey, the first Lieutenant-Governor of Griqualand West, vainly tried to apply the liberal laws of the Cape Colony to the position of native labour. From the beginning public opinion was emphatic that the native was an unskilled labourer and had no higher place. Industrial Kimberley joined the rural Great Trek in its insistence that the town as well as the country be based upon an economic as well as a racial distinction between white and black. The servile tradition of the farm was introduced into industry. It was a crude political economy that exploited the ignorance and the poverty of the natives, and at the same time per-petuated these defects. It also demanded vagrancy laws and complained of 'idle' natives in the reserves and locations.

Before ever the diggers were themselves reduced by capitalistic mining companies to the status of employees, they had decided that no other place was open to the natives than that of low-paid and unskilled labour.

Till his recall in August 1875 Lieutenant-Governor Southey, with the tacit support of the High Commissioner, Sir Henry Barkly, strove to establish the power of government over the diamond industry and to protect the interests of the individual digger against mining companies and organized wealth. He passed several ordinances designed to protect the small claim-holder against the proprietors of the mining ground, to prevent the engrossment by individuals or companies of more than ten claims. But the diggers weakened the Government's strength by quarrelling with its liberal native policy and, with the short-sightedness of their kind, by evading the regulations framed for their protection. Southey's ordinances were frowned upon by the mid-Victorian economic thought of the Colonial Office as an attack upon the rights of capital and property and were disallowed. Had the administration of Griqualand West been wealthy and powerful enough to retain the services of mining experts and to set up the technical authorities to govern the industry, it might have prevailed against 'big business'. Actually the administration was so poor and its income so insufficient that its solvency was at the mercy of banking interests. It was forced to yield the development of mining to companies and organized wealth.

The nature of diamond mining also militated against the individual digger. Elsewhere diamonds had usually been found in alluvial deposits of sand and gravel which could be worked with primitive equipment. Here on the veld were alluvial deposits too, but the greatest proportion of diamonds was found in the unique geological formation of pipes of blue ground running deep into the earth. This meant that at the Kimberley mine, for example, where there were at one time 1,600 claims, some of them as small as 7 square yards, hundreds of separate pits were being dug into the same limited pipe. In the four great mines, the Kimberley, the De Beers, the Bultfontein, and Dutoitspan, there were over

3,200 full claims, many of them subdivided. The attempt to drive each claim and part of a claim hundreds of feet down, by individual methods of working, with every claim-holder trying to preserve the original integrity of his claim at the bottom of a fantastic excavation, could only produce confusion and waste. On the surface the same confusion prevailed in the sale of diamonds. There was cheating and thieving, and presently, because the market was oversupplied and depressed, there was a serious fall in diamond prices. When depths of a hundred feet were reached in the mines the roadways between the claims disappeared. It was no longer possible to haul the blue earth to the top in buckets, and instead a tangle of wires ran down from the rim of the craters. The buckets of earth were raised and lowered first by panting natives, then by horses, and finally by steam-engines. Thus mining advanced from the simple to the exceedingly complex, from muscle to machinery. Upon the digger the burden grew ever greater. At the bottom of the mines floods of water collected which compelled collective action and the use of machinery. A Mining Board was appointed in 1874 to secure a greater measure of co-operation. But the Mining Board, largely because of the weakness of Southey's administration, had neither the finances, the technical skill, nor the authority to impose order upon the throng at the bottom of each pit. When depths of 400 feet were reached mining became dangerous and wasteful. Great falls of rock and reef buried claims and took their toll of life. For every load of diamond-bearing ground many more loads of useless debris and thousands of gallons of water had to be removed. A crisis had been reached. The time had come when organized capital had to take the place of individual resources, and science and administrative skill had to be substituted for personal ingenuity. From 1874 onwards a steady process of amalgamation had been taking place. Before ever capitalists like Cecil Rhodes and Barney Barnato began their famous inclosure movement of the diamond claims, many of the claims, rather like the uneconomic strips on a medieval manor, had been joined together into larger holdings. When the expensive shafts and the intricate procedures of underground mining were adopted in 1882, the digger was doomed. Mining now called for an order of skill far above the competence of the average digger and for capital in amounts beyond the reach even of partnerships. Here Cecil John Rhodes found his opportunity. In his success there was a measure of accident. There were others in the race, men like Barney Barnato, Alfred Beit, and Julius Wernher, who had resource and skill. But Rhodes stood out from his rivals by his strength of imagination and by his power to elevate it above fantasy by daring action.

It was not his achievement to eliminate the little digger. Water and falling rock and bankruptcy had done that. Rather was it his achievement to reduce the three score and ten companies which existed in 1881 by progressive amalgamation till finally each mine was operated as a unit, and all the mines were consolidated under the famous De Beers Consolidated Mines Limited. The final stages of this consolidation are a tale, with chapters both sordid and ringing, of the triumph of this country parson's son over an East End Jew, a Paris diamond merchant, and a Hamburg buyer, all of them very remarkable men. With what purpose high finance had invaded the land of ox-wagons and fat-tailed sheep was seen when the name of Rothschild was invoked in Kimberley, and when the price of a single company's capitulation to the will of Rhodes was £5,338,650. In 1888 Rhodes's De Beers Consolidated Mines swallowed Jules Porges's French Company and Barney Barnato's Kimberley Central Mining Company. In 1889 Rhodes obtained control over the Griqualand West Company and the Bultfontein Consolidated Company. By acquiring the Premier Mine in the Transvaal in 1890 his gigantic trust, with control over all diamond mining, was completed.

Under the spectacular movements of finance there were other important realities. The reward of consolidation was efficiency and economy in mining and selling. As consolidation progressed so did costs fall. But falling costs alone might have punished the industry by glutting the market and causing a serious drop in prices. Rhodes enabled a single company to control output and to regulate the flow of the annual production of some four million carats in a uniform and stable manner. Company mining also found it to its advantage to maintain the difference between white and black upon which the diggers had insisted in the days of their independence. Labour in diamond mining was, therefore, divided into two classes. One was a large body of black labour earning low wages; the other was a much smaller group of white labour earning high wages. This division, so endlessly important in the subsequent social and industrial development of South Africa, must be clearly understood. It was not simply the result of the prejudice of colour. The natives who came to the fields had no skill to sell. Expertness and craftsmanship were the natural monopoly of the white workers. The natives came and went, for their homes and their hearts were in their kraals, whither they returned when their short contracts expired. By contrast the whites were a permanent population, bound by many ties to the place of their work. They had a compactness and self-consciousness which native labour, drawn from many tribes and speaking several tongues, could not have. The white workers stood out still more sharply because they were for the most part not of South African birth. Except for its wagon-builders South Africa simply had no skilled workers upon whom the mines could draw. Hence the special position of skilled labour was made still more emphatic because it was imported labour. Thus the apartness of white and black labour was the result of many circumstances. One other most important peculiarity in the pattern of labour in the diamond mines must be observed. Labour in most modern industry may be likened to a ladder with skilled workers at the top and unskilled workers at the bottom. Between them are the rungs of semi-skilled occupations by which men through their effort and the increase of their experience may mount upwards. In South Africa the emphatic separation of white and black in industry eliminated this intermediate region. It became a doctrine of South African labour economics that skill and high wages were a privilege of the white race, while the heavy labour and menial tasks were the province of the black race. The position of each group was guarded by the

absence of competition, for into the area between them the
one did not sink and the other did not rise. Such a disposi-
tion of labour conferred a great advantage upon the diamond
mining industry. It was the advantage of being able to
employ each year on an average of 10,000 native workers at
rates of pay which were low and, because native labour was
voiceless and constrained, did not vary from year to year.
South Africa's new prosperity was not built up on diamonds alone nor upon the gold whose discovery was at hand.
Of the resources which permitted South Africa at long last
to take its place beside the Australian colonies, New Zealand,
and Canada in the economy of the world, native labour was
one of the most important. What an abundance of rain and
grass was to New Zealand mutton, what a plenty of cheap
grazing land was to Australian wool, what the fertile prairie
acres were to Canadian wheat, cheap native labour was to
South African mining and industrial enterprise.

The author of a *Handbook of the Cape Colony*, published in
1875, declared that 'The resources of the Colony were thus
sealed-up and lying dormant, and its comparatively thinly-
scattered inhabitants idle spectators, during the great movements of labour and capital from the Old World to the New.'
Native wars had caused, it is true, a compulsory investment
of money, energy, and life, but it was for the most part an
unprofitable investment. Private capital found Canada,
Australia, and New Zealand attractive. Kimberley, with its
Saturday night brawls, its black prostitutes, its mud huts, and
Havana cigars changed all that, as it changed so many things.
It was Kimberley that introduced the Industrial Revolution
to South Africa.[1] Diamond mining carried forward what
wool had begun but had been unable to carry to completion.
It provided a greater incentive and more substantial means
for the modernization of the lumbering transport system. It
attracted population and capital to the country, diversified
the life and broadened the opportunities of young men and
women, and gave strength and purpose to political life.
Cape self-government was fortunate in the capacity of men

[1] In 1865 there were less than a score of towns in all South Africa with
a population of more than 1,000.

like Molteno, Merriman, Hofmeyr, and de Villiers, who
steered the Cape Parliament through the shoals and shallows
of its experimental years. Cape self-government was, however, doubly fortunate that it was launched on the tide of
rising prosperity. Because responsible government and prosperity came together, the Cape Colony, unburdened by a
heavy debt or expensive commitments, was limber and
athletic and able to enter strongly upon its new career. How
strong the Cape was in its new-found prosperity was evident
in the fact that the opening of the Suez Canal in 1869 was
not a disaster to the port of Cape Town. The returns of
shipping entered inwards for 1870 showed a decline of only
10 per cent. from the average of the previous ten years. In
the following years the brisk importations for the diamond
fields enabled Cape Town to regard very lightly the fact that
it no longer commanded the only sea route from Europe to
India.

The total imports through Cape and Natal ports were
£3,058,042 in 1871. In 1875 they were £7,000,157. The
total receipts of the Cape Treasury in 1872 were £1,161,548,
double what they had been in 1869. With no alteration in
the tariff, import dues were also doubled in the same period.
In the first dozen years after 1870 the mines exported a
greater value in diamonds than the agricultural and pastoral
industries together had been able to export in a period three
times as long before the discovery.[1] After liquidating £259,900
of its public debt, the Cape still had a surplus in 1872 of
£425,000 and could therefore afford the unaccustomed
luxury of meeting current expenses on public works from its
own resources. In 1874 the public debt was again reduced
by £546,966. This meant that the Cape's debt was hardly
greater than the revenues of a single year and that interest
charges were amply secured by the surplus of income over
expenditure. Far more significant was the Cape's strength
and position on the London money market. The capital
which before 1870 had been reluctant to come at 6 per cent.,
now was glad to come first at 5 per cent. and then at 4 per

[1] During a period of 67 years, between 1869 and 1936, diamonds
valued at £320 millions were produced in South Africa.

cent. Quite easily the Cape Colony could afford the imports of capital which were indispensable in developing all the great colonies of the nineteenth century, and equipping them with the means of modern existence. In the days of Governor Wodehouse a debt of less than £2,000,000 threatened the Cape's solvency. Now a public debt became the instrument of modern progress, enabling the Colony to spend £14,000,000 on the construction of 1,000 miles of railway by 1886. The Cape was able to increase its debt at the average annual rate of about £1,500,000 between 1875 and 1890. A low public debt, so necessary in the sixties, was no longer wise, for the time had come to knit this sprawling land together and to bridge, in more ways than one, the gap between the coast and the interior.

In 1870 there were sixty-three miles of railway between Cape Town and Wellington; in all the rest of the sub-continent there were only six miles more at Durban. The men and the equipment that suddenly demanded to be taken inland caused a partial collapse of the country's primitive transportation system. Its efficiency depended upon roads and grass. A load that was beyond the strength of a team of oxen on a poor road could be doubled and drawn with ease on an improved road. Poor grass weakened the draught animals; good grass gave them strength. That was why ox-wagon loads cost £15 a ton when the roads were fair and the animals well nourished, and £30 a ton when the roads were wretched and the animals emaciated. Behind the serious breakdown of transportation in Natal in 1874 is the story of beasts straining up its countless hills, of brakes groaning down the sides of unbridged gullies, of oxen stumbling along muddy roads, their sufferings made greater because of the overcropped grass and too often ended by redwater and the other diseases that were the scourge of the land.

Till the growth of Kimberley the railhead at Wellington had been poised to strike without, however, any spot to govern and direct its aim. Yet had it not been for Kimberley, it is almost certain that the railway would have followed the coastal belt of reliable rainfall to the Eastern Province, where there were wool, hides, and latterly, mohair. But diamond mining exerted a more powerful attraction. If the industry were to be made efficient it imperatively needed the aid of modern transport. The organization of diamond mining was not the work of Rhodes's genius alone. Without railways, which reached Kimberley in 1885, he could hardly have substituted the impressive equipment of the De Beers Company for the shovels and buckets and hand-made derricks of the diggers.

In the sparsely peopled colonies of the Empire railway building was not usually as attractive to private investors of capital as in the closely settled British Isles and Europe. Private capital was timid, or demanded high rates of profit, onerous guarantees against loss, or special concessions of land and mineral rights. In Natal, for example, the tiny line between Durban and the Point was built in 1860. Then during the next fifteen years various speculative interests attempted to control Natal railway development by angling for guarantees on land and mineral concessions. In the Cape, also, private capital built the line between Cape Town and Wellington and failed to go any farther. As in Australia and New Zealand railway building in South Africa was mostly the achievement of government enterprise and the public purse. Even the Canadian Pacific Railway needed the stimulus of an Imperial guarantee before it could be completed. South African railway building had to contend both with the great distances, the thinly peopled and desert regions common to Australia, and the steep gradients and curves of New Zealand. The climb from the coast to the interior plateau made the first hundred miles as difficult to build as the following five hundred. The lines from Cape Town and Port Elizabeth to Kimberley run for only very short distances in the more fertile regions of dependable rainfall and comparatively close settlement. For the greater proportion of their distance both traverse the great arid expanse of the Karroo, where the average rainfall ranges from 5 to 15 inches per annum. To build railways with any dispatch through the thirst lands of the Cape or over the countless hills of Natal, the public income and credit of the Cape Colony and Natal were alone not powerful enough.

South Africa's railways were like Australia's railways in one further respect. Because of the separateness of Natal from the Cape, and of the British colonies from the Republics, they were drawn deeply into a tangled political and economic rivalry. The steel that was to conquer physical space and bind one community to another was actually guilty of increasing disharmony and ill-will. It was clear that the way to economic progress was blocked by a lack of political co-operation.

In the early years of the seventies there was a widespread and genuine hope in both the British colonies and the Republics for some form of effective co-operation. Thomas François Burgers, elected President of the Transvaal in 1872, was torn and finally broken by the conflict in his mind between a united South Africa under British paramountcy and a single State dedicated to the Dutch race and language. In the Free State President Brand was deeply hurt by the British annexation of Basutoland in 1869 and stubbornly contested the British right to the diamond fields. But he was a member of the Cape Bar; his father was a baronet and speaker of the Cape Assembly; his wife was English, and the education of his children was English. Easily the moral superior of his contemporaries, British and Dutch, the inclination of his mind was to make whole that which was divided. John Charles Molteno, the first Prime Minister of the Cape Colony, was a man of much narrower vision, yet he too felt that in the course of time the Cape Colony might absorb the rest of South Africa. The hope that the rest of South Africa would be drawn within the orbit of the wealthier and self-governing mother colony had also been cherished by Lord Kimberley, who, as Secretary of State for the Colonies, had eagerly pressed responsible government upon the Cape Colony in 1872. Kimberley's successor, Lord Carnarvon, was equally devoted to the idea of South African federation. Unlike Kimberley or Molteno he did not believe that time and the natural prestige of the Cape Colony would together cause all South Africa to crystallize into a single State. He was even inclined to the view that Cape self-government was premature and an obstacle to the federation which only the British Government, as paramount power, could bring about. Ardently and vigorously he sought to guide South Africa in the path that Canada had already taken in the British North America Act of 1867. The explanation which he gave to the Cabinet of his policy reads like a paraphrase of the arguments used by Sir George Grey in his famous confederation dispatch of 1858.

'The advantages of Federation', he informed the Cabinet, 'are very obvious. European immigration and capital flow slowly into countries under small and isolated Governments whose financial solvency is questionable, and where there is no adequate security for property and no confidence in prudent legislation. Federation would greatly improve and cheapen the administration of affairs in almost every branch and greatly lessen the probability of a demand for aid in the shape of Imperial money or troops. But the most immediately urgent reason for general union is the formidable character of the native question, and the importance of a uniform, wise, and strong policy in dealing with it.'

'The Imperial factor' took its first bold step in Natal. There a petty act of disobedience by a chief named Langalibalele had caused a panic in the Colony. The exaggerated emotion and extreme severity of the punishment meted out to the chief and his followers were proof in Carnarvon's eyes of the inability of a single community to contend firmly and fairly with the difficult native problems. Carnarvon availed himself of the crisis to insist that the British Government could not shirk its Imperial responsibility in South Africa. Through the prestige of the Colonial Office and the brilliance and bluster of the specially appointed Lieutenant-Governor, Sir Garnet Wolseley, he persuaded the Natal legislature to increase the number of its nominated members, and thus to increase the power of the Lieutenant-Governor. At the same time, in May 1875, he penned a vigorous dispatch in which he recommended that a conference of delegates from the colonies and Republics should consider 'the all-important question of a possible union of South Africa in some form of confederation'. Lord Carnarvon did not fully understand, in spite of his association with the British North America Act, how sensitive the colonies had become to 'Downing

Street interference'. Molteno in the Cape looked with foreboding upon the abrogation of the Natal constitution. He thought that Carnarvon showed small respect for the rights of self-government in the Cape and was altogether premature in pressing confederation upon South Africa. The attitude which he took would, there can be little doubt, have been taken in similar circumstances by such other colonial statesmen as Macdonald in Canada, Parkes in New South Wales, or Vogel in New Zealand. On the other hand, Molteno's vision was confined to the Cape and did not extend to those common South African interests which could be seen in better perspective from Downing Street. There can be no doubt that, even without any local experience, Lord Carnarvon saw more clearly than President Burgers, President Brand, or Molteno that the different governments could no longer with safety carry out their separate social and economic policies. As long as the coastal colonies selfishly refused to share the customs dues collected at the ports with the landlocked interior communities, as long as the Cape and Natal were engaged in cut-throat competition for the trade of the interior, as long as there was no common understanding whatever in the vital native policy, neither progress nor peace could be assured in South Africa.

Carnarvon, it is fair to say, was a good statesman but a poor politician. After the Cape's refusal to join him in his plans for an early confederation he moved forward in a still more vigorous manner. In 1876 he made his peace with President Brand by paying the Orange Free State a sum of £90,000 in recognition of its claims to the diamond fields. His more peremptory policy was encouraged by the Lieutenant-Governors of Griqualand West and Natal. Sir Richard Southey was an ardent imperialist and no lover of republican independence. As the head of a weak and impecunious government he was better placed than Molteno to appraise the serious disadvantages of disunion. In the stream of native labourers who came to the fields from every part of South Africa he recognized very correctly a new complication of an already serious problem. Sir Garnet Wolseley in Natal was a soldier and little more than Carnarvon's agent. But he was a brilliant man and saw that Natal's fear of a great and disastrous native uprising, headed by the Zulus, was not unfounded. He also saw that diamonds were but the first of important mineral discoveries to be made in the interior. The centre of economic gravity was about to shift from the coastal colonies to the interior.

In Carnarvon's mind a number of motives urged him to take a compelling step. He felt a humanitarian concern for the natives. A sense of impending crisis caused him to fear both for the peace of South Africa and the pocket of the British taxpayer, who had already borne the heavy cost of many South African wars. The elimination of separate States would be a personal triumph and a worthy achievement to set by the side of Canadian confederation. To hoist the British flag over all South Africa would be an Imperial triumph. In 1877 he took a radical step which has ever since been the subject of debate. He annexed the Transvaal.

While the Orange Free State, Natal, and the Cape had prospered after the discovery of diamonds, the Transvaal was drawn ever more deeply into crisis. It did not have the prosperous sheep industry of the Free State, nor its profitable transport riding. Because the more intractable elements of the Great Trek had settled in the Transvaal its history had been fuller of contention. Government was weaker and far less efficient. The incessant clash of personalities had prevented the emergence of such a man as President Brand under whose direction government in the Free State was as stable and efficient as in the British colonies. Amongst the leading causes of the weakness of the country was its prodigal land policy. The largesse of promiscuous land grants was a process which alienated the land resources without returning to the State adequate compensation and benefit. Because the State so carelessly dissipated its rights to the land, the new owners were equally careless in recognizing their obligations to the State.

In 1875 President Burgers paid visits to three European capitals. In London he assured Lord Carnarvon of his devotion to the ideal of confederation. In Amsterdam, however, he made it clear that he did not necessarily envisage

confederation under the British flag. He attempted to float
a loan of 3,600,000 guilders. In January 1876 the *Diario do
Governo* of Lisbon made the purpose of the loan clear. The
Portuguese and Transvaal governments proposed to build a
line to Delagoa Bay. A· railway from the Transvaal to
Delagoa Bay, as later events amply proved, was not only
feasible but the shortest and most efficient route to the sea.
With such an independent outlet the Transvaal could escape
from its thraldom to Cape and Natal ports. It would also
step from beneath the shadow of British paramountcy.
Unfortunately Burgers's move was altogether premature.
More than two-thirds of the debentures of the Transvaal loan
remained unsold. The Portuguese Government also failed to
turn even a single sod.

Then in 1876 the artificial shortage of land caused the
farmers to fall foul of the Bapedi tribe under Sekukuni. The
war placed a burden upon the finances and the administration of the Transvaal under which both collapsed. The
collapse of credit and the failure of the war let loose an outcry
against the Transvaal. Opponents of the Republics, financial
and commercial interests, and other more generous elements
who longed to end disunion joined together in a demand for
British intervention. In England Carnarvon had made up
his mind to bring the Transvaal under British influence
before he knew how utterly the government of Burgers had
broken down. The demoralization of the Transvaal enabled
Sir Theophilus Shepstone to annex the Republic to the
British Crown on 12 April 1877.

The opinion of competent historians is divided on the
merits of the annexation. Some maintain that the abrupt
extinction of republican independence could only be visited
by failure. Others hold that a wiser and more generous rule
of the annexed territory would have won the favour of
Transvaal sentiment and brought confederation within
reach. But the British administration of the Transvaal was
the victim of many errors and much misfortune. It failed to
win popular support and alienated the Transvaal leaders, of
whom Paul Kruger was the most influential. Despite an
Imperial loan of £100,000 it made the mistake of hurrying

the Transvaal too rapidly into solvency and of compelling the farmers to pay the taxes and arrears which they had paid grudgingly even to their own republican government. The errors of a narrow and autocratic administration within the Transvaal were finally turned into disaster by a British Cabinet crisis, by drought, by three of the worst native wars of the century, by a world-wide financial depression, and by the vagaries of a British parliamentary election. In February 1878 Carnarvon left the Cabinet after a disagreement over Russian policy. His successor, Sir Michael Hicks Beach, had neither his conviction nor his energy. During 1877 began the severest drought which South Africa had known in a generation. On the Eastern Frontier the drought revealed as never before the overcrowding of men and the overcropping of animals. In South Africa the heat of drought easily becomes the fever of war. Against the Eastern Frontier natives, colonial and Imperial troops fought a difficult and expensive war, beginning in October 1877, accompanied by a serious constitutional quarrel between Molteno and Sir Bartle Frere, Governor of the Cape and High Commissioner. When peace was secured in June 1878, the Transvaal was at war again with Sekukuni, and the war with the Zulus, which Natal had feared for a generation, was imminent.

In Natal, Zululand, and parts of the Transvaal successive years of drought, too, had burned the country-side, starved its animals, and tortured the inhabitants. There was apprehension amongst the Europeans, and the greatest restlessness amongst all the native tribes. Amongst the native tribes the Zulus were especially powerful and well organized. After his experience of the war on the Eastern Frontier Sir Bartle Frere came to the conclusion that British control over the native world was essential if all South Africa were to be united. A victory over the powerful Zulu military organization would increase British prestige, strengthen its control over the Transvaal, and brighten the hopes of the confederation to which Frere was as ambitiously devoted as Carnarvon himself. The discontents of the Zulus and the exigencies of Carnarvon's confederation policy brought about a Zulu war.

In their wars the natives were usually helpless against

European arms and discipline. But once or twice they won victories that rang round the world. At Isandhlwana the Zulus annihilated a British regiment and turned the tide of British public opinion against Disraeli and a forward policy in South Africa. The Zulu War exposed South Africa's disjointed political framework, for while Imperial troops fought their difficult campaign in Zululand, the Transvaal leaders sulked in their tents, and even Natal often spoke and sometimes acted as if it were neutral. Economically the Zulu War revealed even more. All the millions of acres in Natal were unable to provide enough forage or food for colonists and troops. All its beasts, all its roads were not enough to meet the needs of the forces. The half-starved transport animals fell an easy prey to lung-sickness and red-water; those that escaped disease often perished of the over-work which desperate commissariat officers were compelled to throw upon them. Therein lay the story, not simply of the campaign and its disasters, but of uneconomic land-holding, of backward agriculture, of political disunion, and of economic disorganization. Carnarvon had hoped to cure these evils through confederation. From them Disraeli's government now drew another conclusion. By refusing to annex Zululand and placing it under the rule of thirteen petty chieftains with small authority and less prestige, it announced the bankruptcy of Carnarvon's policy.

A swift victory over the Zulus, with a lovable and brilliant character like Sir Harry Smith to proclaim it, might have rescued confederation and saved the Transvaal. But Lord Chelmsford, the victor of Ulundi, hated South Africa. Sir Henry Bulwer had never been happy as Lieutenant-Governor of Natal. Sir Garnet Wolseley, who succeeded Chelmsford and was made High Commissioner for South East Africa in June 1879, was the advocate of firmness and a big stick in dealing with the Boers of the Transvaal. Sir Bartle Frere understood far more what was amiss in the Transvaal, but neither the Colonial Office nor South Africa any longer had confidence in him. The discomfiture of British policy was the opportunity of Transvaal discontent. There an administration that had become still more arbitrary and cheese-paring lost what popular favour it had had. If the collapse of the Republic had been due to a weak administration and lawlessness in fiscal matters, the collapse of the British administration was, in part, due to an excessive haste in correcting these faults. Men like Kruger and Joubert demanded that the Transvaal should be returned to independence because its acquisition had been unjust and its governance unprosperous. In their discontent was born a new and powerful patriotism. Yet their discontent was also the protest of an economically backward and poorly organized community against a modern government that insisted on solvency and obedience. The haphazard and loose organization of Boer society did not gladly accept the discipline of regular and prompt tax payments and accurate monthly returns from local officials. Nor did men who counted their wealth in land and cattle comprehend the ways of a government which kept its books like a government office in Whitehall. The quarrel, therefore, between the Transvaal Boers and the British administration was a quarrel between a backward subsistence economy and a cash economy. The influence of the diamond mines, the modernization of government, the procedures of finance and banking had, all of them, invaded the seclusion of the Transvaal. True, the declarations of Paul Kruger were couched in the language of patriotic sentiment and the rights of the Boer people. To these declarations, genuinely made and deeply felt, the Boers, and finally British policy itself, hearkened. Yet Boer patriotism had an economic foundation in the attachment to an order of life that had not yet learned to accept without question the rule of law, the efficiency of administration, the solvency of public finance, the revolution of modern science and industry, and what Carlyle called the 'cash nexus'. The later history of the Republic proved that it was not the power of the British Government as such that weighed upon its life. The withdrawal of the British Government would not mean the withdrawal of the forces of the new age. Even though the British flag flew no more over the Transvaal the struggle would still go on between the old and the new, between cattle and cash, between the farmer and the engineer, between the ox-wagon and steam, between self-sufficiency and the interdependence of modern industry and commerce.

Of these truths British policy was only indistinctly aware. Meanwhile its setbacks continued. Gladstone's triumph in the Midlothian campaign was the sharpest rebuke to the Imperial policies of the Conservative Government. In September 1880 the Cape Government rebuffed the Imperial factor. It decided to complete its victory of 1878 over the Eastern Frontier tribes by disarming the Basutos, declaring that a Basuto war was no concern of the Home Government. Tact and patience might have succeeded in bringing about the disarmament which was certainly in the interests of South Africa. But the Cape Government acted peremptorily and drove to revolt a people already tormented by drought and overcrowding. In the long and unsuccessful struggle not a British soldier fought. The Cape Government would have it so. The war was a warning that British policy could not depend upon the sympathy or support of the leading colony. It seemed therefore wise for the British Government to step softly and limit its responsibilities.

Then the Transvaal rose in December 1880. British regiments were defeated and presently marched unavenged out of the Transvaal. Gladstone had at first hesitated to abandon the Transvaal even after the Midlothian campaign. Now he concluded the Pretoria Convention with Kruger and the Boer leaders. The Transvaal received 'complete self-government, subject to the suzerainty of Her Majesty'. Suzerainty in effect meant that the Transvaal's foreign relations and native policy were under British control and that the Transvaal could not change its boundaries without British consent.

Disunion ruled once more; separatism was triumphant. The Republic was reborn in an atmosphere of recrimination. A division existed between Boer and Briton far greater than the century had known. In the Cape the Afrikander Bond appealed for support on frankly racial and anti-British grounds. Political gloom was deepened by economic reverses. The first result of the British evacuation of the Transvaal was a collapse of credit and confidence. The diamond market, not yet safeguarded by Rhodes's organization of De Beers, collapsed. Droughts and the background of depression made the first six years of the eighties the blackest period South Africa had ever known. In those six years the British Government was to learn that it may be given to governments to make amends for the past, but that they cannot thereby deny the future. Bismarck and Kruger and Rhodes and gold-miners, all combined to prove that by shuffling off the Transvaal the British Government was drawn more deeply into the mill race that began with diamonds, was accelerated by gold, and finally plunged Great Britain into a great war.

Till the Convention of Pretoria the affairs of South Africa had been family affairs, openly discussed by the Colonial Office and Parliament as if they had been beyond the interest of foreign Powers. It had been tacitly assumed also that beyond the limits of actual possession in Southern Africa there was a wide area of British influence closed against foreign encroachment. It had never occurred to the Colonial Office that because it refused to annex territories like Zululand or the land beyond the Orange River they were, therefore, abandoned to the ambitions of other Powers. But Russia's search for empire in Asia, Leopold's Congo Free State, and the *Kolonialmenschen* in Berlin altered all that, challenging the 'irrevocable rule which gives Empire alone to British race and tongue'. In 1883 Germany invaded the remoteness of South Africa and immediately made the affairs of South Africa, like the affairs of Egypt or the Fiji Islands, the subject of international debate. Bismarck's sudden annexation of Angra Pequeña in August 1884 is a well-known incident in British foreign policy. Granville's ignorance of German colonial ambitions, Great Britain's need of German support against France in Egypt, and a feeling that Germany was after all entitled to colonial enterprise caused the British Government reluctantly to acquiesce in the German protectorate over Namaqua-Damaraland, more familiarly known as German South West Africa. Yet the German triumph was only partly due to the astuteness of Bismarck

or the bad diplomacy of the Foreign Office. Actually Angra
Pequeña became German because the British and Cape
Governments could not agree whose duty it was to protect
British interests in that region. Since 1868 the annexation of
at least the coast-line had been mooted. The British Government claimed that Namaqualand was no different from
Galekaland. Its annexation was the business of the local
government. And after the refusal to annex Zululand in 1879
and the abandonment of the Transvaal, the British Government was still stronger in its determination not to increase
its burdens in South Africa. Thus, with the exception of the
harbour of Walfisch Bay, which the Cape Colony had
annexed in March 1878, Namaqua-Damaraland shuttled
between Cape Town and Westminster till it fell into the lap
of Bismarck.

The arrival of Germany in South Africa was one more
proof that Great Britain could not turn its back upon South
Africa and leave Republics, natives, and now Germany to
work out their own fate. Mineral discoveries were drawing
South Africa into world economy; the Partition of Africa had
drawn it into world diplomacy. And the Transvaal of 1881
was no longer the Transvaal of 1877. The resentments of
the annexation had provoked a self-consciousness which the
Republic had not had before. The triumph over British
arms fed a new spirit—the spirit of the Dutch race and of
Transvaal nationalism. The Transvaal saw the weakness of
British policy but did not discern the liberal spirit without
which its independence could not have been regained. The
British withdrawal, instead of being an inducement to co-
operation, was therefore an unfortunate incentive to attack
the restrictions which the Pretoria Convention had imposed.
The Convention, for example, forbade the Transvaal to
extend its borders. In reply the Boers of the Transvaal began
once more to press against its frontiers. The shortage of land
caused a new trek to march once more in 1881 and 1882
against the lands of the surrounding native tribes. Into
Zululand, defeated and now ineffectively ruled by thirteen
kinglets, creaked the wagons of a new generation of pioneers.
On the Western Frontier of the Transvaal the hand of the

Boer reached out again to seize the vital watercourses and
fountains. This new movement of the Boers was much more
than a protest against the Pretoria Convention. It was a
demonstration of the powerful hold which the habits and the
aims of the Great Trek still had upon the Transvaal population. In July and October 1882 the two little Republics of
Stellaland and Goshen were formed on the western border
of the Transvaal, athwart the road of Livingstone and
Moffat, of hunters and traders into the interior. The new
republics were substantially what the Great Trek had been,
a spontaneous swarming of a migrant band on to new land.
But to the petty Republics of Stellaland and Goshen there
were weighty objections. It was serious enough that Stellaland and Goshen had made a drastic inroad upon the best
land that earlier encroachments had still left in native hands.
Much more serious was the great strategic importance of the
road which they threatened to block. A rainfall map shows
that the road lay just within the belt of rainfall averaging
15 or more inches per year. Very soon to the west began
the dry and uninhabitable waste of the Kalahari Desert. It
was Cecil John Rhodes who from Kimberley perceived most
clearly and proclaimed most loudly the importance of the
road. Because it was squeezed between the Transvaal border
and the desert he aptly called it a bottle-neck. Leading into
the interior it expanded into the great unannexed territories
of the Matabele and the Mashona tribes. Rhodes, from this
moment on, became the most important political as well as
financial figure in South Africa. Paul Kruger alone could
match him in importance. He was not one man, but several
men who blended their dissimilar and incongruous traits into
a firm and successful union. The biographer is yet to appear
who can do justice to the contradictions of the loftiness to
which he could rise and the baseness to which he could stoop.
As an imperialist of remarkable vision he saw that the loss
of the road would put a stop to further British expansion into
the interior. His mind conceived the project that Cape
Town and Egypt could be joined by a continuous band of
British possessions through the entire African continent.
Rhodes saw, what John Philip and Bartle Frere had each

seen in their day, that the hump, or interior plateau, was the
most desirable part of South Africa's anatomy. Most of it
was already held by the Republics. Their appetite for more
of the interior must be denied. Indeed, the logic of Rhodes's
thought demanded that they must, in the goodness of time,
restore South Africa to its wholeness by accepting a common
allegiance with all men in the sub-continent.

It was with misgivings that Downing Street and the
Cabinet watched men like Rhodes in South Africa and Kirk
in East Africa raise the banner of the new Imperialism. It
was with reluctance that they followed. The Home Government agreed that the restless Transvaalers could no longer
be permitted to carve for themselves new farms and new
frontiers. The entire instinct of British history cried out
against allowing any more of the coast-line from falling into
alien hands. That Delagoa Bay was Portuguese and Angra
Pequeña was German was damage enough. But the Home
Government tried to insist that the Traders' Road and the
unannexed coast-line were, like Kafirland itself, the direct
concern of the colonists and not of the Imperial Government.
Such a distinction had been difficult enough to maintain in
the days when Briton, Boer, and Bantu had lived alone in
the land. It was the inability of the Cape and Home Governments to agree whether Angra Pequeña was an Imperial or
colonial interest that had opened the door to German settlement in South Africa. The Home Government was loath to
be a cat's-paw for its colonies. But Angra Pequeña had been
a severe lesson, and reluctantly the Home Government took
the initiative. The policy of withdrawal had failed. In
December 1884 the British flag was raised at St. Lucia Bay
as a sign that no interference on the coast between Natal and
Delagoa Bay would be welcome. A month later a protectorate was proclaimed over the Pondoland[1] coast. The
Traders' Road was secured by the creation of the
Bechuanaland protectorate in March 1885 and the Crown
Colony of British Bechuanaland in September. In 1887
Zululand, much lessened by the New Republic which the

---

[1] Pondoland itself was not annexed till 1894, when it was annexed to
the Cape.

Boers had cut out of it, was placed under the Governor of Natal.

Almost the entire coast was in British hands, and the Republics were all but surrounded. Now that British influence had been so greatly expanded, the problem of republican independence was once more raised. As late as 1884 the British Government had still been willing to diminish its authority and influence in South Africa. Under the Convention of London in 1884 Lord Derby, as Secretary of State for the Colonies, had agreed to abandon the Queen's right to veto native legislation, and had given the Transvaal the same internal autonomy as the Free State. The right to withhold Her Majesty's consent to any treaty with native tribes or any foreign power save the Free State was maintained. Yet within eighteen months of the Convention the independence of the Transvaal was again in doubt.

The new activity of British policy, if it was not to be mere selfishness or a greed of land, could be justified only if it aimed at composing South Africa's divisions and restoring its unity. The signs, even in a period of deep economic depression, were not unfavourable. The conjuncture of Rhodes, the Englishman, and Hofmeyr, the Afrikander, was especially promising. Rhodes was great by instinct; Hofmeyr, by taking thought. Rhodes comprehended grandly but carelessly; Hofmeyr, narrowly but more deeply and meticulously. Hofmeyr, who was to the end of the nineteenth century what General Smuts was to the beginning of the twentieth century, recognized one truth very often overlooked in the history and politics of the Empire. To Great Britain's command of the sea did Australia, New Zealand, and South Africa, if not Canada as well, owe in large measure the opportunity to devote themselves, at leisure and unmenaced, to their political and social experiments. Hofmeyr knew that the British connexion, grievously though British statesmanship might blunder, was a bulwark against any foreign immixture in South Africa. He would not, therefore, lend his name or his influence to those elements of the Dutch population who, taking their cue from the Transvaal, preached the removal of a united Dutch race from all British control. He led the Afrikander Bond from the anti-British and racialist path which it first took, and prevented the Dutch of the Cape Colony from being swung into the orbit of Kruger and his embattled Transvaalers.

Not the least of the signs pointing to a further extension of British influence was the weakness of the Transvaal, the shapelessness of its government, and the poverty of its exchequer. On a minute paper an important member of the Colonial Office wrote in 1885: 'That the Transvaal would be able to maintain itself as an independent state I have never thought probable.' It was a reasonable prophecy, and yet a false one. The Transvaal did maintain its independence. Indeed, it suddenly began to go from strength to strength. Ten years after 1885 it was the most prosperous part of South Africa. A change so unforeseen and a development so unprecedented were due to the discovery in 1886 of the greatest gold-mines of all history, ancient and modern. From 1886 the story of South Africa is the story of gold.

V

THE WITWATERSRAND AND THE BOER WAR

'Gold is the child of Zeus; neither rust nor worms can corrupt this metal, which doth astonishingly excite the mind of mortals.' SAPPHO, *Fragments.*

IN a region of low hills and eroded valleys, scanty vegetation, and a few poor streams was a treasure of gold of which not even modern mining science has been able to compute the magnitude. Beneath formations of extreme geological age lay deposits that made the Witwatersrand the leader of all the other great names of mining history—California, Comstock, Alaska, Yukon, Ballarat, Calgoorlie, and Yenisei. From that one area was destined to come, in the short space of fifty years, three-quarters of the amount of gold that the world produced during the four preceding centuries.

From the days when Egyptian granites and Nubian sandstones were mined, gold has been traditionally associated with the African continent. The tales of the Queen of Sheba, of the Land of Ophir, and of King Solomon's mines are based upon the real existence of gold deposits throughout the whole continent. Prince Henry's successors brought it back in considerable amounts from the east and west coasts. Later still the Portuguese conducted a confused and planless search for the mythical kingdom of Monomotapa. The first Dutch governors sent one forlorn expedition after another into the trackless interior to find new fields or the old workings of legend. But the King of Monomotapa proved less real than Montezuma, and the city of Vigitti Magna less substantial than the great city of the Aztecs.

The discovery of the Witwatersrand gold-fields was not accidental. That the Transvaal was rich in minerals had been known for at least a generation. The great American and Australian gold strikes directed attention to South Africa. Men had been scratching in gullies and digging in the hills for twenty-five years before the brothers Struben finally located the Witwatersrand deposits in 1884. Indeed the existence of gold on the Witwatersrand seems to have been known by Boers as far back as the fifties. But this gold-bearing region was not like any other great mining region. There were no glittering Australian nuggets, or laden Comstock lode, nor the meteoric burst of the Yukon placers. The spectacular yields of California and Australia came from deposits concentrated by alluvial action. They were a 'geologic cream' that was soon skimmed off. The Witwatersrand ores, on the contrary, were contained in reefs buried deeply in the earth.

The Witwatersrand rocks, sedimentary in origin and of pre-Cambrian formation, contain the gold-bearing reefs. The reefs are a conglomerate composed of rounded quartz pebbles embedded in a quartzitic matrix, which is fine-grained and extremely hard. The gold particles, which are found in the matrix, are microscopic in size, and are usually intimately associated with grains of pyrites finely scattered in the conglomerate. A cosmopolitan host of scientists has still not settled the problem of the geologic origin of the Witwatersrand gold. The gold-bearing reefs, whose weathered outcrop first attracted prospectors, dip obliquely under the surface of the ground, reaching depths so great that part of the ore will probably never be reached by mining operations. The geological formation of the Witwatersrand beds is about 170 miles long and 100 miles wide, and although only a fraction of this area supports profitable mining, geologists and mining experts have periodically revised their estimates of the extent of mineralization. It is perhaps sufficient to know that such an extent of gold-bearing rock exists nowhere else in the world. It is also important to know that the ore is remarkably uniform. The history of mining is full of mining camps that rose and were left derelict, of pockets and veins heavy with gold that abruptly failed. But here in the heart of the veld the gold-mines were destined to be one of the great and enduring industries of the modern world.

The Witwatersrand deposits are at once the richest and the poorest in the world. They are the richest because the number of tons of ore is wellnigh incalculable. They are the poorest because the average gold content per ton is low. In none of the other great gold-producing centres of the world is the average gold content of ore so low. In the United States the average richness of the gold ores is three to six times as great. It is, however, the poor ores, those on the margin of profit, which yield the great outputs of gold. This is because in gold-mining the abundance of poor ore greatly exceeds that of the rich ore. Rich ores are actually rare. The problem of mining, ever since the discovery of the Witwatersrand, has not been to find the rich ore but to make the poor ore pay.

In the days of Cortez and Pizarro the Witwatersrand gold reefs would have been little better than barren rock. The Spaniards who worked the great mines of the sixteenth and seventeenth centuries in Central and South America would have stood helplessly before the gold deposits of the Witwatersrand. Even the methods of the 'forty-niners' in California could hardly have been successfully used in the Transvaal. But for the great forward steps taken by technology and chemistry many of the problems of extracting gold from low-grade reefs that thrust deeply into the bowels of the earth could not have been solved. Science turned barren rock into profitable ore. There was no place here for individuals with pans or hand-made sluice boxes. Heavy machinery and railways, engineers, technicians, scientists, and large volumes of capital—these were imperatively needed by Transvaal mining.

This dependence upon the most recent achievements of industrial and chemical science, and upon complex financial direction, inevitably made the Witwatersrand the centre of a revolution. In the midst of a slow-moving rural people there sprang up a startlingly modern industry, world-wide in its importance. The unusual demands which the gold-fields made, and the vivid contrast between them and the rest of the Republic were a fertile source of the great difficulties which preceded the Boer War.

Fortune smiled upon the early development of the gold industry. Mining began in a period of low prices, and at a time when the world's demand for gold was critically in excess of the prevailing supply. Before Transvaal gold began to reach London the possibility of an unsettling drop in the world production of new gold was not remote. In the fifteen years before 1886 the average annual world production of gold was only about £20,000,000 per annum. Now the Transvaal mines were a guarantee that the currencies of the world would not be readily disturbed by violent fluctuations in the supply of gold. The Rand secured the victory of gold over silver in the 'battle of the standards'. The declaration by the American statesman William Jennings Bryan in 1896: 'You shall not crucify mankind on a cross of gold', was the last bitter outcry against the victory of gold over silver as the principal basis of the monetary systems of civilized nations.

The great machines without which the ore could not be mined needed a ready source of energy. Although there was upon the Witwatersrand little wood and no water-power there was fortunately plenty of coal. Coal was as kind to gold in South Africa as it had been to iron in eighteenth-century England. At one point the outcrop of the reefs actually dips beneath coal measures. Abundant coal, of good quality and cheap, was of the greatest importance in the economy of gold-mining. Gold-mining, furthermore, leapt upwards on the shoulders of the diamond mines. Money and experience were there in Kimberley, ready to spring into action. The men of financial means were men on the spot with a knowledge of local conditions, able to judge and to act swiftly. Mining upon an important scale began within a few months of the official proclamation of the fields in 1886. In 1887 one mine paid a dividend of 57 per cent., and another of 25 per cent., to amazed shareholders. There were naturally bogus companies and wasted effort; there was the grossest speculation and there were resounding failures; serious errors in judgement and the difficulties of mining in the wilderness produced severe setbacks. It took several years to learn that the gold reefs, even less than the Kimberley pipes, could not be successfully worked by a large number of small and competitive companies. Mining that demanded the precisest knowledge of its scientists and the fullest skill of its engineers, also demanded the application to its problems of the most up-to-date business and financial organization. The deeper the mines went, the more refractory the ores became, the more faults and dykes complicated mining operations, the more imperative did carefully planned and organized mining become. Men like Rhodes and J. B. Robinson, with the experience of Kimberley behind them, were swift to bring order into chaos. Although it had taken Rhodes nearly twenty years to found the De Beers Consolidated Mines, within six years the Consolidated Gold Fields of South Africa was an accomplished fact.

The great changes already initiated by diamonds were multiplied and pushed more ardently forward by gold. A land that had seen boat-load after boat-load of emigrants for New Zealand and Australia pass it unheeding by now saw men tumbling on to its wharves and hurrying up country to the mines. Most of them were English, but amongst them was more than a sprinkling from Riga and Kiev, Hamburg and Frankfort, Rotterdam and San Francisco. More spectacular yet was the increased energy of economic and commercial life. The most stagnant of colonial regions suddenly exploded into activity. Figures are hardly sufficient to describe the greatness of the changes that the smallest village and remotest kraal experienced. In 1884 the Transvaal was barely solvent; three years later, in 1887, its revenue of £638,000 approached that of Natal; two years later again its revenue of £1,500,000 was in hot pursuit of that of the Cape. For every reluctant pound which the Transvaal had to spend in 1883 it had twenty-five pounds in 1895, gathered from stamp duties, land transfers, concessions, property and claim licences, and customs payments. The fairy godmother was clearly gold; for in 1896 gold accounted for 97 per cent. of Transvaal exports. No less than the Transvaal were the other communities stimulated to an activity which they had never known. The depressed years between 1881 and 1886 had been filled with anxiety for both the Cape and Natal. Both British colonies had loaded themselves to the breaking-point with debts for their railways and other modern improvements. They had neglected their agriculture and their natives and had fallen into a damaging rivalry with one another. Now a healing hand was laid upon them. The effect of imported foreign capital and increased credit facilities was evident in bounding import trade figures. In the Cape a revenue of £1,990,000 in 1886–7 increased by over £500,000 in 1889–90; the Natal revenue of £478,000 increased by £320,000 in the same period. Even the Free State's modest revenues increased in almost the same proportion.

The task of providing South Africa with the equipment of the modern age was still more aggressively undertaken. The splendid stepping ox, the pride of every farmer who had a well-trained team, became a lumbering beast that impeded progress. The country discovered that it had too few banks and too little credit, too few railways and too little trade. Abandoning the way of gradual transition it strove to secure in the shortest possible time the means of modern transport and commerce. Capital and enterprise caught up at last with the Great Trek. A spirit of innovation showed its impatience with the age-long ways of the veld. The shock of falling earth in the diamond mines, and the blast of dynamite in the gold-mines were felt in farm-house and kraal. The inhabitants of the Republics caught a glimpse of what forces were at work in their midst when the price of draught oxen rose from £3 to £12, when firewood could sometimes be sold for more than the value of the land upon which it grew, and a wagon-load of potatoes could be sold for twice the value of the oxen that drew it. Land itself rose in value. Although speculative traffic in land was already the bane of the country, prospecting fees and mining fees turned speculation into a fever.

The rise of gold-mining in South Africa was like the rise of the same industry amongst the original Mexican settlers of California. It brought confusion to an unprogressive rural society. The frontier of capital and industry did not follow the cattle frontier of the Great Trek gradually, mixing with it slowly, and finally forming another society by the fusion of the old and the new. Instead this frontier of money and machinery leapt into the Boer midst, bringing with it an aggressive and incompatible population. A country-side that was more sympathetic to tradition and uniformity than to innovations and initiative could not suffer gladly the new-comers who wanted to build, to organize, and to exploit. These new-comers put forward their demands vigorously. They demanded high returns and security for their investments. They demanded freedom to carry out their schemes. Often they were careless of the slow pride of the Dutch population and indifferent to the social and spiritual values of Dutch society.

A community dependent on money and machinery could not exist without friction within another community dependent on land and cattle, nor could the objectives and habits of each be readily made to coincide. An industry narrowly dependent on a world market was intolerant of the localism of the Republics. A simple society which had embraced the wilderness in order to protect its habits of living was challenged by a complex order in which there was a variety of industrial and commercial pursuits. The freedom which the Boers genuinely prized was limited to themselves. They had defeated thus far all efforts to extend it to the natives, and were reluctant to see it extended to men who knew not their ways or disapproved of them. Because they had little art, less architecture, and no literature, they depended upon their farms, their Bibles, and their blood to set them off sharply against the native and the outlander. All three loyalties strengthened their resistance to change and affirmed the inertia that was natural to their sluggish economy. It was natural that a landholding society should resist the challenge of men whose claims were based on their place in industry and commerce.

Had the Transvaal been the friendliest community acknowledging Her Majesty's Imperial rule, the invasion of its non-industrial society by the highly developed industrialism of Europe would have been rude and unsettling. In the Transvaal, and to a lesser extent in the Orange Free State, a series of events, from the British annexation of Basutoland in 1869 to the high-handed annexation and humiliating restoration of the Transvaal, had provoked resentments and emotions that were fused into a self-conscious and determined racial patriotism. It was at the moment when political and racial separatism had become a creed with a large section of the republican Boers that the new forces of trade, capital, and industry entered into their midst. Incompatibility was inevitable between men who had entered the interior decently by ox-wagons, and the new hasty generation of men who would not be content till they could travel the same road by train. The natural disharmony between the old and the new economic groups, the one homogeneous, rural, and becalmed, the other cosmopolitan, urban, and aggressive, was intensified by the political and moral disagreements that divided English and Dutch.

The policy of racial patriotism which Hofmeyr rejected in the Cape Colony was adopted by Kruger in the Transvaal. Resentment at the British annexation, triumph over Majuba, and well-justified anger at the selfishness of the British colonies stimulated the feelings of Transvaal patriotism. There came to his aid men from Holland and Germany who hailed the idea of an independent Dutch Republic, free of British control. These men spoke the language of European diplomacy and applied its practices to South Africa. Some of them were frankly opposed to British influence. The years between the Congress of Berlin and the crisis of Fashoda were not a period of British popularity on the European continent. Kruger's advisers helped him to formulate his programme of an Afrikander national State. Their effort was to interpret the relationship between Dutch and English as equivalent to the relationship between separate European national communities. To this end they encouraged the devices of diplomatic strategy. Tariffs and foreign loans and appeals to foreign Powers were some of the means which they used to assert the Transvaal's independence. Already before the discovery of gold the Transvaal had tried to play off Natal against the Cape Colony and to embarrass colonial commerce by means of tariffs. But the Transvaal's power to take an independent line was limited by its own great financial weakness and the British monopoly of the coast-line. With the extension of railways the British colonies controlled commerce and communication even more completely than before, greatly increasing the dependence upon them of the landlocked Republics. In 1883 an American named Mc-

Murdo revived the project of a railroad from the Transvaal to a non-British port. He floated a company to build a railway from Delagoa Bay to the Transvaal border. In 1884 the Netherlands Railway Company was formed to continue the projected line from the border to Pretoria. But capital was shy of schemes that appeared so certain of trouble and so uncertain of profit. With railways moving inland from the Cape and Natal a third railway seemed a doubtful enterprise. In 1885 Kruger, admitting defeat, offered to enter into a customs union and prepared to accept the continuation of the Kimberley line into the Transvaal. It was a critical moment. Such an offer of a South African Zollverein, so full of political promise, would not be made again. But the fault of the Cape ever had been giving too little and taking too much. Knowing herself strong, she was not disposed to yield a share of her customs to other communities. Even with Natal her rivalry was keen. The problem of South Africa never was simply one of inducing the Dutch Republics to abandon their aloofness; for the British colonies were themselves engaged in an economic and political rivalry that was responsible, no less than the separation of the Republics, for the disharmony that disfigured the last decades of the nineteenth century. Once again, therefore, the Cape obeyed the voice of her own interest, and gave no encouragement to a customs union.

Ever since the birth of the Republics the British colonies had selfishly refused to share with their neighbours the dues collected on imports. So little had Natal, for example, developed its agricultural and pastoral resources that its revenues were possibly the most parasitic in the Empire, battening on native taxation and duties on goods destined for the native and interior trade. The responsibility of the British colonies for the financial weakness of the Republics and for the harmful effects of that financial weakness was very great.

Gold was an ideal form of wealth to be discovered in an unprosperous State that had never known genuine solvency. Gold enabled Kruger to renew the search of former presidents for an independent outlet to the sea and to have a survey made of the line from Pretoria to the Portuguese border by the end of 1887. Gold enabled the Transvaal to spurn the Cape's belated willingness in 1888 to call a customs conference. The Transvaal was able, at long last, to indulge its sense of grievance and to punish the coastal colonies for their selfishness. So long defenceless against their superior commercial and financial advantages, it now could forge its own powerful weapons of attack. A tariff for a tariff, a railway for a railway, and a port for a port. For every sleeper laid from a British port to the Transvaal there was laid another sleeper from the Transvaal to the Portuguese port of Delagoa Bay. In 1887 the Transvaal tried to induce the Orange Free State to enter a federal union, linking both Republics to the Delagoa Bay line and closing their borders against penetration by railways from the British colonies. With borders that met the Transvaal, the Cape, and Natal, President Brand's Free State was of great strategic importance. The intimate linking of the two Dutch Republics would be the shrewdest blow that could be delivered against a customs union or political confederation. No man stood higher than Brand as a champion of republican independence. But it was his singular virtue that he could be a champion of the Free State without being an enemy of the British colonies or the British flag. His personality and his State were the core round which the Transvaal and the British colonies might yet group themselves in economic and political accord. In the beginning of 1888 the Free State took the first constructive step towards composing the war of tariffs and railways. Delegates from Natal, the Orange Free State, and the Cape Colony met at Cape Town in a customs convention. The Transvaal already had its gaze turned towards Delagoa Bay and was unwilling to receive concessions or to yield them. The Cape offered to reduce the *ad valorem* rate of its duties from 15 per cent. to 12 per cent. and to grant 9 per cent. to the inland communities on goods in transit through Cape ports. But the Natal rate was only 7 per cent., and Natal refused to abandon the advantages of a low tariff by an increase as great as 5 per cent., which would be necessary if there was to be a uniform rate at all

South African ports. The Orange Free State rescued the conference from utter failure by accepting a customs union with the Cape Colony and giving the Cape Colony the right of way for a railway line through Free State territory. Till Brand's death in July 1888 the Orange Free State remained within the orbit of the Cape Colony. His death made way for the Transvaal sympathizers. His successor, President F. W. Reitz, believed that all Boerdom should stand united against the British paramount power, finding strength in their race, their language, and their ideal of one sovereign Dutch State. Under the influence of Reitz the Orange Free State partly undid the good work of the customs union with the Cape by entering into a defensive alliance with the Transvaal in 1889.

In spite of natural difficulties and the resistance of the Cape and Natal the Transvaal border was connected with Delagoa Bay in 1889, and the first train ran from Pretoria to Delagoa Bay in 1894. The Natal line reached the Transvaal border in 1891, while the line from Port Elizabeth to Bloemfontein reached the Transvaal border in 1892. The Cape line was connected with the Rand in 1892, the Natal line not till 1895.

It would be vain to relate in further detail the quarrels over tariffs and railway rates in these years. The promise that telegraphs, roads, bridges, and engineering would forge the links that politics had failed to do was not kept. The Cape and Natal had played into the hands of Transvaal separatist feeling by failing to compose their own rivalry. In the economic struggle between them the Cape had more capital, a larger population, and better harbours; Natal had shorter distances and lower tariffs. Natal operated a single line; the Cape had the expense of three lines from Cape Town, Port Elizabeth, and East London. With a single line the Cape Colony could far more easily have met the challenge from Natal. The most efficient and business-like single line would have been not from Cape Town but from Port Elizabeth, which was the centre of the wool trade and many miles closer to both the gold and diamond fields. But the Cape had to satisfy the rivalry of Port Elizabeth with Cape

Town, and of East London with Port Elizabeth. The separateness which was the bane of the entire land was thus revealed again in sectionalism within the Cape itself.

The greatest rival of the British lines was the Netherlands South African Railway Company. It controlled the Rand end of all the lines and used its power to adjust rates and divert traffic for its own benefit. When the Cape line, in desperation, drastically cut rates on the section under its control, the Netherlands Company tripled the rates on the continuation of the line up to the Rand. The Cape thereupon transferred goods on to wagons at the Transvaal border. Kruger peremptorily closed the drifts[1] in August 1895, and before he opened them again South Africa recognized that in these quarrels over tariffs and railways there were the makings of a general South African war.

In the Cape Hofmeyr kept alive the hope of co-operation between Dutch and English, while his ally Rhodes continued to labour for a customs union and political confederation. Hofmeyr did not waver in his belief that the formula for self-rule need not be sought in hostility to the British connexion. With his followers he believed that the spirit of British colonial policy was to loosen rather than to bind, to free rather than to subject. He continued therefore to persuade the mute Dutch electorate of the Cape to use more freely the priviléges which the Cape constitution permitted them. Under his leadership Dutch opinion became a powerful force in Cape politics. In 1882 an amendment of the Constitution Ordinance permitted the use of Dutch in Parliament. At the same time instruction through the medium of the Dutch language was introduced in certain grades of schools. In 1884 Dutch and English were placed on an equal footing in magistrates' courts, and all public bills and papers were submitted to Parliament in both languages. In themselves they were not sweeping changes, but they served to indicate that the future of the Dutch language and race was not blocked under British self-governing institutions. To President Kruger Hofmeyr made a suggestion in 1889 which was good statesmanship and even better economics.

[1] Fords over the Vaal River.

Let the Transvaal drop all tariff rivalry with the colonies. Let trade and communication follow natural channels. The Cape railway from Bloemfontein was looking for a way to the north whither Rhodes's Imperial vision was striving. The proper way for this railway to take was through the Transvaal to the gold-fields and thence to the Limpopo River and to the territory beyond. Otherwise it would have to skirt the Transvaal through the unproductive scrub land of Bechuanaland in order to reach the land between the Limpopo and the Zambesi, where there were grass and water and maybe new gold-fields as great as the Rand itself. But in the Transvaal Volksraad were men far more opposed to co-operation with the British colonies than even Paul Kruger himself. Their decision not to tolerate even the bond of a railway line with the Cape Colony affirmed the separateness of the Transvaal, plunged Kruger and his anti-British advisers into deeper recalcitrance, and started in Rhodes the train of thought which ultimately led to the Jameson Raid.

Spurred on by the stubborn temper of the Transvaal Rhodes set to work to seize the Transvaal still more tightly by spheres of British influence. In 1889 the Transvaal could still expand to the north into the land of the Matabele and Mashona tribes and to the east into Swazi territory. Having defeated the Transvaal bid for the vital Travellers' Road in 1885, Cecil Rhodes now forestalled Transvaal expansion into the land between its northern border and the Zambesi. In 1889 the British South Africa Company was formed under Royal Charter. In 1890 a pioneer column made a daring march through Matabeleland into Mashonaland, braving what seemed to be certain disaster. Had disaster come it might have had the same effect upon Downing Street as the disaster of Isandhlwana exactly twenty years earlier, for in 1890 the British Government watched with much uneasiness the tendency of local events to drag it into a damaging quarrel with the Transvaal. It was indeed willing to relieve the Transvaal of some of the weight of British paramountcy. In 1890 it was prepared to vouchsafe to the Transvaal its ambition of an independent outlet to the sea by permitting it to build a line through Swaziland to Kosi Bay, provided that the Transvaal entered the customs union and gave the British Government the right of pre-emption. In 1894 the British Secretary of State, the Marquis of Ripon, decided to permit Swaziland to become a Transvaal protectorate. But the Transvaal in its new-found strength wanted an unqualified control of Swaziland and Kosi Bay. To accomplish this end it decided in 1894 to enter the dangerous channels of *Machtpolitik*. Kruger decided to invite Germany directly into South Africa. Against a background of warnings in the German press to Great Britain to keep hands off the Transvaal, Kruger made a speech in January 1895 which seemed deliberately to invite German intervention in South Africa. The appearance of German officers in the Transvaal, the departure of the State Secretary, Dr. Leyds, for Berlin, and the appearance of German war vessels at Delagoa Bay gave a sinister point to Kruger's speech. The menace of German support for the Transvaal provoked swift British action. The Transvaal lost its protectorate and all hope of access to the sea through territory under its own control. On all sides the Transvaal was now held in a vice which prevented its expansion. The Imperial factor, so reluctant to play a leading part in South Africa that it had granted Natal self-government in 1893, came forcefully back as a principal. Kruger and Germany had provoked the British Government to a peremptory declaration that all South Africa, including the Transvaal itself, was a sphere of British influence.

The remarkable importance of this declaration has not always been appreciated. In effect it once more made the Transvaal a suzerain State, and made its internal affairs the immediate concern of British statesmanship. And upon British statesmanship in its turn was placed the obligation of finding an escape from the frustration and confusion of all South African political life. In a period infinitely more difficult, amidst problems greatly more dangerous, Her Majesty's Government once again confronted the task which Lord Carnarvon had unsuccessfully taken up exactly twenty years before, the task of finding the formula of economic and political co-operation and of persuading South Africa to accept it.

From 1895 onwards the records of South African diplomacy are almost as complex as those in the files of the
Foreign Office. The volume that would do justice to all the
exchanges between high commissioners, lieutenant-governors, secretaries of state, and presidents would indeed be a
bulky one. Yet even as all railways and roads sought the
gold-fields, so did all lesser problems and vexations resolve
themselves into the direct questions: By what means, fair or
foul, soon or late, bloody or peaceful, would the Transvaal
and the States by which it was surrounded recognize that
the gold-mines were South African gold-mines, that its white
and black labourers came from every corner of South Africa,
that the Balkan mentality of Natal politicians, the superiority
complex of the Cape, and the hothouse patriotism of Transvaal politicians were making the land rank with intrigue,
suspicion, and plot? By what means could they be led to
recognize that the gold and diamonds, railways and tariffs,
race and language about which men quarrelled so endlessly
were all the most cogent reasons for not quarrelling? When,
in a phrase, would the unity be found without which no
prosperity could be assured?

In 1895 it was by no means certain that the answers would
have to be given through the bloody process of war. The
moderating voice of Hofmeyr in the Cape and the undoubted
success of Cape self-government in drawing together men of
both racial groups were full of promise. The self-government
which Natal finally achieved in 1893 had been a sign that
Downing Street was still willing to allow the local communities to settle their own terms of association. It is the judgement of competent scholars that at this time the will of the
crusty old president was not yet the prisoner of his advisers,
and that he might still have been won for the foundations
of a lasting accord. Though the matters of conflict were
numerous, the frontiers of conflict were still imperfectly
defined. In the ebb and flow of opinion and judgement
there was still opportunity for discussion and adjustment.
These years of South African history have placed a stigma
upon Imperial statesmanship from which it is not yet, in
the opinion of many, free. The name of Joseph Chamberlain,

Colonial Secretary since 1895, has become evidence of a
sinister alliance between the British Government and capitalistic finance to destroy the independence of a proud people.

Imperial statesmanship has suffered from many illusions
and many faults, but the illusion of omnipotence or the fault
of an ill faith that walked deliberately into bloodshed were
none of these. Yet there took place an event in 1895 which
cast the gravest doubt on the honour and good faith of
Imperial statesmanship. The Jameson Raid is one of the
most notorious incidents in the history of the British Empire.
Of the unhappy aftermath of the Raid, of the suspicions and
animosities which it provoked, of the setback which it gave
to those elements that were seeking one another out in a
spirit of concord, the story has been frequently told. It
thrust men into conflicting camps, justifying their prejudices
and confirming their antagonisms.

The principal cause of the Jameson Raid was the discovery, which had not been fully made before 1895, that the
Rand mines were as none other. In 1889 and 1890 a slump
boded ill for the future of the industry. Mismanagement and
inexperience had caused much wastage of capital. The
inevitable collapse of companies with insufficient capital or
barren properties brought gold-mining shares into disrepute.
Exhaustion of easily worked outcrops and the appearance of
more refractory ores compelled the industry to spend more
money and undertake new scientific procedures in mining
and management which only brought their reward after
some years. But by 1895 many of the difficulties had been
overcome. The success of deep-level mining proved that the
mines were destined to have a long life and that the great
community which had sprung up at Johannesburg to serve
them would not decline and disperse as the first rich finds
were exhausted. The shafts driving steadily down to sea-
level, the costly machinery on the surface, the interlocking
financial houses that managed the mines, were the signs that
not for a generation would there be any slackening in
activity. And by this time the belief was strong that South
Africa stood on the threshold of other Rands in the Transvaal
and in the new lands between the Limpopo and the Zambesi.

Men like Rhodes and his devoted lieutenant, Dr. Jameson, were pricked in their desire to prepare themselves for this impending empire of diamonds and gold by hurrying South Africa, by force and stratagem if need be, into a single political dominion.

The success of mining focused attention sharply also upon the policy of the Transvaal Government to the mining industry and the mining population. Were the Uitlanders[1] to be treated as Athens had treated its metics, who were privileged to live in the State but were denied the franchise and status of a citizen? In former days a man acquired citizenship when he acquired his farm. The landless men on the mines were therefore naturally handicapped. After 1882 Kruger proceeded to make these handicaps greater, till finally the franchise laws became so strict that new-comers had hardly more chance of obtaining the franchise than the natives of the Transkei. The Transvaal franchise laws ran counter to the habits of South African political life. At least three republican presidents had been British subjects. One had left his office as a republican president to become a member of the Natal Assembly, and another had died a baronet. At all times men had been free to come and go, to buy land and to sell it in both colonies and Republics. When the first Republics were created in 1852 and 1854 there had not been any specific parliamentary legislation, and there existed no test cases such as those which determined before British law the legal and civil position of the former American colonists after 1783. Since 1882 the Transvaal, however, had insisted with growing emphasis on its status as a nation. The term *Het Volk*, or *The People*, had changed its loose connotation to mean more precisely the people to whom the Transvaal was a fatherland. The Transvaal claimed to be a State, and indeed a nation, in which Uitlanders were on the same footing as foreigners would be in Belgium or Holland or Denmark. In South African political life this was an innovation, imported for the most part in the baggage of Kruger's Hollander and German advisers, but none the less firmly applied.

[1] Outlanders or foreigners.

It is easy to convict the Transvaal of a narrow and oppressive attitude. Yet Kruger and the men in his Volksraad who followed him felt that their cause was just. They sensed the greed of the financial interests that confronted their inexperienced government, the cynicism of men who could not understand their simple yet deep patriotism, the crookedness and vulgarity that gold had brought into their midst. What they did not sense with the same clarity was the inevitability of the change which had come, and the impossibility of resisting the revolution of diamonds and gold. The British annexation of the diamond fields had spared the Orange Free State the embarrassment of a self-willed and indigestible population of diggers and enabled President Brand to preserve the character of his State. But the problem of a still more self-willed and indigestible gold-mining population could not thus be solved. Yet to admit the great mining population to the franchise would be to surrender the political dominance of the established burghers. By 1895 there were seven Uitlanders for every three burghers. To give them the franchise was like giving up the Transvaal. For this land they had fought the British might itself; and the glory and grievance of that encounter were a special ingredient in their loyalty to their State. Their attachment was too deep to be lightly denied by an act of legislation. It was not altogether a narrow and short-sighted judgement that impelled them to deny the franchise to men who were richer, more numerous, and of a different manner of living. But the measures which were taken to preserve the franchise were stringent and were accompanied by galling disabilities. It was poor wisdom to deny the English language in the courts and schools, or to refuse the right of public meeting, or to be as rough spoken as the President sometimes was in denying requests for redress.

The hardships of the Uitlanders were greatly exaggerated by British Blue Books on South African affairs. Of those who came to seek wealth or a livelihood in the Transvaal there were many, including even mining magnates, to whom the lack of the franchise was no acute grievance. Nor were all of the Uitlanders in a real sense foreigners. A great many were from other parts of South Africa, who in earlier days would have had little difficulty in taking their place besides the other burghers of the Transvaal. Their influence, even without the vote, modified thought and judgement in the Transvaal to such an extent that a liberal movement slowly came closer to a mitigation of the stiff attitude of the Kruger régime. Till 1895 a liberal majority in the Volksraad and even the Presidency itself were within reach of the party of liberal Transvaalers. Before 1895 the burghers of the Transvaal were far from unanimous in following the ideal of an exclusive and reactionary Boer State. Yet in such a country as South Africa and to such a population as lived upon the gold-fields, Kruger's inflexible attitude on the franchise was bound to provoke resentment. Kruger's policy would have been more permissible had the Rand been an African Pike's Peak rush, or had it been, after the fashion of mining communities in young countries, difficult to govern. Although the Transvaal was of necessity weak in the experience and the institutions required to regulate the life of a swiftly growing and active mining population, the Rand was not remarkable for its disorderliness. The rough work was done by natives. The white miners were a stable group with an unusually high percentage of skilled artisans and trained employees. The large proportion of them were men who intended to spend the rest of their lives on the Rand, and whose children would likewise grow up within view of the white hills of crushed rock and within earshot of the thundering batteries. Sooner or later the problem of their civil rights was bound to call for settlement. With the doors to legal or constitutional modification so difficult to open, it was hardly surprising that men began to consider means to circumvent the law and the constitution by force.

Uitlander grievances were easily understood and easily exaggerated; political and emotional capital could readily be made out of them. Yet of far greater importance both before and after the Jameson Raid of 1895 was the relationship between a rural republic and the world industry in its midst. It cannot be too strongly or too often emphasized that the gold-fields were not a bonanza with a life splendid but brief. By 1895 men were beginning to guess a little more accurately than before how enormous were the tonnages of gold-bearing rock. But by 1895 it was also beginning to be clear that the ore was sensitive and exacting, yielding its benefits only under certain conditions. Wasteful mining and expensive procedures were promptly punished by lessened returns. Each ounce of gold, finely scattered in the rock, had to be expensively extracted. For each penny of profit there had to be a proportionately heavy investment of money, machinery, and labour. The margin of profit between expenditure and return for each ton of milled rock was narrow. Successful mining called for a great superstructure of capital, machinery, business organization, and scientific skill, and at the same time for a precise regard to economy and efficiency. The concept of an industry that was colossally wealthy, but could be wealthy only on condition that it jealously watched each penny of its expenditure, is invaluable for any understanding of the history of South African gold-mining.

The industry had been born with the extravagance natural to its product. But the costly sinking of deep-level shafts which only slowly proved themselves taught the lesson of economy. To the natural obstacles in the way of profitable mining were added others of men's making. The rates of transportation on the narrow-gauge railways, which had to drag their loads from sea-level on to the high interior plateau, were naturally high. The Cape system traversed hundreds of miles of barren and profitless land. The rates were made higher by the Transvaal's hostility to the Cape and Natal railway systems. High railway rates meant high costs of essential equipment. Tariffs at the coast and Kruger's tariffs on the Transvaal border raised the cost of living and caused inordinately high wages. The mining industry, it is clear, was paying a heavy price for South Africa's political and economic inefficiency. Nowhere could the harmful effects of political bad blood and economic dislocation be more tangibly felt or more concretely measured than in the ledgers of the great mining companies. Upon them pressed also the burden of government monopolies, concessions, and taxes. Although the Cape and Natal, no less than the Transvaal, mulcted the mining industry, it was the direct charges imposed by the Transvaal which most easily drew attention. In consequence there descended upon the Transvaal a blame which should have been shared by the rest of South Africa.

Modern criticism looks more favourably upon Kruger's mining policy. The system of monopolies and concessions enabled the Transvaal Government to tap the industry at various points, and through the vital dynamite monopoly to keep a tight rein upon it as well. In spite of the bitter complaints of the mining companies the result of the heavy charges placed upon the industry were not always harmful. To maintain their profits the companies were compelled to mine more efficiently and to eliminate waste more resolutely. To the burden which Kruger placed upon the mines were due in large measure, therefore, the feats of engineering and business administration which are an astounding chapter in their history. Unwittingly perhaps Kruger prevented organized capital from plundering the reefs, skimming the cream of their deposits, and by their rapacity shortening the life and, in the end, limiting their yield. Much more successfully than the Lieutenant-Governors of Griqualand West did Kruger succeed in compelling the acceptance of the idea that the gold in the earth was a public benefit and not the booty of capitalist enterprise. Thus an old man who in his youth had walked with the oxen of the Great Trek won for himself a meaningful place in the history of the relations between the State and industry. But in 1895 mining capital looked with little love upon Kruger's strict rule.

On Christmas Day of 1895 none could yet say that there was no hope of an early end to the quarrels over railways and votes, tariffs and monopolies. On New Year's Day of 1896 the future was blank of the slightest hope. This was the work of the raid of Dr. Jameson and 500 followers into the Transvaal from Bechuanaland with the intention of enabling the forces of discontent on the Witwatersrand to rise and seize power. The raid is a story woven of such stupidities that it might be dismissed as a farce were it not so tragic in the damage which it wrought. It was inexcusable in its folly and unforgivable in its consequences. No historian has yet

succeeded in solving its puzzles, in making clear the precise
measure of fault of Joseph Chamberlain, the Colonial Secretary, of Sir Hercules Robinson, the High Commissioner, or
of Rhodes himself. That none of these men was entirely
guiltless is clear enough. That Rhodes had helped lay the
train of revolt that would explode on the Witwatersrand is
certain. In truth some elements of success were not wanting
in the plot. A challenge to the President and his policy
coming from the Uitlanders might have broken the deadlock
of negotiation, and provoked a crisis from which might have
arisen a new order in which the franchise for the Uitlanders
and Transvaal co-operation in customs and railway policies
would be secured. That such optimistic considerations
passed through the mind of Rhodes and his associates cannot
be doubted. But the ignominious failure of the Jameson
Raid made its participants look like cheap brigands and the
Transvaal the victim of a plot on its honour. It tainted all
of future British policy, and, what was really worse, it
reached backwards and left a mark of dishonour on earlier
British statesmanship. It served to justify those who claimed
that in their relations with the British Government the
Republics had experienced little but injustice and bad faith.
In the Transvaal the frontiers of conflict were sharply defined. Transvaal policy now hardened about the set views
of the anti-British group who opposed compromise, maintaining that the Transvaal should abate nothing of its
insistence upon its independence.

Once again the whisper of German help was heard.
Whether it came from Berlin no one could prove. But many
accepted it as a promise and steered their courses accordingly. Henceforth British relations with the Transvaal
stumbled through a dangerous terrain of suspicion and resentment. Discussion continued, but the arrival through
Delagoa Bay of German mausers and cannon showed how
close force and the threat of force were to taking the place
of persuasion and compromise. The prestige of the old Cape
Colony in the eyes of the Republics was gone. The vital
alliance between Hofmeyr and Rhodes was destroyed by
the Jameson Raid. The power of Rhodes's name and the

influence of his ideas on closer union were diminished. In the Transvaal the whole incredible entourage of Paul Kruger—Hollander jurists and German gunners, Calvinists and republican patriots—confronted an equally heterogeneous group of company promoters, Anglophiles, liberals, and imperialists. Power and the law of the land were on the side of Kruger. Money and the future were on the side of the opposition.

New laws, the Press Law, the Aliens Expulsion Law, and the Immigration Law were passed against the Uitlander. In March 1897 the Transvaal concluded a firm defensive and offensive alliance with the Orange Free State. In spite of previous disappointments the Republic turned again to Europe for the capital with which to counter British financial power, and maybe obtain control over the Delagoa Bay line and the harbour of Delagoa Bay as well. Perhaps the support of Paris, together with that of Berlin, might be used to shake off the hated weight of British suzerainty; for in Paris Fashoda and Egypt rankled for a short while more bitterly than did Sedan. And because it is of the nature of threats and force to beget force, British war vessels appeared again to warn foreign Powers that the British Government would resist any intervention in South Africa. The expedition of light artillery and a battalion to South Africa was a hint also that the Imperial factor, speaking with the voice of Joseph Chamberlain, had abandoned the hope that it could withdraw from South Africa. In April 1897 a new High Commissioner, Sir Alfred Milner, left England for South Africa to test once again the rule of South African governorships that no man, however great, had thus far been great enough to cope with its problems. Milner did not come with instructions to force the Transvaal to come to terms. Nor was he the tool of mining magnates and financial interests. Upon the manœuvres of the Uitlanders he even looked with a hostile eye. Milner cherished the hope that the weakness of the Transvaal might yet find it out and chasten its obstinate temper. Even now it might be possible for the liberal element in the Transvaal to gain the upper hand. The President himself could not live for ever. The view that represents Milner as the agent of an imperialist Colonial Secretary, bent on breaking the Transvaal's will, does too little justice to the earnestness of Milner's search for compromise, or to the nature of British policy which was now, as always, variously moved, contradictory in its phases, and uncoordinated between its agents. In the same manner is it true that Kruger was aware of the dangers of too obdurate an attitude. Until Kruger, to the dismay of his opponents, was elected to the Presidency once more in February 1898 Milner trod warily, keeping out of sight the 'big stick' of British paramountcy. No historian of feeling can read the records of these years without halting reflectively at many points where the elements of compromise approached one another, where the old President showed that the desire for understanding was alive in his heart, where even mining magnates admitted the benefits of the republican régime and sought to co-operate with it. The anti-Boer, the anti-imperialist, and the anti-capitalist interpretations of the years before the Boer War all do insufficient justice to the complexity of events and to the character of the participants. The picture of the capitalists as men with gold in their hands, brass in their tongues, contempt in their faces, and treachery in their hearts is as untrue as the picture of an Empire robbing a petty State of its independence out of envy for its wealth, or the picture of an ignorant and perverse old man leading his State into destruction rather than yield to a modern age.

The book is yet to be written that will do full justice to the points of dispute in the last years. The Boer War was caused by two broad sets of circumstances upon which depended the numerous individual points of dispute during the last years. The first, quite clearly, was the existence of the gold-mines and the powerful financial and commercial interests whose focus was the Witwatersrand. The Jameson Raid, the Uitlander grievances, the problems of British Indians, monopolies, and tariffs were directly connected with gold-mining interests. Any attempt by the British Government to secure concessions or reforms from the Transvaal Government made it inevitably the agent of the mining magnates. By espousing the cause of the Uitlander, or by seeking to obstruct the Transvaal's use of a non-British port at Delagoa Bay, Great Britain gave its support, whether this was clearly realized in Downing Street or not, to capital and mining investments. Thus far the British policy was a good illustration of what has sometimes been called 'economic imperialism'. But it was by no means capitalist pressure alone that led to the violent reduction of republican independence. A second set of circumstances, more creditable than the first, and an authentic expression of British policy in South Africa and the rest of the Empire, must be placed beside the first. The Boér War was also the culmination of the British Government's léngthy quest for a united South Africa. No one who has read in detail and with care the records of British policy since the achievement of Confederation in Canada can miss the picture of a British Government groping for some means of ending South African disunity. The vision of British statesmanship was often opaque and its manœuvres were clumsy; its procedures were dilatory and its failures disconcerting. Yet since 1867 its problem had been to discern at what moment and in what manner unity might be obtained. Sir Harry Smith's annexation of the Orange River Sovereignty in 1848, Sir George Grey's plea for Confederation in 1858, and Lord Carnarvon's clumsy annexation of the Transvaal in 1877 were failures. Each failure made a peaceful solution less possible. In the end only a great crisis could break the resistance which the events of the century had built against unity. By 1898 the question could not be avoided: could British policy any longer permit the Transvaal to speak without reprimand or act without restraint in matters that affected all South Africa vitally and closely? Where it was so clear that South Africa was naturally destined to unity, could a single community be allowed to deny that unity and to follow a course that made an unhappy separation the chief characteristic of political life? Could the Transvaal's search for alliances with foreign Powers be permitted to draw South Africa into the company of Egypt and Afghanistan, Samoa and Venezuela, each of which held the threat of an international war? The answer was finally clear. British paramountcy must prevail. After Kruger's re-election in February 1898, Milner held a minatory language, pressing more vigorously for reforms and declaring that a 'mediaeval race oligarchy' could no longer have the fate of a great modern industry in its hands. The crisis was brought by gold. That it was brought by gold must not hide the truth that it was also a constitutional crisis. The blood and suffering of the Boer War were also a political revolution which ended the *ancien régime* of separate and conflicting communities. A war is usually judged by its causes. It must also be judged by its peace and the consequences of its peace. That is the lesson of the Great War and the Peace of Versailles.

VI

THE UNION OF SOUTH AFRICA

'The white people of South Africa are committed to such a path as few nations have trod before them, and scarcely one trod with success.' LORD SELBORNE in 1907.

BY 1895 Johannesburg should have been a vantage-point from which the century could be more freshly and clearly surveyed. Unfortunately quarrelsome memories on both sides dug back to the very beginnings of English and Dutch relations and threw their prejudiced findings at one another's heads. More bad history was created in a short time than many years of fair-minded study have since been able to disprove. That history concerned itself too much with the white races and too little with the black. More than any other period in the nineteenth century the last two decades were inattentive to native policy. Yet at no time had the need for careful attention to the happenings in native society been more imperative. White society was too busy building railways and quarrelling over their use to give to native matters the care which they deserved. For fifteen years before the Boer War, and for almost the same length of time afterwards, white society was too preoccupied with its own difficulties to pay constructive attention to the natives in its midst. Great Britain's refusal to annex Zululand after the Zulu War and the Cape Colony's abandonment of Basutoland were the signs that neither the Home Government nor the most powerful and liberal local government were willing to confront native matters with energy and determination. South Africa quarrelled about everything but its native policy. Even the Home Government joined in the conspiracy of neglect. Aware of the explosive character of native policy, it forbore to speak or to act lest there be added to the sum total of quarrelsomeness the outcry that had once been raised against Dr. Philip and Exeter Hall. In a barren sea of neglect and indifference were two reports and one legislative enactment. The *Report of the Natal Native Commission* in 1881 and the *Report of the Native Laws and Customs Commission* (Cape) of 1883 were valuable first steps towards a more scientific understanding of native life and thought. The Glen Grey Act of 1894, fathered by Rhodes, was the most forward move in fifty years. In the Glen Grey district of the native area known as the Transkei it introduced a system of individual land tenure and initiated a system of restricted native self-government. Land tenure was guaranteed against any possibility of European encroachment. Although the overcrowding of too many natives upon too little land gave the Act only a qualified success, it meant much that a halt had been called at one point to the universal pressure upon native land. But the great body of native workers who tramped to the Witwatersrand or rode there on the new railroads were proof that the revolution initiated by the diamond fields had abated nothing of its intensity. The pursuits of peace, no less than the practices of war, placed severe pressures upon the natives, compelling them to abandon their leisure for labour, their country for the town, their tribe for work gangs on railways and mines. Their clothes, blankets, taxes, coffee, and many things besides taught them the value of cash. Cash wages were difficult to obtain on the poorly productive European farms, many of them on the level of subsistence farming. Thus from native areas as well as from land owned by Europeans there commenced a drift to the towns. Loss of land and the insurmountable obstacles in the way of acquiring property in land had produced a native proletariat. Now part of this great class transferred itself to the town and to industry as well.

The last decade of the century brought the natives of Matabeleland and Mashonaland into line with the rest of South Africa. The British South Africa Company, telegraphs, railways, and prospectors looking for a new and British Witwatersrand were all incompatible with the Matabele chief Lobengula and his martial impis. As soon as it was decided to open up the territories of the Matabele and Mashona tribes to white enterprise the destruction of native independence was as inevitable as the rising of the sun. Whereas the Cape Eastern Frontier had had to fight many wars during a whole century before the tribes were finally broken, less than ten years were enough to assert white supremacy in Matabeleland and Mashonaland. In 1893 the Matabele were defeated by machine guns and cavalry. Their best lands were confiscated. A rebellion in 1896 was crushed after seven months of fighting. A Mashona rebellion in the same year took even longer to quell. But in 1897, when the rail-head reached the royal capital of Lobengula at Buluwayo, the tribes of South Africa from the Great Fish River to the Zambesi were a race of men who obeyed magistrates, paid taxes, and were a reservoir of labour for the white colonists.

At the peace which ended the Boer War there were two problems which towered above all others—native policy and political disunity. They had been the occasion of all the bloodshed during an entire century and the most frequent causes of strife between Boer and Briton, white and black, colony and mother country. Now the war had brought every community under the British flag. The treaty of peace was signed at a place optimistically called Vereeniging, which means union. The peace seemed the opportunity at last for a truly comprehensive settlement of South Africa's great problems.

But between the two great problems of native policy and political unity there existed a serious incompatibility. Much of the hesitant and evasive conduct of British statesmanship in the generation before the Boer War could be attributed to the indecision of the British Government between its obligation to the natives and its obligation to the white communities. To grant an unrestricted political liberty to the whites was to fasten social, economic, and political restrictions on the natives. To insist upon a higher place for the natives was to offend the white communities, especially Natal and the Republics, in their deepest convictions. Humanity and liberty became opposites which for long years had paralysed action.

Now, however, the Boer War compelled a decision on native policy. In the terms of the peace the British Government promised that no attempt would be made to alter the political status of the natives before self-government had been granted to the ex-Republics. In that epochal decision the British Government receded from its humanitarian position, and enabled the Boer leaders to win a signal victory in the very peace negotiations which marked their military defeat. Great Britain abandoned the effort to exercise a control over the vital relations between white and black. Downing Street had surrendered to the frontier.

The length of the war gave men in England an opportunity for reflection. The great bitterness against the views of the liberal opposition under Campbell-Bannerman and Lloyd George lessened. Their demand that the Imperial factor should withdraw from South Africa by granting self-government as soon as possible after the war fell on attentive ears amongst the Government's followers. It became clear by the end of the war that Great Britain had fought the Boer War, not to hold South Africa, but to relinquish it, and that a British victory would paradoxically end British influence in South Africa.

Although the war brought all South Africa under the British flag, it still left the country politically divided. The self-governing institutions of Natal and the Cape Colony placed them beyond the control which the British Government exercised over the Transvaal and the Orange Free State.[1] The grant of self-government to the Cape Colony in 1872 had greatly weakened the position of the British Government in South Africa. Through the power of her self-governing institutions the Cape had played an important part in defeating Lord Carnarvon's earlier scheme of confederation. The question was now raised whether Great Britain, having asserted its power over the Republics, could find a short cut to federation by reducing Natal and the Cape Colony to the same status of Crown Colony governments. Then all South Africa would be on the same footing, and the labour of fashioning a common government could be more expeditiously carried forward. But since 1688 it had been the strongest rule of British constitutional practice that what the Crown had once given could not lightly be taken away. Lacking the support of Chamberlain in England, Milner failed to persuade the Cape to yield its constitutional independence.

[1] Called the Orange River Colony 1900–10.

When Chamberlain came to South Africa in December 1902 his mind was above all focused on conciliation with the Boers. There, in his judgement, was the first and greatest task of reconstruction. At the signing of the peace the British Government had promised £3,000,000 towards rehabilitating the population of the Transvaal and the Orange Free State. Chamberlain now arranged for a loan supported by an Imperial guarantee for £35,000,000. The money allocated for relief and compensation was distributed freely and almost carelessly. The British administration seemed determined not to make the mistake of financial severity which had so damaged its reputation with the Boers after the first annexation of the Transvaal in 1877.

Resettlement upon the land and expenditures on houses and equipment were alone powerless to restore the ex-Republics to prosperity. A severe drought in 1902–3 drew painful attention to the poverty of the soil and the backwardness of its population. It was to the mines that Milner looked for help. They must henceforth assume the responsibility so far assumed by Imperial funds. From them must come the wealth needed to maintain the new roads which Milner had built after the war, to pay for the new schools and teachers, to subsidize, at least indirectly, the new municipal councils, and to encourage the immigration of the new British citizens from whom Milner expected much in redressing the balance between English and Dutch.

The mines complained that they could not undertake such a task until they had recovered the native workers dispersed by the war. At the close of the war it was estimated that the mines needed 70,000 additional native workers. The protest of the mining companies that they could not operate successfully without more and ever more cheap native workers provoked a memorable controversy. Not since the days of van Riebeeck had anybody seriously questioned the economics of native labour. Now at this critical moment, when South Africa stood on the threshold of a new destiny, a startling question was asked. Was not the dependence of the white race upon native labour a menace to its integrity? The question was asked by F. H. P. Creswell. In 1903 he was a mine manager. Later, as befitted a man who asked such a question, he became the leader of South Africa's Labour Party. He attacked the assumption that the only province of white labour was the narrow upper layer of skilled occupations, and that the great area of unskilled labour belonged to the natives. He disputed the argument that white labour was too expensive to be used in the place of black labour. By implication he affirmed that the cheapness of native labour was illusory, for inefficient labour, even though its wages were low, could still be uneconomical. It was a demand that the British Government should reconsider the entire question of the relations between white and black. It was the first blow in favour of South Africa's later civilized labour policy, and the first statement of a familiar and recurrent problem.

Milner was in thorough sympathy with the desire to see more white men, especially of British stock, engaged in the economic life of the country. It was, indeed, one of his fondest hopes that the Witwatersrand would be a loadstone for British immigrants. But he believed that the mines were a special case. Their function was not that of a normal industry. Their function was to impart as quickly as possible a stimulus to the rest of South African economic life. They were a treasure-house to be efficiently plundered. Their life was short. It was wise, therefore, not to treat them as ends but as means. If it were true, as was earnestly claimed by the mining companies, that the use of cheap labour would increase the yield of the mines in profits and dividends, then it would be best to employ cheap labour. The place which both Milner and Creswell desired for white workers would be found in more permanent occupations nurtured by the wealth produced from the impermanent mines.

The leading consequence of this order of reasoning was the importation of a first contingent of 10,000 Chinese labourers in 1904, to reinforce the insufficient ranks of native labourers from within South Africa and the Portuguese colonies. The Dutch sulked, but the mines prospered. Company profits and public revenues expanded. Production mounted steadily until in 1906 £24,600,000 was produced and 18,000 whites were employed. Post-war depression lifted, and in the midst of the shanties of republican days began to rise a new Johannesburg of substantial buildings and well-laid streets.

The growing prosperity of the mines was a powerful ally to Milner's great labours of reconstruction. One of his goals, however, they could not help him to win. They did not attract enough immigrants to turn the scales in favour of the British element. As each year passed by it became increasingly plain that in a self-governing South Africa the electorate would be predominantly Dutch. Each year also made clearer the determination of the Dutch that there should be a respected place for their language and convictions. Thus it came about that they resisted the effort of Milner to give an emphatically British bias to the new system of education. It was one of the means by which he hoped to tip the scales in favour of British predominance. The new teachers did well. By 1910 they had established a sound and active system of education. But the Transvaalers and the Free Staters had not lost their sense of race. In them the war had bred an even stronger attachment to the community of the Boers. The war had also restored the bond between the Boers of the Cape and the Boers of the ex-Republics. The richer life of the Cape Boers, especially of the old western districts, and the experience of leaders like J. H. Hofmeyr, affirmed Boer self-consciousness throughout the land. Milner's schools and English teachers were countered in the ex-Republics by some 200 independent schools, under local committees of parents. Against the superior teachers, the better equipment, and the financial strength of the government schools the Dutch 'Christian National Education' schools could not prevail. Their importance was nevertheless great. They served notice that the Boers would not abandon any of their attachment to their language and tradition. The elected school committees were a sign that the burghers did not intend to remain voiceless. By 1905 most Boer leaders were firm in their attitude that an early establishment of self-government was the best and fairest proof that the British Government could give of its policy of conciliation.

The Balfour Government fell in December 1905 and fell heavily. In the following year Campbell-Bannerman made good the pledge of self-government to the Transvaal. Self-government was granted to the Free State in 1907. The outcome of the elections in each colony proved that the political future of South Africa was in Dutch hands. Everything depended, therefore, on the attitude of the Dutch and their leaders. Ever since the days of the Great Trek Dutch society had been divided into two fluctuating groups, the one amenable to compromise and responsive to generous treatment, the other uncompromising and resistant to alien influence. Smuts and Botha from the Transvaal, and Hertzog from the Free State, had fought till the end. Would they and the other leaders now accept the testimony of Hofmeyr and the Cape leaders that Dutch patriotism could flourish within the Empire? Or would the memory of the Republics and their independence never be effaced from their minds? It was the proof of their genuine capacity for leadership that they recognized that a high place could be found for themselves and their followers in the new order. Boer names found an honoured place in the annals of Imperial statesmanship.

Self-government for the ex-Republics was in one sense a backward step. Once again South Africa contained four separate and autonomous communities. Once again it learned how great could be the friction bred by separate governments and divergent policies. Even before the introduction of self-government there had been quarrels over railways and customs. But it was in the field of native problems that the first crisis came. A petty Zulu chief rebelled in 1906. Behind the rebellion was the familiar story of land, taxes, and labour. When the rebellion was over South Africa had learned again the lesson, which it had known for fifty years, that the relations of each community with the natives was the immediate and vital concern of all South Africa.

The same lesson was brought home by the difficulties caused by Natal's Indian population. For the sake of a sugar crop which was too uneconomical to compete in the open world market South Africa had acquired a permanent Indian population. Of these there were upwards of 100,000 in Natal. The Indian Government had refused to permit their compulsory repatriation upon the expiring of their indentures in

Natal. Were these to be permitted to establish themselves freely in South Africa? Could they be permitted to follow the movement of labour and population to the Transvaal? Their growing number in the Transvaal, already eager to rid itself of the Chinese, moved the Transvaal legislature to peremptory action in order to exclude Asiatics. One of the earliest acts of the new Transvaal legislature was to pass the Asiatic Law Amendment Act of 1907. This was an effort to curtail immigration into the Transvaal of Indians. Through the use of passive resistance Mr. Gandhi brought about a compromise. But the difficulty was not solved. It was plain that neither Natal alone nor the Transvaal alone could deal with a problem which concerned both the Imperial and Indian Governments.

Railways once again were a fruitful cause of strife. The interests of the Transvaal alone were best served by the railway to the Portuguese harbour of Delagoa Bay. It was the shortest and the cheapest way to the sea. It was from Portuguese territory that came an indispensable proportion of native mine labourers. But what was gained by the Portuguese was lost to the railway systems of Natal and the Cape. The moral was obvious. All South Africa depended for its prosperity on the mines. If a proper share of that prosperity were to be assured for all communities, then the Transvaal could not be permitted to follow the lines of its own economic interests, especially if they led to a foreign port. The complex quarrel over railway traffic from and to the Rand reproduced faithfully the atmosphere and some of the dangers of the worst years before the Boer War. There was the same resentment by the Cape of Natal competition, the same rivalry between Cape Town, Port Elizabeth, and East London. Quarrels over the Customs Convention were proof the more that if there continued to exist independent units able to reach separate decisions on matters of common concern, it might still happen that the Boer War had been fought in vain. The country suffered from a no-man's-land of problems upon which no community could encroach without the certainty of quarrelling with its neighbours. It was plain, even as it had been plain in America by 1787, in Canada in

1867, and in Australia in 1900, that the country could not live without a central regulating power.

In 1910 was achieved the political union which every statesman during the last half of the nineteenth century had known to be South Africa's salvation. Natal, the Orange Free State, the Transvaal, and the Cape Colony became the Union of South Africa. Southern Rhodesia, still not sure of its position between Downing Street, the Chartered Company, and its own settlers, remained outside. The National Convention which prepared the terms of union overcame difficulties so great that J. H. Hofmeyr had expected its deliberations to end in failure. Each group now admitted its common allegiance to the Union. Neither was alien within it. The individuality of the originally separate communities was respected by the creation of provincial councils with authority over education other than higher education, hospitals, and municipal institutions. Pretoria was made the executive capital, Cape Town the legislative capital, and Bloemfontein the judicial capital. In the vital matter of languages the Convention declared that 'both the Dutch and English languages shall be the official languages of the Union and shall be treated on a footing of equality and shall possess and enjoy equal freedom, rights, and privileges'.

The principal guarantees of the Act of Union were for the white population. Although Great Britain retained the native territories of Bechuanaland, Basutoland, and Swaziland under its protection, the Act of Union was dedicated to the European community. Had the British Government sought to gain really significant guarantees for the native population, or to reserve a place for the Home Government in the new constitution as the protector of native interests, then the labours of the Convention could hardly have ended in close union. 'There was no part of the Constitution', wrote one shrewd critic at the time of Union, 'which the Imperial Parliament was bound to scrutinize with more care, or with which it was more certain that it could not interfere, than that relating to natives.'[1] In other words, the Union Constitution, in native policy at all events, represented the triumph

[1] R. H. Brand, *The Union of South Africa*, Oxford, 1909, p. 97.

of the frontier, and into the hands of the frontier was delivered the future of the native peoples. It was the conviction of the frontier that the foundations of society were race and the privileges of race.

The new Union Government was confronted by responsibilities of unusual complexity. There was so much to do to meet the great social and economic problems which a century of frustration and deflected purposes had thrust upon her. There was so little time in which to do it, as the World War was only four years away. The Boer War had broken out at a peculiarly unfortunate time. Between 1873 and 1896 the world had suffered from a protracted depression in trade and industry. In the last few years of the century the tide turned, and the world entered upon nearly two decades of rising prices and growing prosperity. New Zealand, Australia, and Canada pulled their feet from the slough of depression. With rapid strides they placed dairying, sheep-raising, and wheat growing on a modern and profitable basis. South Africa was prevented from availing itself of this favourable turn of the tide. The years of uncertainty before the war, the dislocation and damage of the war, and the labour of reconstruction were a serious loss of time and opportunity at a most critical moment in economic history.

In so many things the Union lagged behind the other dominions. It could not even be sure yet of the loyalty of its citizens. While Canadians or Australians or New Zealanders were born, South Africans had to be made. To become South African, men born to Dutch and English parents had to learn to rise above the exclusive traditions of their race, to forswear the special appeals of their blood, to have no indignation, if they were Dutch, over the concentration camps of the Boer War, to feel no contempt, if they were English, of the Afrikaans tongue. Such an achievement could not be easy, nor could it be entire.

Industrial life lacked the order and regulation in which the pioneering work had been done in the other dominions. Agriculture was primitive; the system of land-holding was inefficient. There was land-hunger amongst black men and white men; there was sweated labour and rural impoverishment.

There were railways and schools to build. There were passions that had not yet grown cold. These were great problems, on which it is easier for the historian to be dogmatic than wise. The effort to erect a modern European civilization in an atmosphere and amongst conditions which are more alien to Europe than in any other dominion requires the patient and tolerant understanding of historical and social students. The new Union Government was faced by problems which could not be solved, and by relationships which could not be altered without a continuity of effort and an extensiveness of planning especially difficult in a democratic system. The easy name of the 'native question', it must already be clear, veiled a tangle of conflicting interests, of antagonistic feelings and inflexible situations. Some of the problems were so difficult that they seemed incapable even of inferior solutions. In a land like Australia with a homogeneous population all social and economic problems were relatively simpler than they could be in a country like South Africa. Every problem, before it could reach the plane of ethical or economic principles, must run the gauntlet of keen racial feeling and social prejudice. The relations of advanced to backward peoples must always be fraught with the greatest difficulties. Liberal minds, sensitive to the disabilities of a subject race, were often too harsh in their condemnation of native policies, or too swift to discern sinister motives where there was in reality perplexity and hesitation. Racial problems are by their nature the sport of fear and suspicion. More than two and a half centuries of neglect had given South Africa an economic and political life so knotted that native policy could scarcely be otherwise than compromises and patched adjustments. It is not given to any people, however wise or rich, to extricate itself simply from the disorders and maladjustments that history has produced in its midst.

VII

GOLD MINING

For gold the merchant ploughs the main
The farmer ploughs the manor.

ROBERT BURNS.

SOUTH AFRICA, it is often said, has a smaller population than
Australia or Canada. In reality its total population is
greater than that of any other dominion with the exception
of Canada. The habit of using only the number of the white
population for purposes of comparison with other dominions
is often misleading, for it obscures the truth that South Africa's
place in the economic life of the Empire and the world depends upon the activities of the entire population. It is only
by taking into account the numbers of both white and native
residents in the towns that the remarkable urbanization so
characteristic of Canada and Australia may also be observed
in a country which still regards the rural ox-wagon as its most
characteristic symbol. The concentration of population in
the capital cities of Australia is unrivalled amongst the
dominions. The five towns of Sydney, Melbourne, Brisbane,
Adelaide, and Perth were estimated in 1937 to contain
3,165,400 out of a total population for the Commonwealth
of 6,866,590. But Australia has trodden a path closely followed by the other dominions. In 1931 Canada had 22·44
per cent. of her population in towns of 100,000 and over.
In the decade between 1921 and 1931 Canadian urban communities absorbed nearly 77 per cent. of the total increase
in population. In 1901 only 37·5 per cent. of the population
was urban; in 1931 the proportion was 53·7 per cent. In
South Africa the census report of 1936 revealed a markedly
similar development. Forty-five per cent. of the white population was resident in nine principal towns, headed by
Johannesburg and Cape Town. The white and native
populations of the same nine towns were one-quarter of the
total population of the Union. Johannesburg, Cape Town,
and Durban had in 1937 a combined population slightly less

than that of Sydney, but in South Africa they occupy the same commanding position as Sydney and Melbourne in Australia, or Montreal and Toronto in Canada.

Amongst South African towns Johannesburg stands apart. In 1936 it was the largest European town in all Africa, and with a total population of 519,268 was exceeded only by Cairo and Alexandria. Though it rested upon a thin layer of half a century of development, it had changed remarkably from the struggling appearance of a great mining camp of one-storied buildings and galvanized iron roofs and fences to take on an appearance unlike any other town in the sub-continent. Instead of spreading out into the surrounding veld as the population increased, Johannesburg began, more like a modern American city, to grow upwards. It was a town that not merely sprang up, but continued to grow, to equip itself with new devices and amenities, to rebuild itself, changing its face twice in the generation since the Boer War. The traveller to New Zealand, Australia, or Canada can step from the ship into the great centres of population at Wellington, Sydney, or Montreal. That Johannesburg is reached over a great distance of veld, thinly peopled and poorly productive, imparts to its bustle, its speculative and enterprising spirit, its automatic traffic controls, its electric trains and omnibuses, a sudden and ringing character. And Johannesburg is but the centre of a string of towns along the line of the gold-bearing reef which together had in 1936 a population of over one million inhabitants.

There are fashionable suburbs of Johannesburg set in quiet valleys that give no inkling of the existence close by of a great world industry. But to the south from the high buildings of the central business district are visible the immense 'dumps' of white crushed rock. Upon those parts of the town that are within earshot of the roar of the crushing mills, the sudden winds of August drop their charge of fine white dust, carried from the dumps. The dumps are the physical sign of the Witwatersrand's great dependence upon the gold which makes men live constantly in the present, with their eyes on monthly statements of gold production, their fingers on the pulse of stock exchanges, and their ears cocked for news of

international happenings that affect the price of the commodity which is the basis of their existence.

The Rand, it is true, has become more than a gold-mining
area. When the crash of stamp batteries and the roar of
tube mills are stilled and the bustle of black and white
mines is over, Johannesburg will not sink back into the
veld like so many another famous mining town. It has
drawn to itself the life and activity of a great surrounding
area. It lies within the so-called maize triangle and is an
entrepôt for the agricultural, pastoral, and mineral production of the High Veld. Within fifty miles lie immense coal
deposits and iron resources which may sustain the Rand
towns, although on a lower level, when the gold ore becomes
depleted.

The gold-mines are the life-blood of the Union. Mining,
especially of gems and precious metals, has played an important part in the economic life of all the dominions. Valuable
mineral products are, as it were, concentrated forms of wealth,
easily converted into the money and the credit upon which
young communities so greatly rely. Whereas in Australia and
New Zealand gold at an early moment gave way in importance to wool and pastoral products, the economic structure
of South Africa continued to rest upon gold. Economists
have tried in various resourceful ways to measure the extent
to which the economic life of South Africa is dependent upon
the Witwatersrand. The most refined techniques of economic
analysis do not yet seem to be able to lay bare the precise
anatomy of a country's economic life. It has been pointed
out that the number of people directly engaged in agriculture
is much greater than the number directly engaged in mining,
and that the net income from agriculture is greater than the
net income from mining. Agriculture in such a view supports
more people and makes a larger contribution to national
wealth than mining. But in careful research done for the
Gold Producers' Committee of the Chamber of Mines, Professor S. Herbert Frankel concluded that one-half of the
population obtained their livelihood directly or indirectly
from the gold-mining industry, and that one-half of the
finances of government were derived directly or indirectly

from gold mining. No arrangement of figures or ordering of statistics can disturb the fact that the place of gold in South African life is at least as important as the place of wool in Australia, and greatly more important than the place of mutton in New Zealand or of wheat in Canada.

Here was an industry which feared neither locusts nor cattle diseases, neither drought nor summer floods. Its product always commanded a ready sale in the financial centres of the world. War or peace, depression or inflation—none seemed to affect the demand. Under an international gold standard there existed a constant and reliable demand for gold at established prices. Even the compromised position of the international gold standard after the Great War did not alter the favoured position of gold. Indeed unlike maize, tobacco, wool, mutton, or wheat it could exploit falling prices and distressed currencies to its very signal benefit. Gold, in consequence, did many things for South Africa. It stabilized revenues and preserved national income from violent fluctuations. It gave firmness to foreign trade because it was by far the principal article of export, accounting since 1910 for more than one-half of total exports. Although very intimately a part of the world's economic system, South Africa was spared the worst effects of the fluctuations and crises that occurred between the Great War and the war against the Germany of Hitler. The number of fine ounces won, the expenditures in wages and salaries, foodstuffs and stores, taxes and repairs moved between exceptionally narrow limits. Like a great flywheel the mining industry gave stability to a country that otherwise would have been singularly sensitive to movements in world economy. Farming, so sensitive to world conditions without, and to drought and pestilence within, found comfort and strength in the lee of the Witwatersrand. Were South Africa suddenly to be bereft of its gold-mines, the effect upon its economic system would be catastrophic.

The incomparable advantages of the Witwatersrand are, it has already been pointed out, the huge mass and the uniformity of the gold ore. The ore has for this reason been likened to coal measures where expert calculations can be made of the tonnage of profitable coal, of the expense necessary to extract each ton, and of the profits which invested capital might expect. This ability to establish a highly dependable relationship between investment and return, and the assurance of a remunerative rate of return, made the Rand an enticing field for the capital of the world's money markets. The great constancy of the average yield was a form of honesty from which mining drew much benefit. Otherwise the capital could not have been so readily forthcoming for sinking shafts, exposing the ore, erecting the surface machinery, the houses and buildings, which altogether cost enormous sums and entail years of development work before a single ounce of fine gold is ready for export. After the first spade of earth was turned on the Brakpan Mines on Empire Day 1905, it took six years before the batteries started to crush the first ore. That the methods of collieries could be applied to gold mining permitted them to reach a high level of efficiency. The gold-mines were a spectacular demonstration of how far a capitalistic industry working for profit could go to increase efficiency of management and operation.

Until 1890 so many of the secrets of the gold-fields were still buried in the earth, and so many other difficulties still awaited solution, that no man could speak with assurance of their future. In all the world there was no comparable deposit to guide judgement. Only gradually it was discovered how strangely the gold reefs behaved beneath the surface, for from the line of the outcrop which runs from west to east, the reefs dip underground in a southerly direction. At some distances from the outcrop, therefore, new mining operations had to be undertaken. Expensive vertical shafts had to be driven into the ground to tap the reefs several hundreds of feet below the surface. That was but the beginning of shafts that would finally reach depths of a mile and more, and of underground workings with a combined length of thousands of miles. In the same manner there was a transition from sweat and muscle to science and machinery. At first the ore was thrown up by black workers; then it was drawn up by bullocks, like the buckets of blue earth in the diamond mines; then came wooden derricks and little engines that to the modern age seem to belong to the days of Watt. The first ore, too, was crushed as the Egyptians might have done, by raising and dropping heavy weights.

In 1890 came a severe crisis in the industry. The crazy superstructure of companies was alone enough to produce a depression. At one time there were upwards of 450 companies, most of whom never paid a penny of dividends. Of the nineteen companies which had paid large dividends in 1889, eleven failed to pay any at all in 1890. But the crisis in mining was due to more than South Sea Bubble schemes. Every foot of reef became more difficult and expensive to mine, demanding more workers, more machinery, and more scientific procedures. In the reef there were normal and reverse faults; there were dykes and variations in the dip of the reef which obstructed operation. The deeper ores were pyritic and more refractory. The gold content was also lower than that of the outcrop ores. Where the first calculations had been made in ounces per ton, now they had to be made in pennyweights to the ton. Not more than 60 per cent. of the gold could be recovered by the process of amalgamation with mercury, and no refinement of this process could prevent over one-third of the gold from being lost in the tailings. High transport costs added to the mounting cost of mining. In 1889 transport costs by ox and mule wagons were £1,500,000. But mining was saved from its embarrassment by a series of happy circumstances. Lying intimately over parts of the reef were great quantities of coal which could be easily mined. Though Witwatersrand means literally the Ridge of White Waters, there was no water power, and the wood of the veld was too soft and too scarce to be used as fuel. The existence of cheap coal was again one of those windfalls upon which South Africa seems so much to have depended, for the coal of the Transvaal not merely facilitated the change from shovels, crow-bars, and picks to power machinery, but was one more valuable inducement for the different rail-heads to seek the Witwatersrand. Just at the moment, too, that the deeper-level workings began to send up the intractable pyritic ore there was discovered the cyanide process. First applied in 1890 it proved remarkably well adapted to the Witwatersrand ores. The fortunes which had been thrown away in the tailings were recovered, and instead of 60 per cent., 90 per cent. of the gold content of the ore was extracted.

Efficiency and economy continued to be the inexorable law of gold-mining operations after the Boer War. Every cubic yard of reef that was exposed made more emphatic the truth that the vast bulk of the gold ore lay close to the level of prevailing average working costs. Though the fine gold, when once it had been extracted, was secure against the vagaries of the market, the gold while still in the reefs was acutely sensitive to all the influences which bear upon the costs of extraction. Efficiency and economy were two factors which multiplied the tonnage of payable ore. Inefficiency or increased expense condemned a part of the ore to virtual barrenness. Mining since the Boer War used the most refined calculations and the most modern procedures to lower working costs or to keep them from rising. The ore body must be extracted with the minimum of effort, and development work must be related to final profits in the most beneficial manner. Too little development work might leave undisclosed rich bodies of ore; too much, especially when conducted at depths of 6,000 feet below the surface, might make damaging inroads upon profits. Thus in the search for efficiency and economy light stamps were replaced by heavier stamps; tube mills which crushed faster and more finely than stamps made possible a still more complete extraction of gold. Improved machinery within the mine and cheap central power-stations on the surface helped in the incessant war against high working costs. The replacement of hand drilling by machine drilling before the Great War increased output and cut down labour costs. By means of the old heavy reciprocating type of machine drill the amount of rock crushed in the first six months of 1914 was about 250 tons per native. After the Great War was introduced the light jackhammer drill fitted with drills of better shape and improved steel able to bite more keenly into the hard quartz rock. In a similar period of time in 1930 the amount of rock broken was nearly 800 tons.

Any industry as dangerous to life and to health as mining

must bear the heavy charge of compensation. Accidents and the dread disease of miners' phthisis or silicosis took a heavy toll of profits. In gold mining the temptation was great, especially in the early days of the industry, to hasten the production of gold. Bonuses encouraged the miner to mine more and to mine faster. One shift of workers followed the other. There were sometimes three shifts every twenty-four hours so that the underground air was never free of the dust and fumes of blasted rock. Accidents caused by carelessness and haste were frequent. And every schoolboy on the Witwatersrand was acquainted with the scourge of silicosis. He saw its cause in the whitish-grey dust upon the clothes and faces of the miners as they returned from their work; he heard its damage in their coughing, and saw its effect in frequent funerals. Between 1912 and 1930 15,000 awards of compensation were made under the Miners' Phthisis law. But the great burden of phthisis compensation, estimated at £750,000 in 1932, was greatly lightened by improvements in ventilation and spraying. The single-shift system permitted the dust-laden atmosphere to become clear and lessened the number of accidents. In certain mines there have in recent years been introduced air-conditioning apparatus for improving conditions of labour at great depths.

How resolutely the ideal of efficient and economical operation was pursued was seen most clearly in the organization of the gold-mining industry as a whole. In diamond mining Cecil Rhodes replaced the confusion of individual diggers and competitive companies by a single company. Because the Witwatersrand gold deposits are not alluvial or surface deposits, the small miner with pick and shovel and prospecting pan was out of the question. From the beginning company mining was therefore the rule. From an early moment, too, consolidations were undertaken between companies. But the entire monopoly of diamond mining exercised by the De Beers Company was not achieved in gold mining. Because the price of gold was not affected by competition there was not the same reason to bring all the companies under a single control. Instead there developed in the gold-mining industry the 'Group System'. The groups are great corporations, composed of a number of subsidiary companies. Each group is responsible for the administration of the companies which it controls. Each group maintains a staff of consulting engineers, metallurgists, and other experts upon whose advice the individual companies may draw. Thus the highest order of skill is at the disposal of the companies, and at the same time their policies and methods are directed and supervised in the interests of efficient and profitable operation. The sharing of overhead expenses, collective buying, and similar common policies helped to lower the cost of production and, by the magic wand of economy, to turn millions of tons of low-grade rock into profitable ore. Although mines went deeper and were more costly to operate, working costs over a period of years showed a progressive decline. In 1897 average working costs were 29s. 6d. per ton milled. Forty years later in 1937 they were 18s. 11d.

The principle of collective action was given still further emphasis by the association of the groups in the famous Chamber of Mines. The Chamber is a body which takes care of many interests common to the whole industry. Labour problems and mining regulations, legal problems and health conditions, taxation and statistics—these and other interests were co-ordinated and supervised to the great benefit of the mining companies. The Native Recruiting Corporation Limited, one of several companies established by the Chamber of Mines, undertook the difficult and vital responsibility of recruiting native labour. A single recruiting agency eliminated competition between companies for the available supply of native labour. Other companies such as the Rand Refinery Limited, the Chamber of Mines Steel Products Limited, and the Chamber of Mines Building Company secured active co-operation throughout the industry. In close dependence upon the Chamber of Mines are also the Rand Mutual Assurance Company, which assumes liability for all claims for compensation, the Transvaal Miners' Phthisis Sanatorium, and the South African Institute for Medical Research, which carries out research into the important problems of health under mining conditions. It is due to this impressive organization for common effort that the accident death-rate, for example, fell from 4·64 per thousand in 1904 to 2·11 per thousand in 1934, and that the incidence rate of new cases of miners' phthisis fell from 1·9 per cent. in 1927–8 to 0·80 per cent. in 1936–7. In 1905 an American mining engineer calculated that the prevailing operation costs of mining could be cut if railway rates and import duties were reduced and if governmènt regulation were curtailed. In the twenty years that followed prices rose by nearly 50 per cent. There was a rise in railway rates and in the tariff. Government regulation increased. Yet operating costs fell from 22s. per ton milled to 19s. 3d., a remarkable tribute to science and management.

Australian economists have frequently noted the extent to which the direct burden of taxation and the indirect burden of tariff rates bear upon the great primary industry of wool production. Rich primary extractive industries such as gold mining or rich primary agricultural industries such as wool production, which are dependent upon the world market, cannot pass the burden of direct and indirect taxes to the consumer. Upon them there tends to rest an especially heavy load of the costs of social and economic policies. Australian sheep-farming has indeed been likened to 'one enormous sheep astride a bottomless pit, with statesman, lawyer, landlord, farmer, and factory hand all hanging desperately to the locks of its abundant fleece'. Even so did South Africa look to its mines for heavy contributions to the revenue and to the costs of social and economic policy. Opposed to the purely commercial attitude that the duty of a mining company was to earn the largest possible profit for its shareholders there was, ever since the days of Paul Kruger, the conviction that the mines were a national asset, and that their wealth might very properly be made to contribute to the health and welfare of the entire community. Government, therefore, progressively extended its control over the industry. The various Miners' Phthisis Acts alone numbered nine between 1911 and 1925. The State railway systems taxed the mines by placing heavier rates on goods and stores required by them. In 1932 the mines were charged more for the transport of coal than the cost of the coal at the pit-head. The rates for the transport of mining machinery were almost twice as high as for agricultural machinery. Mining thus became a source of subsidy to the transport system and the agricultural industry.

It is well known that primary industries working for the export market derive the least benefit from tariffs and protective duties. Gold mining felt the incidence of tariffs not merely in the duties upon machinery, materials, and stores which were imported from abroad, but in the increased costs of local goods, labour, and other services due to tariffs. In the fiscal year 1935–6 direct taxes upon mining industry, including diamonds and base metals, accounted for 26·95 per cent. of the entire revenue. Of the direct taxes 54 per cent. were paid by the mines. In addition to revenue from income taxes, from an Excess Profit Duty, collected since 1933, and from a Gold Profits Surtax, collected since 1935, the revenue benefited from profits of government ownership of mining properties. In 1936 there were twenty-one companies operating in areas leased from the Government on the basis of participation in profits. The profit was, in some cases, expressed as a direct percentage of profits; in other cases it was calculated upon a sliding scale, ingeniously devised so that the company received a fixed proportion of any extra profits resulting from greater efficiency or economy. Until 1936 the total government share in such profits was £43,556,232.

Of the expenses involved in the extraction of gold the greatest single item in most years was for wagés and salaries. In 1930 the value of gold won on the Witwatersrand mines was £45,500,000, while the amount spent in wages and salaries was £15,726,173, exceeding the total of dividend and tax payments. In 1936 the amount expended in wages and salaries was £25,704,865. Where such large amounts were spent on labour it followed that the industry should seek to make the most economical use of its labour force. The ability of the mining industry to draw upon the cheap labour of the native population was unquestionably the greatest single source of economy. How greatly the entire extractive industry, including the mining of coal and base metals, availed itself of cheap native labour was clearly evident in the fact that in the three widely separate years of 1915, 1925, and 1935 the percentage of European labour was 10·3, 10·7, and 10·76. In 1936 there were 394,323 non-European labourers in the entire mining industry out of a total of 441,413. The cheapness of native labour was most clearly revealed in comparative figures of European and native earnings. In 1936 the salaries and wages of 47,090 Europeans in all the mining industries of the Union amounted to £16,694,821 or an average of £345. 9s. 2d. per head, while the earnings of 394,323 non-Europeans were £12,483,258 or an average of £31. 13s. 2d. per head. This meant that the average European wage in mining was nearly twelve times as great as the average native wage. Translated into the language of everyday life these figures showed that mining depended upon a small group of highly paid white workers and a preponderant group of lowly paid native workers. In South Africa the organization of mining labour rested upon two sharply separated levels of skill and reward, and the separation between the levels was marked and confirmed by the differences of race and colour.

To an industry abidingly in search of economy a division of its labour supply into two opposite groups, the one cheap and the other expensive, was embarrassing. What was the most profitable proportion between skilled white men and unskilled black men? How could the disadvantage of expensive labour be corrected by the advantage of cheap labour? Although expensive labour may often be the most economical labour because of its efficiency, the gold-mining industry was organized on the basis of the maximum employment of natives and the minimum employment of whites. Roughly speaking, more whites meant less profits and more natives meant more profits. More profits, it has been seen, meant more payable ore and the promise of a larger life for the mines. The appetite of the mining industry for native labour was therefore great. It was an appetite that very often could not be satisfied.

In spite of its great native population South Africa has always suffered paradoxically from an insufficiency of native labour. Even the seventeenth century imported slaves and

East Indians. After 1843 Natal complained that it was over-crowded with natives, yet when it began to grow sugar (in 1860) it imported labourers from India. When it began to build its railways the Cape Colony, too, came close on several occasions to a decision to import Indian or Chinese labour. So acute was the dearth of native labour after the Boer War that the gold-mining industry succeeded in persuading Lord Milner to permit the importation of Chinese labourers. These came in 1904 to the noise of angry comments in England, New Zealand, and Australia. In 1907 their number was nearly 54,000. Economically their use was justified by a great and profitable increase in mining activities. Socially their presence in a land such as South Africa was most unwise. By forbidding further import licences in 1906 and by re-patriating all Chinese mine labourers in 1910 the British Government spared South Africa a further complication of its already complex social life. To obtain native labour the gold-mines also went beyond the borders of the British terri-tories. In 1901 was signed the first of a series of agreements with the Portuguese Government which permitted the import of labourers from Portuguese territories. In 1936 more than 89,000 natives from Portuguese territories were employed on the mines out of a total of over 340,000. The great use of native labour by the mines became a social and economic problem of the first magnitude. It was the new race frontier of the twentieth century.

Although the great proportion of natives never left the ranks of unskilled labour, a certain number crossed the fron-tier into more skilled work. When the rock in the mines was drilled laboriously by hand, it was accounted native work. When machine drilling was introduced, natives learned to use the machines efficiently and were not replaced. The graduation of natives from unskilled to semi-skilled opera-tions expanded the use which the mining companies could make of cheap labour. To extend the use of native labour was a better economy than remission in taxation or a reduc-tion in customs duties. But such encroachment by natives was not pleasing to the white miners. They felt themselves menaced in their monopoly of skill and high wages. As the first generation of men from overseas died or returned whence they had come, their place was taken by South Africans. In 1912 nearly 35 per cent. of the white miners were born in South Africa, and the percentage increased very rapidly until in 1936 three-quarters of all miners in the Union were of South African birth. They brought into industry still more emphatically the thought and the distinctions of the frontier. Black was black, white was white, and it was intolerable that the two should meet in equality over a machine, a drill, or in a railway carriage. In 1911 the essential similarity of industrial and rural thought was made manifest by the passage in a Parliament, composed overwhelmingly of rural members, of the famous Mines and Works Act. The colour bar was legalized. In addition to the protection afforded by their skill, their efficiency, and the force of public opinion, white labour now obtained the protection of a statute as well. In the interest of health, safety, and discipline the use of non-Europeans in many employments upon the mines was forbidden. In reality the Mines and Works Act curbed the use which the mines could make of cheap labour, and placed upon the mines the burden of a social policy which aimed at maintaining the economic superiority of the white race.

In the social and economic history of the Union the Mines and Works Act holds a most prominent place. Of the laws governing native labour in the colonies and Republics the main purpose had been to increase the supply and tractability of native labour. The competition between white and black had been for land and water, and not for labour. Now almost within the first year of Union an Act of Parliament recognized that a new social and economic frontier had taken the place of the old frontier of land and settlement. Where once the natives were extruded from good land and ample water, now they were kept afar from skilled labour and high wages. Where once the natives had been driven from the land to labour, now men began to consider the possibility of driving them from labour back again to the land.

Upon the new industrial frontier there came face to face the poor whites and the poor blacks. The two elements of the agricultural revolution were engaged again in the industrial revolution. Each had been driven by the agricultural revolution to seek the means to live in the industrial towns. The Union was confronted with the task not simply of adjusting the relations between skilled men and unskilled men, but between two groups, different in race and language, similar in their lack of skill and industrial training. Could the opportunities of industry be shared between poor white and poor black? Did the increasing participation of white South Africans in industry make necessary barriers against the entry of black Africans? Could a social and political policy of white supremacy be compatible with an economic policy of cheap labour? The answer to these questions is the greater part of the history of the Union.

In 1913 the ranks of skilled labour looked to their defences. In July the familiar roar of the crushing batteries suddenly ceased. Their silence revealed the dependence of every man, woman, and child upon the successful extraction of the ore beneath their feet. The strike revealed also the explosive qualities of industrial life. Only after riots and some loss of human life did the white miners win the right to organize in trade unions. It was a battle that had long since been won in Australia and New Zealand. Yet South African labour fought its battle on two fronts. It fought the characteristic vanguard action of labour in the Western world against capital. It differed from other labour movements by fighting a rearguard action against a group of a different race and a lower order of skill, without organization or political support, but which belonged nevertheless to the labouring population. In that population the trade unions were an *élite*, a self-conscious and self-regarding group.

The strike of 1913 was not a local strike in a single industry. Because the mines are the Union's life-blood, and because the active economic life of the country is indissolubly bound up with them, mine disputes are national crises. Quarrels between labour unions and mining companies affect labour relations everywhere. Wages paid in mining set the standard of wages, not merely in closely related industries, but in every urban industry throughout the Union. Legislation affecting the mines affects the economic life of the whole Union. The truth of this was seen in a general strike, involving railways and mines, called by the Federation of Trades in January 1914. The strike was in reality a continuation and an extension of the strike of July 1913, for its purpose was to testify to the common purpose of all white labour to protect its interests. Though the machine guns of the Government's Defence Force stiffened the resistance of the mining companies and defeated the strike, it was clear that the interests of South African labour went beyond the interests of Australian and New Zealand labour. What was at issue was the whole immense problem of social and economic relationships between industry and labour, between skilled and unskilled worker, between white and black. Thus did the desire of the mines to make the most economical use of their labour become a problem that touched the life of the country at every point. That men in the Government's uniforms had taken up arms meant simply that the question of how men should live together was not merely the concern of capitalists and trades unionists. It was not a question that could be hastily answered, nor could any single session of Parliament set it right.

Social programmes undertaken in 1914 had small hope of being carried significantly forward, for in 1914, shortly after celebrating the fourth anniversary of Union, South Africa became a belligerent Power, ranged with its sister dominions against the fierce might of the Central Powers.

It was just twelve years after the Peace of Vereeniging. The generation of Boer War generals and their followers was all but intact, and Spionkop and Magersfontein and the burnt homesteads were still vividly remembered. Had the Kaiser belatedly given Boerdom its chance after all to fight the Boer War over again, and to regain the independence that had been lost? Was the invasion of Belgium not the intervention of European Powers for which Paul Kruger had once yearned? For answer two Boer War generals put behind them the past and stepped heroically beyond the limitations of their own land and race. They stepped into the future which, so men said, the British Empire and its Allies were fighting to defend. The two Boer War generals were Botha and Smuts. Under their command South Africans fought in

German South West Africa, in German East Africa, and in Flanders. True there were those who did not see with the eyes of Botha and Smuts. A drought, such as had once set the tribesmen to burning and pillaging, inflamed present discontents, and caused old wrongs to burn anew. Beyers, de Wet, and de la Rey were names which all the world had known at the turn of the century. True to loyalties they had never abandoned, they rose in rebellion.[1] Rebellion was a duty which they owed to their hearts, and they absolved it in defeat, for the vigour and strength of Botha's Government forces were too great. In the same month in which Italy entered the war South African forces began finally to move against the Germans in South West Africa.

Fully engaged in the tide of war, South Africa bore its share of its losses and costs. And like the rest of the Empire it did not come fully to a realization of those costs till the war had been won. It experienced the misleading post-war boom of Great Britain and the United States. When the United States returned to the gold standard in May 1919, and Great Britain did not follow suit, gold abandoned the depreciated pound and went to a premium. The revelation of a commission appointed in June 1919 that half the gold-mining industry was working at a loss or was uncomfortably close to the margin went unnoticed as prices rose again and profits increased. For a moment it seemed as if the unpredictable magic of gold would protect South Africa against the post-war collapse, as it had softened the impact of the war itself. It was not to be. The premium shrank as gold prices fell from 130s. per ounce in February 1920 to 95s. in December. And with the crisis in gold came depression and all its evils. Like the rest of the Empire and the Allied nations South Africa saw for the first time the true magnitude of its war burden. Its unproductive debt had practically doubled since 1910. The expenditures of the Union and Provincial Governments had doubled since 1914. Commodity prices, wages, railway rates, and taxes had all risen. And the drought which had made hard South Africa's entry into the war reappeared again, accompanied by destructive swarms of locusts, to make

[1] De la Rey was accidentally killed before the rebellion.

its exit harder still. Retrenchment in the towns was matched by crop failures on the farms. Poor whites from the country swelled the numbers of the unemployed in the towns. Nowhere was the crisis more acutely felt than in the mining industry. That mines were a wasting asset, and that they could not go on for ever had been understood. But that the weaker mines might not die gradually through a depletion of their deposits, but be stricken to death suddenly by an economic crisis was a shocking revelation. The meaning of the report of the Low Grade Mines Commission of 1920 came into focus. The Commission had strongly recommended, as an important means of cutting working costs, an increase in native employment and the removal of the legal colour bar in order to open up to cheaper native labour certain activities formerly closed. The recommendation meant the substitution of more cheap native labour for expensive white labour. It meant renewed trouble on the industrial frontier of black and white labour.

The effort of the mining companies to carry into effect the recommendation of the Low Grade Mines Commission thrust an irritant into the heart of the country's greatest problem. The cry ran through all the ranks of white labour that the Chamber of Mines was debasing white men to the level of black men. The ideal of a white South Africa was being sacrificed by an unholy alliance between foreign capitalists and a corrupt government. An industry which had produced over 8,000,000 fine ounces of gold each year since 1909 could not be permitted to abandon its responsibilities to civilized men. The strike which started in the coal-mines of the Transvaal on 2 January 1922 spread immediately to the near-by gold-mines. Violent men raised their voices. That they were heeded was seen in the drilling of commandos in open places. The word 'republic' was heard, and the cry for a White South Africa was loud, so that men wondered whether violence would be used against the natives or against the form of government itself. On 6 March, amid scenes of mob violence, a general strike of all Union industry was called. Although the strike was not unanimous, law and order on the Witwatersrand broke down completely. On 10 March fighting became general. Martial law was declared. Cannons roared in the streets of Johannesburg; Lewis guns spat from aeroplanes; soldiers and special police charged against barricaded strikers. The end of bloody fighting was the end of the strike. The demands of the mining companies prevailed.

A Mining Industry Board concluded that economy was the first need of the industry. In the calm after the storm it gave South Africa a wise lesson in economics. To obtain the greatest benefit from the mines the white workers must not insist on the employment of the greatest number at the highest wages. The road to the fullest possible white employment lay through economy. The abiding problem of mining was to make the vast body of low-grade ore profitable. The greater the body of ore mined, the greater would be the power of the industry to spend and to hire. The wretched average of less than seven pennyweights per ton of ore could be multiplied into millions of fine ounces by the means of economy. The economy of native labour was the most important pillar of white employment. In 1925 another commission[1] spoke with no less firmness on the same subject. The demand for skilled and responsible workers depended upon the magnitude of mining operations. It was by economies such as the employment of cheap native labour that a great revenue was created. And this revenue was the source of wages and taxes and of the demand for the products of farming and other industries which depended upon the Witwatersrand for their market. Whatever reduced their revenue imposed both an economic sacrifice upon the country and an ultimate sacrifice through the necessity of leaving unworked millions of tons of low-grade ore.

The economies which were introduced after the crisis had a clearly stimulating effect on gold mining. A large proportion of native labour, lower white wages, and new labour-saving devices preserved the industry from a destructive crisis. Salaries and wages, which had been £17,463,281 in 1920, had dropped to £13,918,545 in 1925. Average earnings per white employee of £485 in 1920 had dropped to £375 in 1925, and the amount of fine ounces on the Witwatersrand was increased from 7,949,084 to 9,341,049.

[1] *Report of Economic and Wage Commission* (U.G. 14 of 1926).

In 1929 the world endured the second and far more severe instalment of the post-war crisis. South Africa suffered with the rest. The diamond trade collapsed. World agricultural prices dropped, dragging South African farm prices after them. Exports shrank, and with them shrank the capacity to pay for imports. It was as if the seasons had the cunning to discern South Africa's plight, for a drought that came and would not go added misery to the sufferings of the agricultural and pastoral industries. To bring some money into the pockets of its stricken farmers the Government announced in October 1931 a 10 per cent. subsidy on all exports except gold, diamonds, and sugar (which was already protected). To pay for the export subsidy it levied a general duty on practically all imports. Three months later the export subsidies were doubled in a further effort to sell more and buy less, and thus to improve the balance of trade. But South Africa was not alone in such a return to the economics of the seventeenth century. As each nation struggled to save itself, the finance and industry of the world sank down into the black depths of 1932. In September 1931 the English pound yielded to the pressure against it and went off gold. Capital in South Africa grew alarmed, and a serious flight of capital from the Union menaced the stability of the currency. Once again a Low Grade Ore Commission announced that the gold-mines were in danger. The story which it told was the familiar story of rising expenses and falling returns, of mines that were sinking below the margin of profitable operation, and of vast resources of ore that could not be saved from barrenness without economy. With new facts and figures it reiterated the old arguments of the great dependence of the entire Union upon this single industry. Expert opinion had come to the conclusion that technical and administrative efficiency could do little more in reducing the working costs of the mines. And yet small changes in working expenses would have startling results. A reduction of 2s. per ton of milled ore would, it was estimated, increase the future average life of the gold-fields by at least 50 per cent. A reduction of 4s. per ton would increase the life of the gold-fields by at least 100 per cent. Small wonder that the proposal was strongly made to the Commission that the poorest mines should receive a subsidy on the principle that unless a little gold were fed to the goose it would cease altogether to lay its golden eggs. The Official Year Book of the Union announced that the long-dreaded moment of rapidly falling returns had in all likelihood come at last. After a production of £43,600,000 in 1932 the yield of the Witwatersrand gold-mines would drop to £20,100,000 in 1942 and to £10,000,000 in 1948. The decline which had come to Victoria and California and the Klondyke was within sight on the Witwatersrand, too.

The depression which began in 1929 should have been a windfall to gold mining. The great drop in the cost of commodities should have meant lower prices for the stores and supplies needed by the industry. But increased taxes, export subsidies, and special import duties stood between the mines and the benefit of low commodity prices. The stubborn refusal of the Government to follow the example of Great Britain in abandoning the gold standard caused an overvaluation of the South African pound, and still further prevented local prices from adjusting themselves to the level of world prices.[1] An agitated debate followed Great Britain's abandonment of the gold standard. Men remembered the mark and the franc and for a brief period feared that the pound might not be able to check its downward movement. Was it fitting that a sovereign and independent State such as South Africa had become by the Statute of Westminster should compromise its political status by too servile a dependence on the British pound? On the more real and immediate grounds of economic expediency the debate was hottest. Argument faced argument while capital seeped out of the country. Inflation, it was claimed, would reduce working costs on the mines and increase both profits and the tonnage of workable ore. The benefits of inflation, it was countered, were only temporary. Soon enough a rise in costs equivalent to the amount of inflation would nullify the benefits of inflation. The establishment of parity with the depreciated British pound, it was optimistically affirmed, would increase employ-

[1] In relation to world prices the South African pound paid too much for labour, foodstuffs, repairs, and dynamite.

ment, stimulate the investment of fresh capital, and send an invigorating stream of wages, expenditures, and profits through the economy of the whole country. The pessimists retorted that the problems of unemployment and labour unrest could only be made worse by the adverse influence of currency depreciation on costs and purchasing power.

Just as the depression after the Great War had led to the downfall of the Smuts Government, so did the new depression undermine the support and popularity of General Hertzog's Government. There were quarrels over the relationship of the two official languages. Natal, the most English of the provinces, spoke of secession from the Union, and finally, as the black year of 1932 neared its end, the flight from the pound became a stampede. On 27 December South Africa abandoned the gold standard and prepared to watch the effects of its action.

The effects were startling. The ebb of money back to South Africa became a spring tide. Credit and confidence flowed again through the economic system. Withdrawals turned into deposits. Plentiful money lowered short-term rates of interest. The mines benefited from generous offerings of capital. The industries and occupations which were dependent upon them took heart as well. Not even the strongest advocates of an abandonment of the gold standard had expected such a powerful and energetic stimulus to be given to economic activity. Once again South Africa enjoyed a windfall, the greatest perhaps of its career. Import prices and the local cost of living showed no marked inclination to follow the movement of inflation. Existing mines extended their operations. New investment and increased profits provided the money for driving new shafts and exposing new ore bodies that a year before had been beyond the reach of profitable exploitation. The conversion of the interest rate in 1932 on £2,000,000,000 of British Government Loans and the fall of interest rates on American Federal and State securities caused the boom in mining to be unusually attractive to investors. There was money for great air-cooling plants in the bowels of the earth that were unique in engineering history. The working profit was 8*s*. 6*d*. per ton in December 1932; in

January 1933 it was 18*s.* 7*d.*, and this meant that it was possible to mine a substantially lower grade of ore and yet show a profit. Huge quantities of ore that in 1932 had to be treated as waste could now be profitably mined. Thus rich mines became richer; failing mines were stimulated back to health. Entirely new mines were opened up, and new companies floated. Operations were conducted at depths once considered unpracticable. Deep-level working beyond 8,000 feet made available further millions of tons of ore. In two years government revenue from the mines rose by 210 per cent.[1] In spite of a heavy tax, dividends rose by 76 per cent. The increase in salaries, wages, and expenditure on stores was most striking. A large capital expenditure on improvements and development of new ore bodies still left room for the accumulation of reserves of great importance for the future. Five million more tons of ore were crushed in 1934 than in 1932. Some critics estimated that the life of the industry had been doubled. Johannesburg and the other towns of the Witwatersrand began to rebuild themselves. Architects and contractors vied with one another in modern designs, appropriate to such prosperity. From the air parts of central Johannesburg began to look like Chicago or Saint Louis. There never had been so much business for the railways, and the streets of Johannesburg became crowded with motor-cars like an American town. Even the bitterly stricken agricultural and pastoral industries benefited from an increase in the price level of their products.

The truth was that the abandonment of the gold standard had not simply restored a former prosperity that had been temporarily lost. It raised South African economic life to a new level. In the words of a former Government Mining Engineer, Sir Robert Kotze, South Africa was witnessing the opening up of what was practically a new gold-field, larger

---

[1] The excess Profits Duty Act No. 33 of 1932 imposed a tax of 70 per cent. on the premium of gold, i.e. the amount of the price of gold in excess of the former standard value of 85*s.* per fine ounce. In 1935 a Gold Profits Surtax imposed 2*s.* in the pound on the profits of the gold-mines. These taxes follow ingenious rules calculated to graduate the tax burden according to the special problems of each mine.

than any other field in the world outside the main Witwatersrand gold-field itself. What was virtually a new industry, with new conditions and new prospects, had come into being without the encouragement of lowered taxation, or subsidies, or wage reductions.

Almost alone amongst the modern governments the South African Government enjoyed a series of budget surpluses, amounting to almost £19,000,000 between 1933 and 1937. This permitted a salutary reduction to be undertaken in the gross public debt from £272,133,000 in 1933 to £254,937,000 in 1937. In 1934, although debt repudiation was the order of the day in international affairs, South Africa repaid a war debt of £8,000,000 to the British Government. The repayment of a significant proportion of public and private debts held abroad began a fundamental and salutary change in the position of South Africa as a debtor country. The internal debt grew relatively larger, and the external debt relatively less, which meant that local capital was becoming more able to satisfy the country's needs, and there was less dependence upon foreign capital. An important degree of financial independence gave new meaning to political independence.

In 1932 the gold-mining industry had faced the danger of a rapid decline. Its problem, it seemed then, had been to make such a decline as gradual as possible, lest too sudden a stroke bring widespread disaster. The higher price for gold, which indefinitely extended the life of the industry, removed the fear of batteries that would stamp no more ore, and 'dumps' that would slowly be worn away by keen August winds. But the boom was born of international confusion. The basis of the boom was the shifting and uncertain equilibrium between the major currencies of the world. The gold standard which had once ruled all the important currency systems in their relations with one another had yielded to exchange restrictions and 'managed' currencies. The America of Franklin Delano Roosevelt was glutted with gold; the Germany of Adolf Hitler adopted the most desperate financial and commercial expedients, and yet remained starved of gold. Before 1932 the searching question had been how long the ore resources of the Witwatersrand would last. As South

Africa towards the end of 1939 took its place with the Empire against Germany's resurgent might, the question was how long the world's demand for gold would last. Another chapter in the full and exciting history of gold still had to be written.

VIII

POOR WHITES AND POOR BLACKS

'These are subjects that never will be understood from the speculations of the mere farmer, or the mere politician; they demand a mixture of both; and the investigation of a mind free from prejudice. . . .' ARTHUR YOUNG: *Travels in France.*

WITHIN the British Empire can be studied most of the problems which the struggle for existence on the earth entails. The Australian must struggle against the heat and dryness of his continent. The Canadian must battle against cold and the inhospitable North. Newfoundland must find its harvest in the treacherous sea. New Zealand must match its science and enterprise against its isolation from the markets of the world. Yet it is South Africa that is clearly the most complex and arresting of the British dominions. Australian droughts are like South African droughts; there are distinct reminders of South Africa in the relations of British and French in Canada; British Secretaries of State once spoke of Maoris and Bantu as equally troublesome; only in Ireland does there exist the same tradition of political and military conflict. In certain southern States of the American Union there is the same dependence upon black labour; some South American republics confront similar problems of race mixture. But in the end South Africa is unique. It belongs to two societies, white and black, and stands upon two cultural levels. Its education is devoted to two languages, one a great world tongue, and the other a vigorous dialect, nurtured by Dutch patriotism. Nowhere else, not even in French Algeria, does there exist the same phenomenon of a self-conscious white community, endowed with great industries, and all the amenities of modern civilized life, living in intricate and vital dependence upon the labour and obedience of a subject race. In spite of this dependence there is perhaps no other society where the relationship between the white and the black races is so intractable. While North America and New Zealand drowned the aboriginal tribes in a flood of white settlement, South Africa failed to attract a preponderant white population. The South American solution of Indian problems by miscegenation might perhaps have been possible in the eighteenth-century Cape Colony when the numbers of white, slave, and Hottentots were more nearly even. But the nineteenth century violently disturbed this proportion by bringing white society face to face with a far greater mass of Bantu tribesmen.

The great Bantu race refused to follow what one Australian governor called the 'natural progress of the aboriginal race towards extinction'. The South African natives, it would seem, possessed some principle in their blood that fought the contamination of drink and disease, some special virtue of the loins that enabled them to multiply in spite of wars and droughts and the loss of most of their best ploughing lands. These facts alone are enough to justify a leading place for the natives in these pages. The greatest phenomenon of South African history most emphatically is not, in spite of all appearances, the rivalry between Boer and Briton. Nor is it, in spite of many and costly native wars, the antagonism of natives and colonists. The oppositeness of black and white, or the antithesis of European civilization and tribal culture, is not a sufficient clue to the relations between black men and white men. A century and a quarter ago colonists and natives were still separate societies. But for a generation now economists and historians have increasingly abandoned the attempt to discuss the natives and the whites as distinct groups, for they have come to recognize their close and inseparable relationship to one another. It is true that the great prejudices which race and colour engender hide the close weaving of the strands of black and white. It is true also that a variety of things such as language, diet, legal and political status, education, and much more besides, suggests a wide gulf between white and black races. The language of public discussion and political debate freely uses such terms as 'native question' and 'segregation', as if native questions concerned only natives, and as if segregation meant a real separation between two distinct communities. Though the use of these terms can hardly be avoided, they must not be taken as an indication that the life and activity of white and black are really separate, or that each can be described within its own sphere without prejudice to the other.

The truth is quite plain that the native wars of the nineteenth century were unlike the Indian wars of North America. They did not sweep the natives before them, clearing the land for an exclusive white settlement. Transvaal farmers did talk of 'cleaning the land' of natives, and native administrators thought vaguely of resettling the Bantu tribes in some undefined northern land beyond the limits of white settlement. Actually the native wars were a process which gave the white communities more than possession of the bulk of the best land. It gave them a considerable measure of control over the services of the natives. The land wars were also labour wars. In other words, the natives lost free access to the land, but were permitted to draw sustenance from it as labourers, herdsmen, tenants, or renters. South Africa's frontiers were not pushed in front of an advancing wave of white settlement until they disappeared in the desert or tumbled into the sea. They were opened up by encroachment and blown up by wars, so that the communities on either side could enter into more intimate and interdependent relationships with each other. History has commonly regarded miscegenation and intermarriage as the clearest indication that two originally separate societies have become fused. Yet two societies do not have to open their blood-streams to one another in order to grow inextricably together. That the nineteenth century in South Africa successfully maintained the purity of the white race did not prevent the entry of the natives into the arteries of economic life.

How a large body of the native population became first a rural and then an urban proletariat has already been discussed. Dispossession and the collapse of the tribal system, erosion and drought, cattle diseases and taxes, new needs and old clothes—all these conspired to accelerate the change from independent tribesmen to a servile group. Because the nineteenth century created a great class of black workers upon the farm and in industry, the impression was easily created that white society had won a special position for itself, elevating all of its members beyond the reach of the forces which governed the life of the natives. Such an impression was strengthened by the doctrine of racial superiority which was drawn from the Bible and reinforced by the popular interpretation which the nineteenth century placed upon Darwin's theories. Religion and science each seemed to lend the weight of its peculiar authority to the elevation of one race over another. Indeed the two Republics were, in one point of view, societies of landholders deliberately organized to maintain 'proper' relations in Church and State between white men and men of colour. Until the days of Kruger's discriminatory franchise laws, a white skin made a man the equal of all those similarly endowed. Equality in the Republics was an equality of privilege, and democracy was the benefit of white society.

It was at the turn of the century that it became evident that white society had developed within itself disturbing inequalities. At the base of white society had gathered, like a sediment, a race of men so abject in their poverty, so wanting in resourcefulness, that they stood dangerously close to the natives themselves. Racial equality amongst the whites had not prevented the development in their midst of economic inequality. In 1892 John X. Merriman, Minister for Agriculture in the Cape Government, drew attention to the beggared condition of a large section of the population of the eastern districts. In the following year the Dutch Reformed Church called a conference to deal with the acute crisis of rural poverty amongst its own members. The new Republics, no less than the old Colony, observed that their country-side was seriously afflicted. Before ever the Boer War devastated the Transvaal, the Volksraad debated the plight of the 'poor burghers'. Each year after the Boer War the problem of indigency grew graver. Government commissions and further conferences of the Dutch Reformed Church testified to the concern which the problem caused. In 1923 it was stated on the best available evidence that the ranks of the poor whites contained as many as 160,000 individuals, or approximately 10 per cent. of the white population. The poor whites were peculiar to no province and to no climate, nor were they the result of any special set of causes. They were equally to be found on the barren Kalahari and in the well-watered malarial Bush-veld, on the treeless Karroo, and in the damp forest of the Cape coastal area. Some were of nomadic habit, others were still attached to the land, even though by a cord so shrivelled as to give them the scantiest nourishment. The century had, in other words, produced a race of 'poor whites' and a race of 'poor blacks'. If the economic historian could adopt the classification of the botanist or the biologist, he would say that the poor blacks and the poor whites belonged to the same economic species. All the investigations which public and private bodies have conducted since the Boer War into the causes of the economic and social degradation of a large proportion of the white population have tended to the conclusion that poor whites and poor blacks are the result of very similar causes. The poor whites are the South African equivalent of the 'crackers' and 'mean whites' of the former slave States of America. There, too, during the very same period was bred a marginal population of poor whites, kin to the landholders by race, kin to the negro population by their economic circumstances. The study of the origins of South Africa's proletariat is an essential passage of its economic and social history.

The tradition that the best and most vigorous elements of a young colonial society seek the frontiers of settlement is not always true. Amongst those who dared to face the hazards of frontier existence were also men who dared not face the responsibilities of the settled regions. A spirit of restlessness is not always a spirit of enterprise. On South Africa's un-exacting frontier there long remained room for men who were laggard and unprogressive, wanting in the very qualities characteristic of the true pioneer. The Great Trek has become an epic in South African history, and the communities established by the Trekkers have compelled the admiration of the world. Yet in one sense the trek movement was a refusal to accept the stronger social discipline and the stricter rule of law which British governance brought to the Cape Colony. Economically it did not go forth to found a new society, but to continue and perpetuate an old. This conclusion is not incompatible with the existence within the Trekker communities of an important proportion of progressive men. That the trek movement was followed by a considerable expansion in wool exports is but one indication of the vitality of many of the Trekkers. Yet by casting off the control of Downing Street they outran the slow march of education. Still farther from markets, the Boers had less inducement than ever before to change their habits. Their new condition as large landholders, generously supplied with cheap and docile labour, did not stimulate them to apply the effort and the sacrifice and the courage of the Trek to their farms. They were pioneers in their movement, but not in their settlement. The fruit of their victories over Kafirs and torrents and sickness was a greater measure of isolation and the release for another generation from the spirit of modern enterprise. The Republics extended the fundamental errors of land settlement which the British Government had been powerless to correct in its own territories. Land was obtained too easily, so that it came into the hands of too many men who lacked the capital, the energy, or the efficiency to develop it profitably. Such farmers did not ask much of their fields and flocks. It was enough that the land should satisfy their unambitious wants and that their flocks should increase in number. Such farmers could not readily acquire the businesslike habits of modern life, and did not easily learn the commercial principles upon which profitable farming must be based. In the activities of men so placed there was little call to keep books, to study the fluctuations of the market, to correct the deficiencies of the soil, or otherwise to combat the shortcomings of nature. Only the very enterprising laboured to improve the breed of their stock and to lessen the ravages of disease. A small outlay and a small return were the economic rule of most of their lives. They did not have the economic rationalism of the Australian and American farmers, or the money sense which makes land and cattle not ends in themselves but instruments of enrichment.

In a subsistence economy the margin between prosperity and stagnant living is not easily evident. At their level of existence thriftlessness and improvidence and a want of scientific knowledge were not the menace that they become under modern conditions. It was, of course, the sort of farming that time and circumstance called forth. It was natural for Boer society to put its faith in occasional good seasons rather than science, or to tolerate wasteful and inefficient native labour rather than introduce labour-saving machinery. A people that asks little of its environment is less exposed to punishment by the droughts or hailstones or diseases of that environment. Boer farming was not inefficient farming in its own day and age. The satisfactions of Voortrekker life were the simple satisfactions that came from the great wideness of the land, the placid movement of its population, and the absence of the schemes of social reform that agitate an active and liberal society. The slow dust that rose from a neighbour's wagon on the horizon was like the pace of their own lives. They set security in a few things above profit in many, hated taxes and the daily discipline imposed on the lives of those that seek profit and gain. But their way of life also bred characteristic weaknesses. It relaxed the habits of regular work and tolerated a limp and self-indulgent thought on social and economic questions. Voortrekker life was bare of all but the simplest necessities. In many areas a 'wall-house', even though the walls were of sun-dried mud, was sufficiently rare to be remarkable. Less enterprising families lived in 'mat houses', made of woven rushes on a light framework of poles. In the well-to-do houses near Cape Town there had been some fine furniture, solid and well made. But the furniture in the dwellings of the Voortrekkers was rude, often no better than the rough unseasoned timbering of the dwelling itself. The floor was the bare earth to which dressings of manure gave the rich smooth appearance of mahogany. Most dwellings were without ceilings. Locks and window-panes were quite as unusual as novels and newspapers.

Amongst the inhabitants of the interior districts and the Republics there were differences of wealth. Even as early as the turn of the eighteenth century there were significant differences on the frontier between well-to-do cattle farmers and shiftless men who eked out an existence by wood-cutting. But in a non-capitalistic and uncommercial atmosphere these differences did not yet seriously affect the individual's politi-

cal or social standing. With his horse and a rifle the poor
burgher was as good as his richer neighbour. The leaders of
the community, even the President of the Republic, were
accessible to him. Though he lacked the exuberance of those
of Andrew Jackson's followers who spread mud on the chairs
of the White House to prove their democracy, his dislike of
social pretension and class differences was the same.

As long as there was new grass and fresh land to be found
beyond the horizon, Boer society was free to live its life unchanged. Land and flocks were the measurement of their
wealth. They were forms of wealth which the country generously provided. Without them a man lost caste. They were
the portion given to sons, and the dowry given to daughters.
As long as there was new land, sons could have farms and
herds as big as those of their fathers while they were still
young men. In parts, land could be acquired for nothing or
bought for a song. The sale of a bale of tobacco or wool or
a few bushels of grain was more than enough to pay the quit-
rent on an entire farm of 6,000 acres. The Transvaal especially had neither the officials nor the desire to regulate the
alienation of the land in a systematic manner. The land was
the patrimony of the people. That its disposal could be made
profitable to the coffers of the State, or that it should be conserved for the benefit of future generations, was little in their
thoughts. The failure of all communities to overcome the
great dislike of the rural population to direct taxation caused
land to be unduly spared. Because the contribution of the
farmers to the public revenue was slight their inducement
to improve their land was diminished. Most of the land
throughout the country provided little more than a living
for its owners, although there were profitable sheep farms in
the Free State, Natal, and the Eastern Province. Some land
was made to show a profit by the system of Kafir farming.
Widespread land speculation locked up land, which caused
an artificial scarcity and drained into the pockets of speculators the money which might have gone into the improvement of the land. Until the end of the nineteenth century
South African farming was starved of credit. What credit
there was all too frequently was devoted to the buying and

selling of land for speculative purposes. The Cape and Natal banks after 1870 were notoriously involved in land deals.

Amongst a section of the population the sense of ownership even was dulled. In their eyes land assumed something of the qualities of air and water. There was more than enough for the use of all men. Not to own land did not mean that a man lost the right to graze cattle upon it, or to till a portion of it for food. In the distant districts of the Cape Colony and the Republics there was from the early beginnings a group of men unlike their fellows, who used the land but did not seek to own it. They followed the grass and the seasons, fleeing drought and cold. Those of their new neighbours who owned land defended their proprietorship against the Kafirs, but not against their own kind. Thus it could happen that no vital difference was felt to exist between a farmer with land and another without, for none were denied its use. At the very end of the nineteenth century it was still possible to find in both the British colonies and the Republics many families who had departed not one whit from the habits of the eighteenth century. Owning not an acre of land in their own right, they leased land in the manner of their great-grandfathers, or, in a country that was innocent of both fences and the law of trespass, followed the seasons with their flocks and tented wagons.

Eventually the day came when new land was scarce, and it was no longer easy to drive off the Kafirs to make room for decent white settlement. Many acts of British policy precipitated the land crisis. Every effort which the British Government made to influence the relations between the whites and the native tribes was also an effort to restrict the freedom of the whites to possess themselves of whatever land tempted them. The British annexation of Natal in 1843 protected the Natal natives against entire dispossession, and preserved the great native area of Zululand from encroachment for forty years. The annexation of Basutoland in 1869 and the protectorate of 1885 over Bechuanaland, forced the Republics to accept definite boundaries and halted the movement on to new land. But now in the decade of the Boer War the day had come when the population could no longer roam freely or swarm on to new land. Rural society began to reveal its hidden inequalities. Rural society began to separate into classes of landed and landless men. The scarcity of land and the influence of gold caused a rise in land values before the Boer War. The rise was resumed after the Boer War, and prices were firm till the Great War. The rise in land values drew a sharper line between landowners and squatters. Often rising land values were a doubtful blessing to the landowners themselves. They were sometimes content to let a rising market rather than their own industry bring them prosperity. But when the largesse of the land market ceased, the pressure of downward prices squeezed from the land the speculators and others who had neglected the enterprise and skill of the true farmer.

Upon the entire remoteness of the veld the invasion of the instruments and the men of modern industry and commerce had a disturbing effect. The new towns meant a money economy instead of a subsistence economy. The new industries meant the habits of the nineteenth and twentieth centuries instead of the habits of the eighteenth century. Before the tide of economic progress the slipshod habits of a subsistence economy became improvidence, and the old easy-going ways became indolence punishable by bankruptcy and impoverishment.

Between the divorcement of a portion of the white population from the land and the inability of the native areas to sustain their population the resemblance is very clear. The process in the native world was dramatic and plain to see; in the white world it was insidious and slow to reveal itself. How akin the two developments are may be seen in an examination of other causes of white indigence. By the sixties and seventies magistrates in native areas had begun to notice the disappearance of trees, the erosion of the soil, the degeneration of herbage in the native areas, which together were a sign of the extent to which a crowding of men and animals had wrecked the natural balance of soil and vegetation. What took Nature a thousand years to build could be destroyed in less than the lifetime of a single man. In all the great colonial regions of the world the history of the ruthless exploitation of natural resources is a full one. In Canadian Alberta and Manitoba the plough exposed the soil to the rigours of wind and drought; much of its fertility, like that of the States of Kansas and the Dakotas, was disastrously scattered in the spectacular dust storms of the American Middle West. Axe and fire in other parts of Canada reduced immense acreages of forest to lumber, pulp, and ashes. In Australia the nibbling and trampling of millions of sheep weakened vegetation and caused erosion; ringbarking produced gaunt cemeteries of dead trees; gushing bore-holes made serious inroads upon the invaluable stores of underground water. Yet no comparable area in the British Empire, unless it be Australia, was more vulnerable than South Africa to an inconsiderate and unscientific exploitation of its agricultural resources. South Africa has lived to a dangerous extent upon that part of its capital which is represented by its soil, grass, trees, and water. Together natives and whites have dissipated huge resources. The grass-burning that reddened the late winter horizon sent up in smoke the organic matter that should have quickened the soil. When protected by a cover of vegetation, the virgin veld could not be harmed by the most violent deluges that poured upon it. Baked hard by grass fires, trampled down by innumerable hoofs, and laid bare by the grazing of countless mouths, the same veld was helpless before the devastation of thunderstorms. Streams that once came gently from the ground became muddy torrents after each rain. In South Africa rain rarely falls with the gentleness of an English drizzle. Clouds pile in overtopping formations, the heavens crash, and a deluge descends upon the earth. Paths made by stock driven to and from water, cracks produced by drought, valleys that have lost their vegetation are defenceless before the force of rushing water, and become the gullies and 'sloots' that carry off the precious soil. The barer the soil is of vegetation the more moisture is lost to the heat of the sun. Erosion was at its worst in the native areas, but everywhere wind and water carried away a fertility that had never been abundant. The universal destruction of trees left large areas with hardly a bush to relieve the gaunt landscape. In 1841 there was not a tree fit even for fuel within fifteen miles of Pietermaritzburg. Most of the midland region of Natal was treeless. In the air round most farm-houses and native huts hung the familiar reek of manure burnt as fuel. Most men, black or white, failed to recognize that manure in their fields was as bread cast upon the waters. Thus it could be that men who were deeply attached to the soil and who had not the greed for swift profit that devastated thousands of square miles in the 'dust bowl' of America, nevertheless impoverished the land and imperilled their own security upon it.

The improvidence of men found a cruel ally in drought. As early as the middle of the nineteenth century frontier farmers spoke of a special South African golden age of plentiful rainfall and rich grasses. The truth was that regions like the Karroo had been subject to drought for centuries, long enough for the development of the flora characteristic of an arid land. Even other regions like Natal and the Transvaal, which enjoyed a much higher average rainfall, were subject to protracted droughts. In the period between 1882 and 1925 South Africa suffered on an average one severe drought every six years. Between 1878 and 1919 the area of Griqualand West suffered eleven ruinous droughts, of the sort that caused farmers to cut the throats of lambs to save the lives of their sheep, many of whom died nevertheless of the thirst that thickened their blood and burned them with fever. Although there is no conclusive evidence that droughts have become more frequent and severe since the arrival of white settlers, the evidence is very clear that the power of the land to resist drought has been much weakened, as overgrazing and wasteful husbandry weakened its vegetation and drained it of its underground water. The rainfall has probably not decreased in volume, but it certainly has decreased in efficiency. Tumbleweed, prickly pear, rhenosterbos, and jointed cactus invaded the territory of the edible grass and nutritious plants. Through these results of overstocking and grass-burning thousands of square miles of pastoral country have committed suicide. To such land rain, when it fell, did less good, and drought did more harm than formerly. The land retaliated for its neglect by providing less support for human beings and live stock. Farms that could bear ample stock in good years became grossly overstocked in years of drought. In severe droughts cattle and sheep died in the thousands, and crops withered in the fields. Years of drought plunged some men into debt; from others it took cattle, land, and even their attachment to the soil. Men of courage and persistence, who would not break under the first lash of adversity, were belaboured time and time again till their hardihood and their substance gave out together. In the end the years of drought withered their enterprise. In their minds and bodies was the barren apathy of men who believed that it was vain to pit their energies against the weather. It was an almost Bedouin fatalism that accepted good years as providential rewards that could not be tempted by hard work or enterprise. Passively they rode the crests or sank into the troughs of good and bad years. If ambition stretched in one year, hope sagged in the next, till many of them lost all tautness of mind and will.

Even as the natives, so did many white families undoubtedly suffer chronically from an insufficient or unbalanced diet. In the more arid regions of the country fresh foods such as vegetables, fruit, milk, and butter were never plentiful. In protracted periods of drought they were hardly obtainable at all. A diet with an excess of carbohydrates and a deficiency in protein and certain of the vitamins shows its effect in the lassitude of ill health and poor physique, in the mental fatigue and retardation which are amongst the most common symptoms of malnutrition. There are levels of personal misery where it cannot be decided whether men are more victims of themselves or of the conditions which bred them. But by qualified medical opinion it is considered very possible that the vitality of a section of the rural population suffered seriously from generations of recurrent starvation in essential food elements. Between malnutrition and a lowered resistance to disease the connexion is well established. In the hot low veld malaria is endemic. Malaria and bilharzia, which is also called redwater fever, conspired with poor feeding and poor housing to produce widespread physical and mental debility. On the spacious farms of the sun-drenched veld crowded and unhygienic living conditions were still possible. The great fecundity of the white rural population was often compromised by cramped and un-sanitary housing. There can be no doubt that the errant Trekker of the middle of the nineteenth century, who lived in his wagon and shot his own fresh meat, lived more healthily than his descendants sixty years later in the hovels and shacks of the poor whites.

In the old spacious days it had not been necessary for children to wait for their father's inheritance. But when free land became scarce, and cheap land dearer, the father's single farm often had to suffice for the whole family. The Roman-Dutch law of inheritance was the law of Natal till 1863, of the Cape Colony till 1874, of the Orange Free State till 1901, and of the Transvaal till 1902. It compelled the division of a father's property amongst his children. Even where the law was formally abolished it continued to be respected by many of the rural population. Had this process of subdivision of the land been followed by more skilled and intensive farming, it might have conferred upon the country the boon of a thrifty peasantry of small landholders. But irrational subdivision and the same primitive, wasteful, and unsystematic farming as of old harmed both the land and its owners. Few medieval manors could have been more fan-tastically subdivided than some South African farms. Only the pitiful holdings discovered in France by Arthur Young, extending only as far as the shade of a single cherry-tree, were comparable with the 1/148,141 share of a farm of 2,527 morgen to which one heir was entitled. For many families such an inheritance became a sure road to pauperdom. Strips too scattered to be efficiently farmed, or too narrow to be fenced, plots that could not be protected against the trampling of cattle, intermingled holdings that reduced the enterprise of all to the level of its weakest members—these medieval phenomena were inevitable when thirteen indivi-duals owned the same 17 acres of land. The alternative to subdivision, which was collective ownership, often led to the same disastrous results. Lacking the commercial habits and customary observances of a medieval village, groups of owners on the same farm usually failed to achieve the co-operation and common enterprise without which farming fell into profitlessness and wrangling. Whether or not farms were subdivided their occupants were immobilized upon them, living and dying without incentive and without responsibility, without experience of anything save the narrow uncommercial routine of the farm, so that children grew up poorer than their parents and unfitted for anything but the diminished existence of their grudging land. Even after the Great War the traveller could come across such groups of families huddled together on land that could not support them in comfort, condemned to eat the meanest food, so abjectly poor that money was almost as rare as the meat on their plates. To argue whether neediness leads to moral degeneration or whether moral degeneration leads to neediness would be vain, for both propositions can be true. Amongst both the causes and the results of rural impoverishment were a weakening of the moral fibre and a slackening of these impulses that enable men to oppose their character and energy against the forces of their environment. Upon sections of South Africa's population the years immediately before and after the Boer War saw descend a dull apathy, even an indifference to the aspirations of civilized men.

Gibbon Wakefield in his day taught that a colonial government should alienate its land so carefully and at such a price that a proportion of the population, being unable to obtain land readily, would be the labourers in a healthy rural society. In many agricultural regions of the Empire and America the scarcity and the expense of land have produced, since the Great War, a class of labourers for wages and tenants at a money rent. In South Africa, on the contrary, the separation of agricultural society into two classes, the landed and the landless, did not produce a compact class of white labourers and tenants. Instead the depressed group occupied an ambiguous intermediate position, neither wage-earner nor tenant, divorced from the enterprise of ownership yet not wedded to the self-respect of sustained and remunerative labour. This class of squatters or *bywoners*, as they were called, had no parallel elsewhere in the British Empire. At one end of the scale were those who were little more than labourers, earning their keep, an occasional sheep or calf, and, more often since the Great War, some cash as well. At the other were those with rights of grazing and cultivation over an entire farm in return for shares and services. Between them was the great body of landless *bywoners* who eked out an existence by the grace of the landowners. Common to all was some plan of working on shares, whether of crops or cattle. With enough acres for the plough or enough grazing land for their beasts, the lot of some was tolerable. Too few acres and too little grazing land thrust others into a perpetual struggle for existence.

Their position in rural society was made harder by the presence upon the farms of a great body of native labour. Native labour prevented the great body of *bywoners* and poor whites from becoming an established and recognized class of labourers and wage-earners. The cheapness and docility of their labour gave the natives a great advantage over their white competitors. But white competition was not keen. Widespread amongst even the poorest whites was a distaste for 'Kafir work'. There was no corresponding prejudice against all forms of manual and unskilled labour in the other great colonies. In Canadian industries and upon New Zealand farms the bases of skills may be laid by manual labour and semi-skilled activities. Because so much manual and un-skilled labour in South Africa was not 'white man's' work, it could happen that the very foundations of successful farming were abandoned to native labour. Of all skilled occupations farming most surely requires an apprenticeship of calloused hands and a sweated brow. The South African rural poor white finds a close parallel in a well-known section of the population of the former slave States of America. There, too, a system of plantations and large farms operated by cheap and docile labour bred a marginal population of poor white men. And these, despising the negro, kept themselves apart from those who were economically their closest kin. Their effort was to keep themselves above the negro by the virtue of their race and superior political position. In

South Africa in very much the same way the poor white
occupied an intermediate position between the class of
landowners and a servile native population. Their poverty
separated them from the one; their pride separated them
from the other.

Because the *bywoner* was so clearly the product of an uncommercial age of subsistence farming, it followed that his
lot was made worse by the development of modern farming.
Indeed, wherever sheep farmers and cattle farmers learned
the lessons of Australia and New Zealand, wherever the
agriculturalist sought to apply something of the skill and
business practice of an Iowa grain farmer, the traditional
bywoner system was doomed. A more efficient use of labour,
the use of fences, more intensive agriculture, better stock-
breeding, or more economical grazing were incompatible
with the haphazard system of squatters and hangers-on.
Fencing in South Africa, as in Australia and sixteenth-
century England, decreased the demand for human labour.
A fence stood for more rational farming, a greater use of
capital, and modern technique. In more senses than one it
became a barrier against the group which had not adapted
itself to the new age.

In the decade before the outbreak of the Great War there
were still unsettled regions. They were so dry and unattractive that earlier settlement had passed them by. Now the
arid lands of Bechuanaland, of the western Orange Free State,
and the north-western Cape received settlers. But these acres
were altogether incapable of absorbing the excess rural population or of correcting its poverty. It was to the diamond
mines and the gold-mines that a large body of natives had
gone to make good the deficiencies of their rural existence.
It was to the towns also that there began a drift of the white
rural population. In 1904 the white urban population
was 590,926, which was 53 per cent. of the total white population. In 1931 it was 1,119,848 or 61 per cent. of the total
white population. In the same period the percentage of the
rural population dropped from 47 to 39 per cent. As early
as the census of 1904 a decrease of rural population was
observed for the whole of the Cape Midlands. In the census

of 1911 the affected area had widened, stretching into the Orange Free State. Further census reports in 1918, 1921, and 1931 showed that the drain was widespread and continuous. Between 1890 and the Great War a change came over South Africa. With a speed that even the United States could hardly match, thriving towns sprang up where there formerly had been a struggling village or simply the bare veld. Between 1891 and 1911 the urban population increased by more than 200 per cent. In New Zealand, Australia, and Canada industry, commerce, and the movement of population were stimulated by rising prices and an increased demand for goods. But in South Africa these world conditions were spurred forward still more emphatically by diamonds, gold, railway building, and the expenditures of war and reconstruction. Johannesburg especially experienced a growth paralleled by few towns of the Empire. Into the new towns flowed a steady stream of the rural poor.

The growth of towns and a decline in rural population can be, as social historians well know, a sign that a country is becoming more prosperous and more advanced in its economic structure. Since the Great War, New Zealand, Australia. Canada, and the United States, as well as some of the older countries of western Europe, have all experienced an exodus from rural to urban areas. Machinery and scientific methods have lessened the need for human labour on the farms. Urban factories have taken over many operations formerly carried out on farms. A change of population took place even in rich agricultural areas. That it took place in the rich regions was all the more reason why it should take place in poorer regions, where a lesser efficiency and a weaker productivity simply meant a poorer chance of meeting the competition to which agriculture is especially exposed. The rural exodus of modern times is in consequence not necessarily a tragedy, nor a sign that the country-side is suffering from a wasting economic disease. Rural depopulation is in part due to a more efficient distribution of production between town and country. Even South Africa's rural exodus, unique though it is, was a natural response to changed economic conditions. A country which in 1870 was exclusively rural must perforce yield a part of its rural population to other occupations when the country reached a more advanced state of development. Restlessness amongst a people does not always prove that its condition is becoming worse. Sometimes it indicates the awakening of new ambition, so that men change their homes and their way of living not because the old is intolerable, but because the new is more enticing. Some of the dividends paid by the great mining corporations, and some of the profit made in the grain and wool warehouses went into the pockets of the rural community, even of the very poor. Though far behind the towns they too obtained a share of the more abundant goods which South Africa's wealth could buy. But their demands not rarely outgrew their capacity to satisfy them. What the land in its poverty could not give them many sought in the towns. Yet it must remain clear that most of them went to the towns for the same reason that water flows uphill when driven by machinery. Drought and fences, the devastation of the Boer War and the collapse of the ostrich feather industry at the outbreak of the Great War, inefficiency and bankruptcy— these and similar causes do much to explain rural depopulation. When the British army command decided to break Boer resistance by laying waste the land, it destroyed much that reconstruction could never replace. At the Peace of Vereeniging not less than 10,000 individuals had been torn loose from the land which was their way of life and the pillar of their self-respect. The townward drift was only partly, therefore, the country's response to modern industry's call for energetic workers. The country-side's contribution to the towns was not a class of sturdy yeomen thrust forth by laws. A large proportion were defeated men, unable to maintain their hold on the land, destitute in both wealth and energy, drawn into an unfamiliar world of reluctant opportunities and depressed wages. In the towns as upon the land they were caught between the upper and nether millstones of two classes. In the country they had been extruded from the ranks of the landowning and prosperous farmers; in the town they could not enter the ranks of the skilled and well-paid workers, for they had no skill of their own. In the country the system of cheap and tractable native labour gave them no chance of becoming a useful race of rural labourers; in the town the same natives obstructed the absorption of the poor whites in the ranks of unskilled labour. To the English rural poor of the eighteenth century the factories and slums of the Industrial Revolution afforded some relief from the pressure of inclosures. The mines and industries of South Africa did afford a similar relief to the dispossessed and the poor. The real difference was that the black poor were favoured over the white poor.

It is clear that in their landlessness and lack of industrial skills poor whites and poor blacks were close indeed. The forces which, since the Boer War, depressed a section of the European community continued to affect the natives, too. In 1930 an Interdepartmental Committee on the Labour Resources of the Union came to the conclusion that the overwhelming majority of the able-bodied males of the reserves spent a portion of each year in European service. In other words, the twentieth century made still more acute and still more chronic the inability of the reserves to provide for the needs of their population. Even areas that enjoyed good land and good rains grew increasingly unable to meet the food needs of their populations, let alone the taxes, hoes, candles, and other burdens and wants. The official Union Year Book estimated in 1932 that native production of maize was too little for their consumption by 8,000,000 bags per year. In 1925 it was reported that the Transkei, which was regarded as one of the most prosperous and best-favoured native areas, could not support its inhabitants from its own resources, so that at any given moment nearly half the able-bodied men were absent in European employ. From hopelessly overcrowded areas like the Ciskei or Basutoland the exodus of able-bodied men was all but entire.

After the Boer War, as before, native life continued to be punished for its ignorance and neglect. Overcrowding and overstocking of men and animals brought more swiftly than in white areas the retribution of erosion, the ruin of nutritious vegetation, and loss of fertility. There was often such voracious overgrazing that the grass could not throw its seed and yielded place to weeds and noxious growth. Erosion in Basutoland is a geologic habit, for its valleys were phenomenally deepened by ages of erosion. The pressure of men immensely hastened the slow work of nature, and the signs were ever more clearly visible in the denuded hill-sides and the gaping ditches which, like running sores, carried away the health and fertility of the soil. And yet in Basutoland, as in the Natal and other native reserves, men were compelled to demand from the soil more than it could safely yield. In areas which were not simply unprogressive but deteriorating, the number of human beings and cattle continued to increase. It has been estimated that between 1918 and 1930 the number of cattle in native areas increased by 232 per cent. from 1,680,000 to 3,900,000. Compulsory dipping and other governmental effort to control animal diseases threw the burden of over a million more mouths and feet on to the land. This increase was not compensated by any comparable growth in agricultural skill and science. An increase in animals did not mean any economic enrichment. Of inferior quality, poorly herded and wretchedly nourished, they added little milk and less meat to the native diet. Nor did the Bantu ever learn the tender care of the impoverished and overcrowded Chinese for their soil, for they denied the soil the enrichment of their cattle's manure. And the soil punished such neglect by feeding the cattle ever more poorly, till often the oxen were too weak to plough the earth deeply. Part of some reserves were so dry that cattle could be taken to water only once every two days.

To the natives cattle were more than wealth. To sell them or to eat them was a step away from the ways of their fathers against which the spirit of the tribe continued to struggle. They were a cult. Some of the serious economic consequences of 'cow worship' amongst the Hindus of British India could, therefore, also be observed amongst the Bantu. The ban upon killing cattle for food was much less severe in South Africa, but the cattle cult had the same result of permitting many thousands of wretched and useless beasts to batten upon the slender resources of the land. Cattle were hoarded like money. They became more a measure of their owner's dignity than a source of income or profit. Cattle or grazing facilities as payment for native labour on farms were a form of reward that did not enrich the natives. Thus their two principal assets, their cattle and their land, continued to stand in an unproductive and damaging relationship to each other.

Upon their poverty pressed the burden of taxes, direct and indirect. As reluctant as the old separate communities to tax European land, the Union Government continued to levy direct taxes upon the natives. Thus it could happen in the Cape Province that a European did not pay income tax, even though he might own several thousands of acres of land, while a native paid 20s., or 30s. if he had a hut in a reserve. Customs duties severely affected prices of goods intended for native use. In 1930, for example, a duty of £256,037 was collected on imports of beads and cotton goods intended for native trade with a value of £443,952. 'The present burden of taxation on Natives, direct and indirect', reported the Native Economic Commission in 1932, 'is very heavy. It is quite impossible, without serious consequence to Native welfare, to increase it.'

In 1894 the famous Glen Grey Act held out the promise of a gentle but sure transition from an unenlightened and squalid tribal existence to an active and progressive individualism. Through its operation natives would be bound to the land by a new and intimate bond of personal possession and profit. The *Bunga* or Transkeian General Council of 1895 was to be the forerunner of a greater measure of native self-government so that the benefits of Victorian liberalism should be bestowed on Her Majesty's black subjects as well. Within the limits of the Transkeian Territories the experiment showed distinct elements of success. Few modern debates on native policy refrain from complimentary reference to the Transkei. Between 1894 and 1911 the system of individual landholding was extended to seven other districts, in which ultimately 50,000 individual titles were registered. But the Act never lived up to Rhodes's boast that it was the Magna Charta of the native population. Its very corner-stone, which was individual landholding, was imperfect; for there was not enough land for such a system. Each plot that was assigned to an individual, even though it was no more than 4 acres in extent, reduced a portion of the tribe to landlessness till in 1929 there were 11,000 families with no ground of their own in which to plant crops. The crowding upon private land and common land was a brake upon the enterprise of individuals. Indeed it was not the intention of the original Act that the Transkei should become a self-sufficient area, for the Act made provision for a labour tax of 10s. The tax fell into desuetude and was repealed in 1905 because the natives were at no time able to satisfy their needs without a constant and considerable export of their labour to European areas.

The Glen Grey scheme committed the common fault of taking one step and going no farther. It remained unique. The truth was that individual tenure came at a time when native land losses had been so great that the rule of 'one man one lot' was an impracticable dream. There was not land enough. The Beaumont Land Commission of 1915 estimated that the native areas had room for not more than approximately half of the entire native population. Half the population lived permanently outside the reserves and locations, in the towns and upon the land of Europeans. And not all of the reserves enjoyed the arable acres or the reliable rainfall of the Transkei. Since native diet depends so greatly upon maize, it meant much to native life in the reserves that the greatest maize-producing areas were in European possession. Of the production of maize four-fifths was on European-owned land. After Union there were many reserves unable to produce as much as half of the food they needed. Native areas which once had good arable land, like the Witzieshoek location in the Orange Free State, and were able to produce a surplus of grain, lost their fertility so that they were compelled to import grain to make good an annual deficiency. The congestion of the reserves, the backwardness of their methods, the exhaustion of their resources accounted for many things. They accounted for chronic undernourishment under a generous sun, for weakened stamina in the open air.

They accounted for the shrunken enterprise, and for the tightened hand of tribalism. They accounted, together with taxes and tea and hoes and cotton blankets, for the departure each year of a high proportion of the able-bodied men to earn money as labourers. And, as in a vicious circle, the departure of each man robbed the native land of his labour, and threw the burden of production on the shoulders of women and boys. Too poor to stay at home, their going surrendered their land still more to inefficiency and ignorance. The cold facts of native economics prove that the reserves were unable to produce enough to feed their population, pay their taxes and debts, and acquire the cheap manufactured goods that had become necessities. The natives were the victims of too few acres; in some places they were the victims of chronic malaria and of the cattle diseases borne by the tsetse fly. They continued to be visited by drought. In the fourteen years between 1917 and 1930 the district of Willowmore, like the Egypt of Pharaoh's dream, had seven lean years. Still more were they the victims of their own ignorance, for without the benefit of education in farming twice the space would still be insufficient to support them. They were the victims of a railway system that avoided most of their areas, and of a credit system that starved them of capital.[1]

After the Boer War, even more than before it, the native areas were reservoirs of labour for the towns and European farms. Since 1900 the native population continued to flow from areas of predominantly native population to those chiefly occupied by whites, to the towns and the farms alike. Between 1890 and 1921 the white population of the Orange Free State increased by 143 per cent., while the native population increased by 239 per cent. Between 1921 and 1936 the percentage increase of the native population of the Orange Free State was nearly five times as great as that of the European population. Their movement was essentially one of colonization. It is indeed one of the remarkable occurrences of South African history that the advance of white settlement

---

[1] They were an uncertain risk, for there was usually no assurance that they could put money to a productive use. Unfamiliarity and ignorance stood between them and the use of credit.

into the interior did not halt the movement of the native population. Though the tribes were broken and their hold upon the land destroyed, they continued to flow on into regions that had never seen the Bantu race. As servants and labourers they continued the process of distribution which they had begun as independent pastoral tribesmen, denying every effort to confine them or to hinder their movement. In 1916 the Beaumont Land Commission estimated that there were 1,264,593 natives, nearly one-third of the total rural population, who lived on European-owned land. In 1927 their numbers were given as 1,618,000. These were the native squatters, labour tenants, and labourers. They were, economically speaking, the native equivalent of the poor whites.

The presence of such a great body of natives upon European land was a safety-valve for the overpopulation of the native areas. In spite of rightlessness, low wages, exploitation, and high rents, life on European land preserved the familiar rural framework of the tribe and left intact many of the social habits and customs necessary to native happiness. The European landowner was not a hard taskmaster and almost never a cruel one. The great farms, themselves inefficient instruments of production, made possible only an inefficient use of native labour.

In the early days when land was plentiful the farmers could reward the services of their labourers by giving them the use of land on which to grow their crops or graze their cattle. The services which were rendered and the payment which was given were appropriate to a subsistence economy in which land was used wastefully and labour inefficiently. The system had two important advantages, complementary to one another. To the European farmer it provided labour for little cash expenditure; to the native it provided life upon the land for himself and room for his cattle. In these conditions the natives resident upon European land did not become a class of labourers for a cash wage. The great majority occupied an intermediate position between the status of labourers and tenants. Labour tenancy was a form of labour peculiar to South Africa. The labour tenant did not correspond either to the tenant or to the hired hand of Canada, nor to the farm labourer of the other dominions. In return for residence, the right to cultivate a piece of land and graze a few animals, the landowner usually received the services of the tenants in the field and of his women in the household. Between the labour tenant and the medieval serf the resemblances are sometimes striking. There is the same exchange of labour services for the permission to cultivate the land and graze on the common, the same right to cut wood for fuel or building, the same tendency for the tenant's entire family to be bound by his 'contract'. Professor Maitland's assertion that to ask for a definition of the medieval manor 'is to ask for the impossible' applies with equal force to the framework within which the South African farm native had his being. The privileges and obligations of the labour tenant showed extensive variation, being subject to innumerable differences from district to district, and even within the same district. The return to the farmer or landowner might be made in cash rent for grazing rights and a plot to be cultivated, or in the contract to supply labour for a specified period, or yet again in the payment of a fixed share of the crop. Over the greater part of the country labour was given for ninety days in each year. In Natal 180 days were commonly demanded. In former days the farmer could call upon his tenants at any time. Since the Great War an unbroken period of service became more usual, although exceptions remained frequent.

The principal advantage of labour tenancy was permission for the native to live upon the land. The most arduous conditions were often borne, so great was the native hunger for land and cattle. But other advantages were few and uncertain. No industry, however sustained, no thriftiness, however resolute, could enable the labour tenant to acquire land of his own. Even upon the accumulation of cattle limits were set. The verbal contracts and the lack of any uniformity of conditions of tenancy or labour gave the natives no status and little security. The system was uneconomical for the natives. It used his labour intensively for a short period, and tied him to the land in idleness for the rest of the year, or compelled him to accept poorly paid labour elsewhere. It stood between the natives and the solace of tribal existence, or the freedom and opportunities of life in the towns. At its best it gave the natives food to eat and shelter; but poverty and a low level of subsistence were the fate of most. The malnutrition of the reserves was common upon the farms, too. Many pages of details about diet and conditions of living could not reveal as much as the evidence of the District Surgeon for Aliwal North before the Native Economic Commission.[1]

'The farm labourer', he reported, 'in my experience is badly nourished. I have a recollection of a number of post-mortem examinations which I performed on Natives on farms and they had hardly any superficial fat and their bowels were very thin. . . . It seems to me that a Native ages a great deal earlier than he should. A Native in his fifties is pretty well worn out. . . . To my mind, it is entirely a matter of nourishment. If you have a diet of mealie-pap[2] without any fat, the balance is all wrong, and that is the cause of it. . . . There is one point which I have noticed in the gaol, and that is this—I can usually pick out the sheep-stealers, because they are well nourished. . . . An increase in the meat diet would undoubtedly tend to give them better health.'

Uneconomical to the natives, the system was uneconomical to the landowners as well. As in the reserves so also upon European land was there much wasteful agriculture and much overgrazing. With the growth of population and the rise of land values the demand came for a more profitable use of the land. The same intensive cultivation and the same fencing which so clearly affected the white *bywoner* affected the black *bywoner* or labour tenant, too. With the progressive abandonment of subsistence farming the semi-feudal relations of *bywoner* and labour tenant began to give way little by little to relations more fitted to a cash economy. Payment in cash instead of payment in privileges, regular instead of seasonal service were steps towards more business-like and profitable methods of agriculture. In certain districts of the old Cape Eastern Frontier the labour tenant system saw a rapid replacement after the Great War by a system of cash labour. In

[1] U.G. 22 of 1932.
[2] A porridge made of ground mealies or maize; the American corn mush.

others the change took place with exceeding slowness. But sooner or later the crisis of adjustment to modern conditions befell the native population upon European land as well. The drift of natives from the farms to the towns was one proof the more of the common economic condition of poor white men and poor black men. Prior to Union in 1910 it was legally possible for natives to purchase land in all of the provinces except the Orange Free State. There the purchase or the lease of land by natives was expressly forbidden by law. In the Cape Province and Natal natives could acquire land in freehold or in leasehold without any discrimination. In the Transvaal natives could acquire land for which the Government acted as trustee. This meant in effect that natives could not become private landholders. In actual fact poverty, and sometimes social pressure, prevented the native population from relieving the great shortage of land from which they suffered in any significant degree. In 1913 the notorious Natives Land Act undertook to remove the differences in the conditions of native land tenure between the provinces, and to define more emphatically the relationship between white and black settlement throughout the whole country. Its intention was to put an end to the widespread practices of 'Kafir farming' and the commingled habitation of white and black which was the result. Natives on European-owned land were to be labourers; independent agriculture and cattle raising could be carried out only in native areas. Thus suddenly a firm line was to be drawn between white and black settlement. The segregation of which men had been talking for a hundred years was to be undertaken at last.

In young communities such acts of legislation are not uncommon. Not yet three years old, the Union Parliament addressed itself to relationships that were a hundred years old. The success of the Act was naturally very uneven. The provision in the Act that existing contracts between farmers and natives were to run until they expired in the Orange Free State, and could be renewed at the will of the landowner in Natal and the Transvaal, permitted very extensive evasions of the purposes of the Act. The Act was further weakened by a decision in 1917 of the Appellate Division of the Supreme Court that the restriction upon the purchase of land would conflict with the right of the Cape natives under the Union Constitution of qualifying for the franchise by the acquisition of property in land. But by far the greatest difficulty in the way of purging European land of its native squatters and tenants was the lack of any land to which they could move. A Native Land Commission in 1916 proposed that some 17,600,000 acres of additional land be set aside for exclusive native settlement. This land still left the Europeans in possession of the healthiest and most fertile areas. Yet public opinion baulked at the return to the natives of so much land. The result was that the natives reaped few of the intended benefits of the Act and suffered serious disadvantages. The Government, it is true, used its discretionary power to continue to permit the purchase or lease of land by natives in certain areas. On the other hand, farmers were enabled to undertake evictions of natives from their land. After 1913 two streams moved from the European areas, one into the reserves, making congestion greater still, the other into the European towns. This confused movement of the native population from the farms to the towns, from the farms to the reserves, from the reserves to the towns, and from the town back to farms and reserves, indicated the manner in which economics and politics affected every section of the entire population. That the cattle held by natives on European farms increased very slightly between 1923 and 1936, and that the number of goats and sheep of all kinds fell by 24 per cent. in the same period indicates little improvement in the condition of a large proportion of the native population. Census reports are not engaging documents, but their evidence in social matters is sometimes eloquent. While the European urban population between 1904 and 1936 had more than doubled, the native urban population had more than trebled. In 1904 13·4 per cent. of the entire native population was urban; in 1936 the percentage had risen to 22·2 per cent. In 1904 the natives were 29·4 per cent. of the town population; in 1936 they were 38 per cent. In 1921 the number of urban natives in the Union was 587,000. In 1936 it was 1,149,228. Between such a great increase and the conditions of life in the native reserves and upon European land the connexion is clear. It is even more clear that South African rural policies have been instrumental in creating a great native urban population.[1]

[1] For most of these figures I am indebted to Professor Shannon's article in the *South African Journal of Economics*, vol. v, 1937.

IX

CIVILIZED LABOUR

'. . . and the happiness and greatness of the People are by the Ordinary Rules of Arithmetick brought into a sort of Demonstration.'
SHELBORNE's Preface to PETTY's *Politicall Arithmetick*, 1691.

THE large towns of South Africa are few and very far apart. Cape Town is 650 miles from Kimberley and 956 miles from Johannesburg. Durban is 516 miles from Bloemfontein and 494 miles from Johannesburg. Bloemfontein is 263 miles from Johannesburg and 755 miles from Cape Town. Between them, as in Australia and the Canadian West, lie the great solitudes of thinly peopled land. The fine roar of the Union Express between Johannesburg and Cape Town is, for mile after mile, lost in the lonely veld, where each isolated farm-house seems anxious to place the horizon between itself and its neighbour. The white-walled houses of Cape Town, the flower markets and fish pedlars of its streets; the jingling bells on the white-washed legs of Durban's ricksha boys; the fine organ, the University, and the metropolitan din of Johannesburg, accentuate the unusually great differences between town and country. Though the number of farms which used the implements and the wisdom of modern agricultural science increased after the Great War, the greater part of the agriculture of the country made slow headway against the handicaps of nature, against inefficient labour and inefficient methods. Agriculture remained a pursuit that conferred ease upon only a very few, and paid those that served it very poorly indeed. Between the country and the towns there was the widest contrast in incomes, in wages, and the standard of living. The large South African towns, on the other hand, were the homes of high wages and a high standard of living. Not the mines alone but other industries as well disposed of capital, modern skill, and management which together raised the economic level of the town remarkably high above that of the country. In those industries the artisans and skilled workers received wages and enjoyed a standard of living which brought them well within the ranks of the middle classes. Even though high wages caused notoriously high rents and other costs of living, a Johannesburg carpenter could send his son to a secondary school, a linotyper might have a motor-car, a painter enjoy annual vacations by the sea, or a miner own his own home. Even as the skilled worker of the United States did not regard his motor-car as a luxury, so was the South African skilled worker inclined to consider native help for the grosser tasks of the home as a necessary part of the cost of living. Unique amongst the skilled workers of the Empire, the South African artisan revealed his especial rank by being himself a frequent employer of labour. Numerous attempts have been made to compare the standard of living and the wages of the South African workman with those in other parts of the Empire. In 1914 the average weekly wage of a white coal-miner in the Transvaal was twice that of a coal-miner in New Zealand. In 1926 it was observed that 'while in England a skilled engineering artisan's weekly wage is the equivalent of the pithead price of three tons of coal, in South Africa it is the equivalent of from 20 to 25 tons'.[1] Any economist knows how difficult and uncertain such comparisons are, yet most studies agree that the purchasing power of the wages of the average South African skilled worker gave him one of the highest standards of living in the British Empire.

The full meaning of the statement that on the Witwatersrand in 1937 the minimum wage of a linotyper was £7. 12*s*. 9*d*. per week, of a shaft timberman was £1. 3*s*. 7*d*. per day, of a painter was 3*s*. 4*d*. per hour, is seen by relating these to the rewards of other classes of labour in South Africa. For all its gold and diamonds South Africa must rank amongst the distinctly poor parts of the British Empire, and indeed of the civilized world. An Industrial Legislation Commission sitting in 1935 found that mutilated Austria and backward Spain had a higher *per capita* income than South Africa. Calculated in gold dollars of 1913 the *per capita* income of South Africa was roughly one-third of that of Australia, one-quarter of that of Canada, and one-fifth

[1] Economic and Wage Commission, U.G. 14, 1926.

of that of the United States.[1] That Johannesburg, Durban, and Cape Town had the standard of living, not of Milan or Seville, but of Montreal, Sydney, or Philadelphia, meant quite simply that they were spending upon themselves an unusual share of the national income. The distribution of income in South Africa, in other words, brought about an abnormal investment of national wealth in fields and facilities from which only a small part of the population could benefit. In other words again, South Africa's skilled workers were unique in their dependence upon an exceptionally uneven distribution of income. Society in South Africa was not so composed that there was a fairly even descent from wealth to poverty, so that classes merged into one another. In a more homogeneous community life, in Australia or New Zealand, where there existed no abrupt gaps between social groups, great contrasts between the well-to-do and the utterly poor did not exist, and no group was denied access to the services and social amenities which were provided by the community. In South Africa the services and amenities of modern life were provided for only a part of the population. There existed two bodies of consumers, far apart in their standards of living and in their purchasing power. A large section of the population lacked the economic means to afford the high price of good food, healthy housing, industrial goods or amusements, and the cost of these was made higher because of the smallness of the group which enjoyed them.

A high rate of income is more than a guarantee of a high standard of comfort. It is also an assertion of racial and cultural superiority. The denial to the native population of access to more skilled employment and a better scale of life is both an economic desire to protect skilled labour against encroachment and an assertion of the superior worth of the Europeans. The roots of race distinction the world over are never purely economic. They are psychological, social, and

[1] Industrial Legislation Commission, U.G. 37, 1935, par. 99. Since these proportions are based upon the 1928 figures for the national income of Canada, Australia, and the United States, and upon the 1923 figures for South African national income, they are not precise.

cultural as well. Indeed, between the white and black frontiersman of a great part of the nineteenth century the economic resemblances were frequently greater than the economic differences. Hence the distinctions of the frontier, of which many were inherited by the twentieth century, went beyond economic rivalry. The white frontier insisted upon religious, moral, and cultural barriers between itself and its neighbours. The frontier sought out differences not to diminish them, but to widen them. To European self-esteem concepts of native debasement, of inferiority and savagery became convenient modes of thought and useful bases for action. 'Untameable savages!' cried Governor Sir Benjamin D'Urban in 1835 when the Ama-Xosa plunged into the Cape Colony to plunder and burn. His phrase was more than exasperation that the natives had broken the peace of sixteen years. It made of the marauding Ama-Xosa beings against whom violence and confiscation could be legitimately used. The history of the nineteenth and twentieth centuries is full of the unconscious propaganda of the white race against the black race. Although the rifle and the burning torch secured the military submission of the tribes, their work was carried on by concepts and attitudes, sanctions, and sentiments which imputed indignity to the natives and increased their submission, till they came sometimes to be regarded as a passive commodity, part almost of the raw material of the country, properly confined to a depth which emphasized the economic and social height of the dominant group.

In the beginning of mining and industrial development the high wages of skilled labour were protected by its scarcity and a certain exclusiveness given by its British or European origin. In gold mining as in diamond mining South Africa was at first unable to provide trained workers and technical experts. It was the immigrant who started South African industries. The first generation of gold-miners were mainly from Cornwall and the north of England. The predominantly British character of the miners and the scarcity of skilled labour both set their mark on the mining industry. The habits of the British workshop and the traditions of the

British trade unions established themselves on the Witwatersrand. The traditions of the miners and the great demand for their services set them apart as a sort of industrial *élite*. This special position was enhanced by their relation with the native workers. They did not become miners in the Australian or Canadian sense of the word, but a group of highly paid overseers superintending a great mass of unskilled and low-paid black labour. Thus in the labour organization of the mines there developed the sharpest differences between skill and the lack of skill. And these differences corresponded so exactly to the inbred attitudes of the country towards race that race and colour became more than ever before the badge of economic status. Racial inferiority was held to be sufficient proof of economic incompetence. More unambiguously yet did unskilled work and kafir work become synonymous terms. For all work performed by natives it was proper to give a low rate of pay. Attitudes such as these took deep root in the thought of the white industrial community. They assumed the validity of self-evident economic truths. The equality which had been denied the natives in the churches of the rural Republics was again denied them in the temples of labour. The country had its low-grade ore, its low-grade land, and also its low-grade human beings. And the ineradicable contrast between these and the whites justified the great economic inequalities between skilled labour and unskilled labour, between rates of pay that were exceptionally high and exceptionally low.

When the supply of local white labour became more plentiful after the Boer War, skilled labour naturally endeavoured to continue the special advantages which it had enjoyed. It drew profit from its organization in trade unions which were in an exceptional degree confined to its own ranks. Its close concentration in a few large cities enhanced its exclusive and monopolistic character. In 1902, for example, the Transvaal Miners' Association was founded and, after a successful strike in 1907, became a powerful organization. The tendency of the trade union to regard its particular industry as the preserve of its own members continued and even sharpened the division of labour into two groups, the one compact and self-conscious, the other formless and hampered. The higher grades of employment became 'non-competing groups', not altogether unlike the guilds of another age. They were protected, not simply by their greater skill or efficiency, but by obstacles opposed to the ready employment of outside workers who were less skilled and less familiar with the self-conscious traditions of organized labour. The creation of artificial barriers to the free movement of labour and the maintenance of gaps between classes of workers affected the status of the trade unions and the political Labour Party. Neither before nor after the Great War did they represent a genuine socialist movement, for their province was not the entire labouring population. The energy of organized labour was principally directed towards maintaining its monopoly. The membership of the Labour Party was confined in an unusual degree to skilled workers, and its constituency to the few large industrial centres. It remained cold to the interests of unskilled labour, and frankly hostile to black labour. The South African Trade Unions and the South African Labour Party sponsored the interests not of all men who laboured for a living, but of a confined membership and a restricted constituency.

Because it was possible to give high rates of pay to only a small proportion of the population it inevitably followed that the remuneration of the rest of the population was unusually low. A high standard of living in the towns and a high level of wages for part of the European population rested directly upon a low standard of living and a low wage level. The striking difference, before and after the Great War, between the maximum and minimum rates of pay in South Africa was without parallel. The rough rule in Great Britain and the other dominions that the wages of unskilled labour must be a generous fraction of the wages of skilled labour was not observed in South Africa.

In 1935 it was found[1] that skilled workers in the building industry received on an average three and one-half times the wages of unskilled labourers. On the Witwatersrand, where differences were greatest, a bricklayer or carpenter

[1] Industrial Legislation Commission, U.G. 37 of 1935, par. 11.

received ten times the wages of the unskilled native who mixed his mortar or held his planks while he sawed them. Whereas in countries like Canada, Australia, and Great Britain the wages for unskilled labour ranged from 50 per cent. to 75 per cent. of the wages for skilled labour, in South Africa the wages for unskilled labour varied from 10 per cent. to 30 per cent. of the wages of skilled labour. In Australia the rates of pay for skilled and unskilled labour after the Great War came to be exceptionally close to one another. Only in a country where the sharpest social and racial distinctions were drawn was it possible for skilled labour to earn three, five, and even ten times as much as unskilled labour. In plain economic language,

'the relatively high wages of white artisans are due to and dependent on the employment of large numbers of unskilled native labourers; and in this the artisan is typical of the whole white community who are enabled to maintain a standard of life approximating rather to that of America than to that of Europe, in a country that is poorer than most countries of Western Europe, solely because they have at their disposal these masses of docile, lowly paid native labourers.'[1]

It was not the natives alone who were depressed in their power to earn. The country could not afford a high standard of living for the entire white population, with the result that, in addition to the native population, a very large proportion of the white population was also depressed to a low level of income and livelihood.

The very contrast between ramshackle farm-houses and neat urban dwellings, between the unreliability of crops and cattle and the dependability of mining, between the low incomes from land and the comparatively high incomes from industry, made the towns unusually attractive to a large section of the rural population, both black and white. The gap between agricultural and industrial incomes, between urban and rural wages, was one cause the more why the rural areas failed to hold all their population, and why, in common with many other parts of the world in the twentieth century, South Africa experienced a marked drift

---

[1] Economic and Wage Commission, U.G. 14, 1926, par. 276.

of unskilled rural labourers to the towns. By their presence they exposed in an unmistakable manner the structure of economic and social life. The *bywoner* of the farm, by becoming the unskilled labourer of the town, showed up the unrepresentative and monopolistic character of organized skilled labour.

Rural society suffered, we have clearly seen, from its own backwardness and poor organization, and its drawbacks were made to appear greater by the advantages of the towns. In Canada and New Zealand railways and roads, motors, telephones, and wireless did much after the Great War to break down the isolation of rural living. In South Africa the changes wrought by these were evident too, but the use of motors, telephones, and wireless is limited where there is little money to buy them. It was monotony as well as poverty which focused the eyes of the sons of *bywoners* on Johannesburg. To many an untravelled 'backveld' farmer Johannesburg held the place that Constantinople must have held in the mind of a German peasant in the eighth century or Paris in the eyes of a French peasant in the eighteenth century. If many a farmer's son was driven to the towns by great hardships, many another went forth eagerly to seek the glamour and see the life of the big city.

The new population of indigents which began to grow up on the outskirts of the towns after 1902 gradually altered the early simple division of the country's white population into urban English and rural Dutch. In the years after the Great War the poor white belonged equally to town and country. The Dutch-speaking community as a whole began to lose, like the French-Canadian population in Quebec, its predominantly rural character, and to achieve new social and economic interests. Although the grievances of the Boer War did not lose their power of exciting sudden debate and passionate utterances, new problems became more real and new political shapes more substantial. The quarrels of republican independence against Imperial co-operation, of Afrikaans against English, remained keen. Yet the Boer lost his unique place as the type of the South African. The miner took his place beside the Boer as representative of South

African economic life. Indeed, the Boer most frequently became the miner. The Union became a new country which still hearkened to many of the old cries from force of habit and because societies, like individuals, cling to their griev-ances. Yet the Union was so changed that any return to the old loyalties of the Republics and Colonies was impossible.

The great qualities of the Voortrekkers belonged to the veld and bush. Physical courage, skill on horseback, marks-manship, and knowledge of the beasts of the field were attributes that enabled them to live the life of the pioneer. In the town, in an environment of business and industry, other accomplishments were in demand. Their attainments in carpentry and the mason's craft, in tanning and wagon building, in soap boiling and candle making had been ade-quate in the unexacting circumstances of farm life, but were below the levels of urban industry. Already handicapped by inexperience, most of them were also handicapped because the language of commerce and industry was English. They were the victims of more than poverty and ignorance. In the towns, as in the country, many were improvident, irrespon-sible, indolent, and credulous. Incapable of skilled labour, their approach to unskilled labour was often grudging and biased. Their race was their title of superiority over the natives, and to do manual labour conflicted with the dignity conferred upon them by their race. To be hirelings was bad enough. To have to do work commonly done by natives was offensive. Such an aversion degenerated, in those who were most demoralized, into a claim to charity as a right. 'Let the Government help us!' was their demand. 'Shall we permit men in whose veins runs the blood of our Voortrekkers to be reduced to the level of Kafirs?' asked sentimental compatriots. More practical and critical men complained of the 'begging spirit' of the urban poor whites, protested against their dependence upon State aid, and affirmed that they were 'demoralized by help'. These com-plaints were in numerous instances not difficult to prove. Yet they did less than justice to the poor whites. The blood of Huguenots, German, and Dutch stimulated some to new and successful effort. City-bred sons and daughters did not always inherit the apathy of their country-bred parents. After the Great War came a noticeable change in the attitude to 'Kafir work'. Neither charity nor the colour of their skin could change the inexorable truth that untrained men, with no resources but the strength of their hands, must bite into the sour apple of menial labour. But the great difficulties which the poor whites experienced in the world of industry were ultimately not caused by their own delinquency or by their own inaptitude. The competition of natives which had prevented the growth of a white labouring class upon the land confronted them again in the towns, an obstacle once more to the growth of a white labouring class in industry.

The forces which had affected the tribes throughout more than a century contain the explanation of the presence in the industrial cities of large native labouring populations. Part of the native population sought the towns because of the conditions of their life in native areas and upon European farms. A little like their prototypes on the medieval manor they denied the traditional bonds of rural life, and migrated to the towns in order to find the mobility and the wages which life upon farms did not yield them. Still others came as the result of the pressures and persuasions which ever since the middle of the nineteenth century never ceased to demand more labour from the native population. Before the rise of towns South Africa had been insatiably greedy of native labour. Then the towns added their demand to that of the country. So impatient were the mines to swell the ranks of cheap labour that, it has already been shown, they imported Chinese, between 1904 and 1907, and each year a great army of natives from beyond the territories of the Union. But the movement of natives to the towns was not always violent and involuntary. Given two societies living side by side in the same land, no power of law or edict could prevent the passage of men and habits from one group to another. When one of the two societies was much greater in its material wealth, more complex in its culture, and more powerful in the means of coercion, then the poorer and weaker naturally sought the higher, for such was the mark of its inferiority. Landlessness and taxes and labour laws gave an irresistible impetus to the already natural urge for the natives to come forth seeking the gifts and wonders of villages and towns. The swelling stream of men coming to the towns and returning from them again diverted the course of old habits and made native life a maelstrom of new and conflicting tendencies. With money in their pockets the young men looked with scorn on the inexperience of those who had stayed behind, and resented the effort of the chiefs and elders to apply the old tribal sanctions to them. Even more than magistrates and missionaries and traders did they bring alien ways into the life-streams of their society. In the minds of native youths the towns bulked as impressively as in the imagination of white youths. To go to the towns was like coming of age. Young men no longer took the same pride in their ox-hide shields, milk-white and taut, or in their manhood rites. A sixpenny clasp knife took pride of place before an assagai, and six months in a mine was a higher initiation than the ceremonies of the tribe.

From communities in which all men lived the same uniform lives they went into communities which contained the greatest differences in habits and occupations. Men who had immemorially tended the same flocks, ploughed the same fields, and reaped the same crops went out, one to deliver milk in a suburb, another to scour pots in a kitchen, another to labour in the dust-laden depths of a mine, another to be a policeman with power to arrest his fellow men. Some worked for Englishmen and some for Dutchmen. Some saved their money and some squandered it, although there was not much to save and little to squander. Some fell foul of the law and lay in crowded prisons. But none of them returned to their kraals and to their kinsfolk without the mark upon them of change, which repeated returns to the world of the white man made more indelible till their very spirits were transformed. The nostalgic appeal of the tribe was, of course, not easily denied. It was a homogeneous group. Its laws were known to all. It drew its discipline and cohesion from within itself. The relations between its members and the obligations of the individual to the group were determined by the usages of the community. Law and morality had held men in a uniform bond. But ultimately the town destroyed the tribe. For many natives the links between the old life of the kraal and the new life of the city corroded and snapped. The binding force of their own native ways dissolved, and the immemorial habits of mind and body yielded to ways of thought bred in the individualistic society of western Europe. A generation of natives grew up who were completely separated from the land, socially closer to the negro populations of Chicago and St. Louis than they were to their own compatriots in the reserve.

It is no longer possible to define in any simple manner the social distribution and the economic composition of the native population. Distinctions between tribalized and detribalized natives, or between urban and rural natives, are useful, but not very accurate. Detribalization occurred extensively in rural areas, while natives who did not sacrifice their tribal loyalties lived in the towns year after year. Each year, and no year ever was an exception, a large body of men ebbed and flowed between the huts of the veld and the shanties of the town, shuttling to and fro in a sorry alternation between town and kraal that thwarted the simple human wish for home and permanence, an indeterminate throng with blankets on their shoulders and trousers on their legs, amenable now to the law of the city and now to the law of the tribe, and representing by their plight the inevitable and irresistible revolution in native life. The urbanization of natives after the Boer War was continuous.

One and a quarter million natives were the indispensable basis of urban industry of all kinds in 1936. They were the counterpart to the much smaller group of skilled industrial workers. Because industry paid such a large proportion of its income to trained white employees, it naturally spent the rest of its income which was available for wages on the employment of a large body of cheap labour. Thus a balance was found in low native wages for high white wages. It was a balance which seemed to correspond to the naturally high standard of living of the one and the naturally low standard of living of the other, each receiving according to his established and traditional needs. Poor native wages or good European wages responded to inherent qualities in each group, which made low wages seem as just for native workers as high wages for white workers. Poverty, in such an order of reasoning, was thus a normal condition of native life, like the infertility of barren land. It was a condition different from the poverty suffered by whites. The mitigation of white poverty, therefore, had precedence over the mitigation of native poverty. Mr. Justice Higgins of the Commonwealth Arbitration Court in a famous decision affecting the standard of living of Australian labour declared that

'the basic or living wage is computed and awarded on the principle that a normal man has a family and must earn sufficient to support it. Nor is the basic wage confined to the money necessary for the main requisites of life . . . it allows something to "come and go on". The wage is based on civilised conditions—the normal needs of the average employee regarded as a human being living in a civilised community.'

In South Africa it was a definition which excluded the natives, for they were not members of civilized society. Instead they had standards of comfort proper to their own level of culture, and reasonable wages for them could be much lower than those for the whites. This connexion between high incomes for a few workers and very low incomes is essential to any clear understanding of South African economic life.

The natives had established themselves in industry in the days when European labour of all sorts was scarce. During at least the last fifty years of the nineteenth century they had held a virtual monopoly of unskilled and manual labour in every part of South Africa, except the regions near Cape Town where their place was taken by the Cape coloured folk. Before ever the drift of poor unskilled whites to the towns had become a serious problem, it was a deeply rooted tradition of economic life that the natural division of labour was between brain-power and muscular strength, between administrative skill and docility, between the few and the many. But a division which appeared so convenient and so fitting was disturbed by the coming of the poor whites.

After the Boer War white labour, once in great scarcity, became more abundant. In what manner could industry open its ranks to permit the entry of these new recruits? The upper ranks in industry were entrenched behind their skill, their solidarity, and their high wages. The lower ranks were protected oppositely by their lack of organization and their low wages. By their race the poor whites belonged to the upper ranks. Their standard of living and their industrial inefficiency were at odds with one another; for the wage warranted by their standard of living was higher than the wage warranted by their lack of skill. They had, therefore, little bargaining advantage. Their coming disorganized and glutted the market for unskilled labour to their own disadvantage. Even whites with some skill and experience found their way blocked by the preference which employers normally showed for black labour, or in the western districts of the Cape Colony, for coloured labour. Amongst the natives there had developed a group of natives equal and often superior in experience and efficiency to the average poor white. Because as labourers they were cheaper and more tractable they normally found more ready employment than their white competitors.

Even before the Great War public opinion had regarded the poor whites with uneasiness. There seemed something ignominious in the sight of men and women who loved the land drifting helplessly to the towns, there to be dragged into competition with men of an inferior race. Something should be done to staunch this bleeding of the country-side. Something should be done to prevent white men from living the lives of black men. Economic equality between members of the white and black races created social equality. The threat was plain enough in the equally wretched habitations of poor whites and poor blacks in Johannesburg's slums. Social equality would break down the barriers of blood and race. The poor whites were the frontier between the European and the native. Through their weakness might pour a debasing stream of uncivilized blood. Race mixture, it could not be denied, took place most naturally in the common environment of poverty and ignorance. The degradation of the poor whites became therefore of vital interest to the entire white population. There was no ideal to which the country was more firmly attached than to the maintenance of a white South Africa. Against this determination even the laws of economics must not prevail. However powerful the opposition of economic arguments, the attempt should be made to raise the poor white population beyond the reach of black intercourse. '. . . A very appreciable portion of our white population,' wrote a leading educational authority, 'is fast sinking below the economic standard of living which we consider a white man should maintain in virtue of his white skin over against the native. . . .'[1] Reasons of public policy outweigh strictly economic considerations. The solidarity of white society and the integrity of its blood were supreme values.

Before the Great War social policy had used charity and provisional schemes of relief in order to mitigate the poverty of unfortunate whites. Based upon sentiment and much ignorance, they did little to widen the opportunities of the poor whites. When South Africa emerged from the Great War the problem had grown manifestly more critical. The year 1921 especially was a shocking year to South Africa. On top of the slump in trade and revenue caused by the post-War depression came the gloomy news and still gloomier forebodings of the 1921 Census Report. Statistics revealed convincingly the drift of population from the poor rural areas of the Cape Colony and the Orange Free State. More startling yet was the hint of a rising tide of native numbers. The hint was unnerving. No other census report had ever made such an impression on public imagination. Critics were, indeed, quick to point out that the evidence of a more swiftly increasing native population was very unreliable. Further evidence in later years fully sustained their criticisms. But the shock had been felt. White society became more acutely conscious than before of its numerical inferiority, against which neither natural increase nor immigration from Europe showed any promise of prevailing.

It was natural that, after the failure of casual charity and

[1] E. G. Malherbe, *Education and the Poor White*, iii, p. 22.

temporary expedients, the attempt should be made to lead the poor whites back to the land whence they had come. The State adopted a policy of direct pecuniary assistance, and helped poor families to build homes and construct fences. The attitude to the repayment of government loans was tolerant and yielding. Men were rehabilitated as farmers on agricultural training farms, such as the Losperfontein farm in the Crocodile River Valley in the Transvaal, and then established as tenants on government farms. At Kakamas in the far north-west corner of the Cape Province, where little rain and a hot sun are the enemies of cultivation, the Dutch Reformed Church nevertheless established a successful settlement for uplifting the poor white. Men were settled on the banks of two irrigation canals, one on each side of the Orange River. Strict and intelligent management secured an important measure of success. But the effort to place men upon the soil was costly. Ignorance and indolence were responsible for unequal success. There was not always sufficient strength in education and rehabilitation to prevail against locusts or hail or drought. 'Under such conditions,' wrote one disillusioned observer, 'farming for profit is a farce that South Africa has played for generations with sad results to her people.'[1] Furthermore, the trend in South Africa and in the world was towards town and industry. Rural rehabilitation of poor whites was but a palliative, and not a cure.

The great industrial upheaval on the Witwatersrand in March 1922 was a bloody sign that the focus of interest was in the towns. The social and economic questions of which poor whites and poor blacks were the centre were more important now than even the burning issues of South Africa's relations with the Empire and the Crown, about which political parties had hotly contested ever since the Armistice. In June 1924 the long premiership of General Smuts and the still longer reign of the South African Party came to an end. The defeat of General Smuts and his followers was not upon constitutional issues but decidedly upon social and economic issues. In the new 'Pact' Government, led by

[1] C. E. Leipoldt, *Bushveld Doctor*, p. 75.

General Hertzog, were included both the Nationalist and Labour parties. They were, in a manner of speaking, a white people's front against the natives. Only the passage of years revealed how thoroughly the change of government in 1924 had committed South Africa to policies conceived more resolutely than ever before in the interests of white society. It would be premature to speak henceforth of South Africa as a planned society. Yet there was manifest in government and legislation an increased unwillingness to leave the movement of society to chance, or to the unpredictable workings of economic or social laws. Better guarantees were sought for the development of a stable up-to-date white society. Means were more energetically sought to secure the political security of the white race as a whole and the economic security of its feeblest members.

The policy of the new government in providing work for the poor whites went deliberately beyond the provision of temporary relief. In 1924 a Department of Labour was created, of which a leading function was to establish areas of employment in which poor whites were protected against native competition. Municipalities and other public bodies were encouraged to employ more Europeans at 'civilized' rates of pay. The employment of European unskilled labourers had begun on the State railway system as early as 1907. In 1921 there were 4,705 white labourers in railway employment. By 1928 the number of unskilled white labourers had steeply grown to 15,878, employed at 'civilized' wages of 3s. to 5s. per day with free housing or an equivalent allowance. The success of the policy of higher wages and protected labour for the poor whites was not small. The conviction that hard manual labour was incompatible with a white skin grew weaker. Thousands of men who had once been 'irreclaimable' were elevated to a level of greater self-respect. Many discovered new resources of initiative and advanced into the upper ranks of semi-skilled or even skilled labour. When economists declared that higher wages were a form of bounty, and that protected labour was uneconomical, the answer was given that the sacrifice was well made if the unfortunate elements in the white population ultimately found an assured footing in modern life. *Laissez-faire* did not contain the stimulus that would compel the demoralized European to use his energies more fully and to increase his skill. Without special protection he could meet native competition only by a fatal reduction in his own standard of living, and that would simply permit the lower civilization to drive out the higher civilization. The colour bar was the result of a crisis. South African society was being comprehensively transformed. A society which was passing from a simple rural order to a complex commercial and industrial organization, and which, furthermore, was undergoing such changes in the midst of an inferior and subject people, could not permit a group of its own members to be lost to itself.

Racial discrimination and an increasing tendency in national legislation to separate the population on racial lines were an inevitable accompaniment of the new policy. White industrial society in the twentieth century had preserved many of the habits of mind of white frontier society in the nineteenth century. Its inclination to interpret its relations with the natives in terms of conflict was strong. The emphasis on conflict, therefore, weakened men's ability to discern the truth that in a society so thoroughly dependent on native labour the natives were not merely competitors but the most important collaborators as well. In the history of colonization in all parts of the world the greatest stress has always been laid upon competition and conflict between white and coloured races. The familiar theme is the success of the white race in sweeping away inferior races to make room for their own settlement as in North America, or in establishing a firm administrative rule over a great native population as in the Dutch East Indies. The popular knowledge of South America, where the development of intimate relationships between colonizing white races and aboriginal races is one of the great events of modern history, stops short with the exploits of Cortez and Pizarro. Of the subsequent creation of new societies in South America in which many men share there is the greatest ignorance, although in South Africa such information would be invaluable. Yet ignorance of another continent is less surprising than ignorance of Africa and the Africans. In spite of the labours of many students of native life, there continued to prevail amongst most classes of white society a remarkable lack of precise and unequivocal knowledge of native life. It was no shame for a legislator to be ignorant of the condition of the greater part of the population. In the absence of full and sustained knowledge the room for prejudice and misinformation was increased. To the ordinary European voter after the Great War the inborn inferiority of the native remained a truth beyond serious contention. Inequality and inferiority were natural defects beyond the reach of enlightenment. In the country-side this truth had the full authority of the Bible behind it; in the towns it was supported by popular scientific beliefs. A belief in an innate and invincible white superiority in turn justified the determination to preserve in South Africa the dominance of the white race. The pattern of society, in fact, was predetermined by the natural arrangement of its parts. Through such a belief the European became invested with a mission to preserve the higher values of Western civilization. White political dominance and white racial purity became, not selfish ends, but trusts to which unfaithfulness would be punished by degeneracy. To diminish white control of the instruments and powers of government in reality dispossessed South Africa of the cultural inheritance which the first colonists had brought, and which their descendants were obliged to keep intact and increase. In this order of thinking racial superiority became a faith, and racial and social segregation became a creed.

The social scientist is not perplexed by gross inconsistencies in popular thought on controversial questions. Because in these questions the heart speaks with no less force than the head concordance must not be expected. Side by side with the view that the natives were an embarrassing obstacle to progress, as might be a swamp or a stretch of desert, was the view that they were a natural resource to be exploited, like a mine or a forest of valuable timber. Side by side, especially, with an insistence on native ineptitude was an opposite fear of the ability of the natives to acquire the skill and expertness of white men. In this order of reflection the natives were likely to profit by a greater equalization of opportunities and by a removal of barriers between the spheres of white and black life. Native education and enlightenment, therefore, achieved subversive and dangerous qualities. Native enterprise struck at the roots of obedience, and ambition dissolved native tractability, weakening the restraint and control of the ruling race. In reality both attitudes, the one based on a judgement of native ineptitude, the other based on a judgement of native capacity, served the same purpose. Whether it be true that the black man threatened unduly to depress the white man, or that the white man threatened unduly to elevate the black man, the conclusion remained unchanged. Both attitudes supported the conviction that the destinies of the two races must be kept from flowing into the same channel.

The calmness of the scientist cannot be acquired by the whole body of citizens. The detachment of the scholar responds less readily to the fears and misgivings of men who are concerned to avoid great changes in their own lives or the future of their children. The natural tendency of any group to defend its integrity and preserve its privileges is a real and inescapable fact of political experience. A purely equalitarian society is like the Heavenly City of the eighteenth-century philosophers. It is still a Utopia or a philosopher's dream. The theoretical and ethical appeal of programmes for racial equality and free competition characteristically ignore or underestimate the tenacity of vested interests and the resistance of the habits of generations. Any approach to an equality of racial opportunity is a challenge to established interests and privileges. Greater opportunity and a higher economic reward for the natives would be at the expense of white income and the white standard of living. It is, it must never be forgotten, the essential poverty of South Africa that makes greater generosity towards the natives so very difficult. If rich loess soil were as broadly distributed in South Africa as it is in the American Middle West, or if the moisture-laden winds of the Atlantic and Indian oceans could find their way regularly to the arid Karroo and Kalahari, then the equalization of the economist or reformer might be more easily attained. Just as in the relations between whites and negroes in the southern States of America, so does poverty in South Africa, too, help to explain the effort of political action to restrain competition and to protect privilege. The economic and political governance of South Africa illustrates clearly how a community can be at the same time democratic and authoritarian.

The formation of the 'Pact' Government of the Nationalist and Labour parties in 1924 led to a more resolute effort to protect white society against the challenge of the natives. Its civilized labour policy spelt the exclusion of natives from certain kinds of work and also from the opportunities for development which depended on them. The exclusion received the popular name of Colour Bar, and the Colour Bar signified the entire complex of obstacles, some of them legal and administrative, others conventional and spontaneous, which were opposed to the rise of the native population in the industrial and economic life of the white community. Its strength came both from the force of statute and the power of public opinion. Though the Colour Bar was established in the native policy of the Republics, its principal statutory basis was the Mines and Works Act of 1911. This Act provided that certain positions of responsibility in the mines of the Transvaal and the Orange Free State must be held by competent white persons. Between 1923 and 1926, after a decision in the Transvaal Provincial Division of the Supreme Court, the Act could not be legally enforced. Yet such was the force of public opinion that the gold-mining industry continued to act as if the Mines and Works Act had never been declared *ultra vires*. A new Act was made imperative by the report of a Mining Regulations Commission in 1925,[1] which indicated that the introduction after the Great War of machinery capable of being worked by experienced natives threatened the place of the European worker in the entire range of mining operations. The Mines and Works (Amendment) Act of 1926, popularly and not inaccurately known as the Colour Bar Act, re-established the chief statutory support of the Colour Bar in mining.

[1] Mining Regulations Commission, U.G. 36, 1925.

The Act of 1926 was only the most important of a number of affirmations of the principle of the Colour Bar. The legal Colour Bar received support from several other enactments. The Apprenticeship Act of 1922, for example, imposed wage-rates and educational requirements for industrial apprentices which had the effect of preventing the entry into industry of natives as apprentices or learners. Native life in the towns was deeply affected by the Native Urban Areas Act of 1923.[1] This Act greatly extended the power of Government to control the presence of natives in urban and industrial areas. For more than a generation the growing body of natives in the towns had been regarded as little more than convenient reservoirs of labour. Since the turn of the century there had grown up in all large towns the disfiguring slums of galvanized iron and rubbish which city fathers seemed content to regard as makeshift and temporary camps. They failed apparently to see that in the sordid environment of these camps there was being bred a new race of native city dwellers. The natives were exchanging the spontaneous discipline and the familiar morality of the tribe for the arbitrary restraints of police and the confused morality of wretched living conditions. With little physical comfort and no social stability, the deadening weight of poverty and lack of opportunity fought against the hope of physical or intellectual betterment. The fruit of insecurity was restlessness. The fruit of neglect was delinquency. The most serious obstacles prevented urbanized natives from achieving an established and self-respecting existence. Though the towns were expanded and beautified, and the amenities of modern life were introduced, the level of native payment advanced very little during the space of more than a generation.[2] The advance was out of all proportion with the demands which life in the towns made upon them. They had, after all, changed from a natural economy where they grew their food and paid no rent, to a money economy where they had to purchase clothes and food, pay rent and taxes and fines.

[1] Amended by Act 25 of 1930.
[2] The average native pay for underground work in 1914 was 2*s*. $\frac{1}{4}$*d*. In 1930, in spite of increased costs of living, it was 2*s*. 2$\frac{1}{4}$*d*.

The cheapness of native labour was not in proportion to their inferiority or inefficiency, for upon native wage-levels there bore the depressing effect of laws which restricted the natives in their freedom of movement and bound them by regulations which did not apply to European labour. A series of laws thrust native working conditions out of the realm of civil law into the realm of criminal law, so that breaches of contract or labour agitation were punishable as crimes.

An advance in the level of native payments was impeded by deadly competition from rural natives. These natives, still attached to the land, enjoyed some of the advantages of a rural economy. With less food to buy and less rent to pay, they could come periodically to the towns and there accept very low rates of pay to the acute disadvantage of their urbanized fellow natives. Temporary workers from farms and native areas and especially the imported native labourers from territories outside the Union kept native urban labour in a state of chaos. There was no chance for the development of a regular class of native labour, able by its reliability, its permanence, and growth in skill to improve its condition. Native rural impoverishment was mitigated by the responsibility which the tribal group assumed for its individual members. The help which father gave son and brother gave brother, the sharing of a cigarette or the payment of a madcap debt, are illustrations of the succour which one tribesman spontaneously offered to his fellow, whether in a tribal fight or the harvesting of crops. But in the towns the detachment of the individual from the group caused his poverty often to stand unhelped and alone. The level of rural native wages, in the opinion of the Native Economic Commission in 1932, was far below the minimum necessary to provide native workers and their families with a diet 'consistent with reasonable maintenance of health'. Their poverty condemned them to living conditions which not even the abundant sun and fresh air of a South African town could make healthy. Their ignorance fastened their poverty more firmly about their necks. On the veld the wind and the rain and the sun had tempered the worst faults of their unsanitary habits. Here in their airless, overcrowded, and promiscuous locations disease and pauperism bred each other in a vicious circle.

In 1918 the influenza epidemic horribly revealed the disease and misery which was bred and sheltered in windowless shacks and congested unsanitary backyards. In the interests of the entire urban population the Natives Urban Areas Act sought to eliminate the more disastrous slum conditions by better building and stricter regulation. Acts directed against slums which ignore the more deep-seated causes of social degradation and poverty can only bring about reform slowly and imperfectly. After 1923, however, better housing, a few hospitals and dispensaries, and other social amenities at least arrested a few of the degraded conditions upon which a number of commissions, such as the Tuberculosis Commission of 1914, had given damaging evidence. Within the Act was also contained, however imperfectly, the prospect of native urban locations as places of healthier physical and social life, more accessible to emancipating and enlightening influences. Native urban settlement achieved an improved status. It no longer was simply a huddled reservoir of cheap labour about which the rest of the town was indifferent provided only the natives worked and kept the peace. The provision for Advisory Boards in each urban location at least elevated the governance of native urban groups above the mere maintenance of order and the enforcement of labour contracts. But the Act established another important principle. Urban areas were European areas in which the residence of natives was permitted only in so far as they served the needs of the European population. Such natives were, as far as possible, to be segregated in special locations. The right of natives to come to the towns was limited, and their status within the towns was severely depressed. Segregation also made control and discipline easier. The extension to all urban areas of the monthly pass system, which required each native to carry a permit to seek work or a registered service contract, was a device to measure the number of natives in each urban area and to limit their numbers; for a leading aim of the

Act was to discourage the flow of native labour to the towns and to reduce their power of competition in the labour market.

Few obstacles to native advancement were more serious than their ignorance and the lack of adequate educational facilities for overcoming it. A discussion of the provision of education for the native population must first of all understand the unusual educational problems which confronted South Africa at the beginning of the twentieth century. Upon the shoulders of the Union Government and the provinces was placed the heavy responsibility of making good the exceptional backwardness of a large proportion of the white population. The Great Trek had taken a large proportion beyond the reach of formal education. The responsibility, moreover, was not simply one of providing formal instruction where little or none had been given before, but also of making education serve the special needs of a society that was being comprehensively and swiftly transformed. In a society passing from the undifferentiated rural order of the Republics to the complex commercial and industrial organization of a modern British dominion, in a society which was undergoing such a transformation in the midst of an inferior and subject people, the urgency of education for the whites was greatly increased. Behind the impressive encouragement of education in South Africa there was much more, therefore, than the democratic feeling which sponsored education in the other dominions. There was also the conviction that to neglect education was to weaken the defences of the white community against the natives.

The natural price of a vigorous sponsorship of white education was neglect of formal native education. But because education is never simply a matter of schools and class-rooms the native population was not entirely without the means of instruction. It was impossible to weaken the life of the tribe without opening the way to new habits and, in the end, to a new culture. It was impossible to drive the tribesmen to mines or into factories without training them in some of the secrets of the white man's world. The effort to draw hard lines between the minds of men who breathe

the same air and draw their nourishment from the same
soil can never be entirely successful. Acute differences between groups that are close to one another must always be
tempered by the power that men have, however lowly their
place in the world, to learn and by learning to change the
ways of their life and the manner of their thought. Every
stroke of a hammer on an anvil, every thrust of a foot on a
delivery bicycle, every pot that was scoured, took the natives
farther from ancestral habits and closer to the habits of a
new society. In their keenness for education many natives
deliberately abandoned the farms or the reserves in order
to acquire reading and writing, in order to reduce the space
between uncouthness and civilization, and in order to hasten
the transition from ignorance to knowledge. Barbarism was
conscious of its own deformity.

Yet between the native mind and its environment the
discrepancy was inevitably great. All the great body of
superstition that stood in the way of better crops and herds,
of better health and a wiser use of time and energy, were
challenges to improvement and correction. It was not simply
the children who needed education; it was the entire native
population which required some release from the handicaps
which their history and social heritage had placed upon
them. If they were to be better adapted to the modern
society into which they had been drawn, the grip upon their
minds of primitive ideas and upon their bodies of inadequate
institutions needed to be unloosed. During the greater part
of the nineteenth century missionary institutions bore most
of the burden and cost of native education. They advanced from the early delusion that the Bible, Shakespeare,
and easy Greek were the road from barbarism to civilization,
to the skilful training for practical living which is found in
modern missionary schools. Yet not all the generosity of
congregations in Great Britain or France, nor all the devotion
of missionaries, could influence more than a small fraction
of the native population. That in 1921 almost nine-tenths
of the native children were illiterate was a measure of the
insufficiency of even the most elementary schooling, of the
lack of public sympathy and financial support for native

education.[1] In 1925 the Native Development Account was established under the Native Taxation and Development Act. Its main objects were to provide elementary education for native children and to train farm and home demonstrators to work amongst their own people. The Account consisted of one-fifth of the proceeds of the Native General Tax[2] plus a fixed contribution of £340,000 a year from the Union Government. The salutary effect of this measure was seen in an increase in schools and enrolment,[3] yet it was still possible for the Native Economic Commission to report in 1932 that four out of every five native children remained without any educational provision, and that the money available for native education was too little by $2\frac{1}{4}$ million pounds. The Native Taxation and Development Act meant that the most backward part of the community was made responsible for its own development, and restricted the expenditure on that development to a portion only of the revenue obtained from the natives. In more purely economic language the Union refrained from spending a large portion of the income produced by the native population on their education, on the tools, the fertilizers, and the reclamation work necessary to improve the standard of life of the natives. The saving was virtually added to the income of the European community.[4]

In the generation following the Great War segregation—industrial segregation, urban residential segregation, and territorial segregation—became ever more clearly the leading principle of public native policy. Laws were amended and old Acts were changed for new in the effort to draw more clearly the lines between white and black. It is a temptation not easily avoided by minds sensitive to any hint of oppression or discrimination to look upon such a policy with disapproval and concern. Racial discrimination and the protection of

[1] The Census report of 1921 listed 3·5 per cent. of the natives who were part of the European economic system as educated or skilled.

[2] Increased to two-fifths in 1937.

[3] 207,621 in 1926; 345,540 in 1935, or an increase of 60 per cent.

[4] The South Africa Year Book for 1937 stated that £8,147,211 was spent on all forms of white education; £677,518 on native education; £658,326 on 'other coloured' education.

white man against black man were avowed purposes of the policy of segregation. Yet it must be noted that such a policy was not inconsistent with a genuine feeling that segregation could be made to confer benefits on each race. The consequences of a Colour Bar need not be oppressive, it was claimed, for it could secure to each race the order of life that was proper and natural to it. The white race properly belonged to a 'highly organized civilization'. The natives equally belonged to a 'privileged class' happily free from the burdens and demands of a complex culture. In 1836 Sir Benjamin D'Urban conveniently discovered the 'untameable savage'; in 1936 South Africa quite as conveniently rediscovered the Beautiful Savage of the eighteenth century.

It is fair, then, to attribute to post-war native legislation a genuine effort to improve the quality of native life and administration. Laws were passed which made life more coherent and administration more consistent. The Native Affairs Act of 1920 created the Native Affairs Commission with the function of advising the Minister of Native Affairs in matters of policy, legislation, and administration. It also provided for the establishment of a number of local councils in native areas of the Cape Colony, the Transvaal, and Natal, which were the basis of a restricted experiment in native participation in local government. The Natives Taxation and Development Act of 1925 established a uniform system of native taxation throughout the Union, and created the Native Development Account which in a short period made valuable contributions to education and agricultural training, to practical improvements such as the building of dams, the sinking of bore-holes, and the breeding of improved stock. The Native Administration Act of 1927 brought an end to the caprice and confusion of the uncoordinated legal and administrative procedures which the Union had inherited from the separate colonies. Few forces had had a more corrosive effect on the system of interdependence and reciprocal obligation by which the individuals of the tribe were held together than the conflict of laws and jurisdictions in the nineteenth century. Of especial significance, therefore, was the declaration in the Native Administration Act

that all suits between natives would come under the jurisdiction of Native Commissioners' Courts administering native
law, except where native laws were repugnant to natural
justice or public policy. There was an end to the anomalies
and arbitrary system which had permitted magistrates to
apply Roman-Dutch law and for natives to appeal to Roman-
Dutch law in the settlement of cases arising from native
customs. Limited jurisdiction was given to chiefs and headmen to try issues between their tribesmen, and two Native
Appeal Courts were established to hear appeals from Native
Commissioners.

Laws and politics are always indissolubly intertwined.
South African native legislation may be legitimately presented as measures of useful reform, and yet may also be
interpreted as political instruments regulating the place of
the natives in the entire society of the dominion. The measure
of laws is always both juridical and political. In South
Africa it is not difficult to discern the political foundation
on which native legislation rests, or the social and economic
interests which they defend. The entire series of native laws
from the Native Affairs Act of 1920 onwards pointed to
further legislation which should still more clearly define the
separate provinces of white and black existence. The Native
Affairs Act with its provision for Native Councils contained
the hint of a separate political compartment for the natives.
The Native Administration Act escorted the natives outside
the rule of law, thrusting them back into a region where the
Government had wide discretionary powers. The declaration that native law was valid only when it did not conflict
with 'public policy and natural justice' brought native life
more than ever before under the rule of administrative
procedures. The decision that the native could not be granted
the same place in urban life and industry as the Europeans carried with it the plain implication that the future
of the native population was primarily on the land. It was
there that they were best fitted by nature to live and grow.
That was why native chiefs were restored to some of the
authority which the nineteenth century had so violently
wrested from them. That was why the native law was made

whole again by the Native Administration Act of 1927. That was why such critical customs as the *lobola*, or bride-price, once reviled by missionaries as the buying and selling of women and the mark of paganism, were restored to their former integrity. Where once Natal colonists and Cape frontiersmen had cried out aloud against the menace of tribalism, now the tribe was seen as the bulwark of native existence, as the vessel which contained it and prevented it from spilling into individualism and becoming assimilated to the ways of another society. Where, it seemed reasonable to ask, could native development be best secured, in the alien atmosphere of towns, where native competition bred resentment and strife, or in the familiar atmosphere of their own land and their own institutions?

The firmer attachment of the native population to the soil and to their own institutions promised to mitigate the asperity of race relations, and to develop a sincerer co-operation between black and white. Capable economists had pointed out that the denial of higher wages and a better opportunity for development affected the welfare of the entire dominion, which suffered from the low productivity and the low spending power of its millions of natives. It was in the reserves that the natives could be taught the skills otherwise denied them by the Colour Bar. It was upon their own land that they could learn without embarrassment to European society to work their fields more scientifically and to tend their herds more expertly, so that, by the increase in their wealth, they might contribute more fully to the welfare of all South Africa.

'*The cure*,' declared an especially competent Commission, '*the proper economic synthesis of our wealth producing factors, lies in a wise, courageous, forward policy of development of the Reserves*. . . . It would be wise to develop the wealth producing capacity of these excellent areas and thus secure a larger amount to go round, rather than to allow a continuance of the present struggle between black and white for a larger share in the wealth being produced from the developed areas. With these areas developed to a reasonably productive level there should be enough to make possible friendly co-operation between the races.'

Two Acts, the Natives Land and Trust Act, the Representation of Natives Act, passed in 1936,[1] were the culmination of the policy of segregation. The first Act[2] sought to make good the deficiency which had turned the Natives Land Act of 1913 into a weapon against native rural life. Recognizing that few forces had been more powerful in driving the natives to the towns than overcrowded reserves and insufficient land, the Act established the South African Native Trust Fund,[3] to be used for the purchase and development of additional land, and for the advancement of agricultural and pastoral industry within the native areas. The Act empowered the Trust from time to time to acquire land within specially designated 'released' areas until a maximum of $7\frac{1}{4}$ million morgen, approximately 15,300,000 acres, was reached. And so the dispossession of native land which had been almost a rule of nineteenth-century policy was reversed in the twentieth century. Exiled men were to be returned to ancestral lands, or at least to some of them. Only the future could reveal whether the history of a century could be changed by the will of a legislative body.

It followed that men who were to be physically segregated should be politically segregated, too. Formerly men had blanched at the prospect of a concerted uprising of the blacks against all white men; now they contemplated a rising tide of black voters who might one day swamp them at the polls. In the Republics the natives had been denied all equality in Church and State. In the Cape Colony there was no legal discrimination against the enfranchisement of natives. The same property qualification and, since 1892, the same educational qualification was required of both European and non-European voters. In Natal the franchise was theoretically open to the native. But the road to qualification was beset by conditions so onerous that the chances of gaining the franchise were, not figuratively but literally,

[1] Amended in 1938.

[2] A third Act, the Native Laws Amendment Act, 1937, controlled the presence of natives in urban areas, native labour, and the acquisition of native land.

[3] This took the place of the Native Development Account.

one in several million. In 1936 Natal contained a single native voter! At the Convention which settled the terms of Union in 1908 the Transvaal and the Orange Free State had made it a firm condition of entry into Union that the franchise should not be extended to their natives. Since the delegates of the Cape Colony were resolute in defending their liberal native franchise, the Act of Union contained a compromise. The Cape retained its non-European franchise on condition that it could be altered by a two-thirds majority of both Houses of Parliament in joint session. The Constitution also declared that the franchise of the Cape natives could not be constitutionally challenged before the end of ten years. The challenge came in 1926 after sixteen years. That it took ten years more before the Representation of Natives Act of 1936 stood upon the statute books indicated the opposition which it experienced. The opposition to the 'Colour Bar' Bill of 1926, which was so strong that the Bill had to go to a joint sitting of both Houses, also declared itself against the limitation of the native franchise. The opposing groups were weakened by the enfranchisement of European women in 1930. Because native women were not included the European electorate was practically doubled. In 1931 the property and educational qualifications in the Cape and Natal were removed for European males, but not for natives. Thus the European electorate was expanded to its maximum proportions. An entire chapter would not be enough to describe the historic controversy of these years. To destroy the Cape native franchise was to destroy the most important bridge between the worlds of the two races. Nothing would so unambiguously define their relations. In 1936 the Representation of Natives Act became the law of the land. It took away from the natives of the Cape the right to be enrolled on the same voters' rolls as the Europeans. Instead those natives who had enjoyed the franchise were grouped into three native electoral circles each entitled to elect one white member to the House of Assembly. This was a concession which only imperfectly concealed the truth that the Cape native franchise had been destroyed, and that with it had disappeared all hope of an extension of the franchise to the rest of the population. The Act further established four electoral areas, the Province of Natal, the Transvaal and Orange Free State, the Transkeian Territories, and the Cape Colony, with an electoral college in each area to elect altogether four white senators. The electoral colleges were composed of chiefs, headmen, local councils, native reserve boards of management, and other similar bodies. These bodies, which were only indirectly representative of the native population and frequently nominated by the Government itself, would each exercise votes in proportion to the number of native taxpayers whom they represented. The four senators so elected were to be in addition to the other senators representing the natives, for whose election and nomination provision had been made in the Act of Union. The Act also established a Native Representative Council, composed of six official members, four nominated members, and twelve other members elected by the electoral college. This council was purely advisory. It had statutory authority to report to Parliament upon all legislation affecting native interests, and it could give advice on the appropriations which Parliament proposed to make to the Native Trust Fund. It was distinctly a body without legislative or financial power.

The Act did not, as some of its opponents had feared, entirely extrude the native population from representation in Parliament, although the native population of the Union as a whole was represented in the Senate which, like most second chambers in the Empire, had been shorn of its independence by the lower house. In the Native Representative Council it created a body which might be regarded as a first step towards a fuller responsibility on the part of the native population for its own affairs. Whether the Native Representative Council could ever have the same career as the early representative councils in the constitutional history of the British Empire remained a purely academic question. The political segregation of the natives and not their ultimate political maturity was the first concern of the framers of the Act.

It was inevitable that the closely connected policies of

civilized labour, the Colour Bar, and segregation should be attacked within South Africa and in other parts of the Empire as an effort to build towers of privilege so high that the natives outside them would never be able to scale them. To place the natives on an inferior economic level and to reduce them to a lower legal status was justified, it was contended, by neither science nor morality. The true cause of such repressive policies was 'prejudice begotten of fear and fed by ignorance'.[1] But the answer was given that as long as the blood and the votes and the competition of the natives menaced the integrity of the European community there could be no accord between the races. It was in a real sense this friction which halted the co-operation between the races. A sense of weakness engendered intolerance; fear was the enemy of restraint and wisdom. Once white veins were secure against native blood, white jobs against native competition, and white political life against the native electorate, European society could take up its proper task of securing the welfare of the natives. Segregation was the indispensable prerequisite to trusteeship. Segregation was the middle road between repression, which condemned the natives to a servile and inarticulate existence, and assimilation, which would cause Bantu, Boer, and Briton to founder in a mutual degradation of race and culture. Segregation permitted men to build planfully upon the foundation of the native's own being, adding the good and useful of European life to the good and useful of native life. To halt the further movement of natives from their own environment to the environment of the Europeans by giving them additional lands would restore their economic equilibrium. Not only would they be withdrawn from the competition with the white race, but in the less hurried and less challenging atmosphere of their own reserves they could more constructively remove the causes of their poverty and backwardness. To such wretched farmers and herdsmen it was more important to learn how to sow seed and breed cattle than to possess the franchise. Side by side with white society there would develop a native society, building its separate culture out

[1] Native Economic Commission, par. 104–5.

of tribal and European elements. Two distinct streams of culture would then pursue their parallel course into the future.

Segregation is one of the most familiar words in South African life. It has a history as long as the history of white settlement, for from the beginning the officials of the Dutch East India Company had striven to keep the tiny settlement apart from the surrounding natives. The history of South Africa since that early day has abounded in proposals of sweeping measures intended to solve the difficulties of racial contact. One after another the efforts to find simple and lasting arrangements failed. Yet in Parliament, in trade-union meetings, and in the debates of the country store, there persisted the same faith in a final solution. The appeal of segregation to the post-War electorate was great. The oppositeness of black and white was, to a popular and uncritical imagination, the clearest justification for keeping the two races separate. Segregation held out the illusory promise that the two communities could be kept separated, each in its proper sphere, like oil and water.

Segregation is a myth, a fancy, anything but a fact. As a word it describes a hope or a policy but not a real situation. It is denied by the sight of hundreds of thousands of natives dwelling permanently in the towns and upon European farms. The census-takers of 1936 found 559,675 more natives outside the native areas than inside them. It is denied by the recruiters of native labour for the mines, by the farmers who possess the vast bulk of good land, by the taxes which compel the natives to go out to earn money by their labour. It is denied above all by the fact that industry has been, in the language of the horticulturist, budded or grafted on to the stock of native labour. It is denied by the fact that the native population was no longer homogeneous. The greatest differences had developed in their ranks. Those, for example, in the towns, who had no roots whatever in the native areas, had developed economic and social habits which in reality brought them closer in many respects to the poorer class of Europeans than to their own tribalized brethren. The raw blanketed native of the reserves was an alien being to the trousered helper in a city foundry or a suburban kitchen. Not even the 15,300,000 acres of 'released' land were enough to permit of the development of the native population as a self-sustaining peasantry. Before ever it was 'released' most of it was already settled by natives. Even so large an additional area was far from being a cure for native landlessness. Landlessness as a leading cause of the urban movement was not removed.[1] What has been twisted together by history cannot be readily disentangled by laws. To unwind the woven cord of native and European life is simply to require history to retrace its steps. It would pretend that no wars had ever been fought, no droughts had scorched the earth, no diseases had stricken the native herds.

In most industrial countries of Western civilization it has long been a leading principle that industrial and social legislation is wise only when it increases opportunities of employment for all men, and removes those barriers that secure privileges for only a part of the population. Such measures are considered economically unwise and socially unjust which impose restrictions upon one part of the community in order to grant corresponding benefits to another. Indeed, a generation of able South African economists has exposed the economic weaknesses and contradictions of native policy. Not one but a whole series of expert commissions have challenged the wisdom of a rigorous Colour Bar. The principles of what Sir William Petty in the seventeenth century called 'Politicall Arithmetick' in national economic affairs made it quite clear that no restraints should be placed upon the economic usefulness or the skill of any part of the population. In strict economic thought native progress was part of the progress of the entire community. Whatever restricted the power of the native population to earn or to increase its capacity to produce also restricted its power to consume. It is one of the simplest axioms of economic thought that the whole of society suffers when any important group within it suffers from excessive poverty, inefficiency, inadequate use of its intelligence, wasteful organization of

[1] Scientific grazing and improved agriculture could, of course, increase the carrying capacity of the native areas.

its labour, or restrictions upon its ability to work and to produce. The belief that native wages should be low not merely froze a large potential purchasing power, but encouraged industry to make a wasteful use of human energy and to disregard the development of greater efficiency. The civilized labour policy was simply the payment of a concealed subsidy to the poorer members of the white population without any commensurate increase in efficiency. While governmental and municipal authorities could employ men under artificial and uneconomic conditions, private industry itself could not economically give preferential treatment. It was, furthermore, a medieval fallacy to suppose that an increase in black employment would decrease the amount of work available for white men. The plain facts of history were that since 1902 the numbers of both whites and natives in all branches of industry had increased. Granted that white workers must receive a civilized wage if white civilization were to be maintained in South Africa, the preferential treatment of unskilled whites ran the risk of perpetuating the existence of a marginal group of all but beggar folk. Willingly exploiting their indigence, they placed the burden of their existence on private charity and public subsidy, and shuffled off the responsibilities of thrift and industry. Quite regardless of all questions of morality or human justice, it was inefficient and uneconomical to pay wages corresponding with differences in colour instead of differences in skill. The very effort to pay uneconomically higher wages to white workers tended to defeat its purpose, for industry would inevitably prefer cheaper black labour when the margin of skill between white and black labour was not very marked. Far more important than the problem of securing special privileges to the European population was the problem of increasing the efficiency of the total labour force and the productivity of all industry, so that all men might share more generously in the expanded resources of South Africa.

The catalogue of the objections of the economists is long. Given their goals, which are the most efficient increase of natural wealth and its best distribution amongst all sections of the population, many of these objections are unanswerable. But it has not been in South Africa alone that the voice of the conventional economist has gone unheeded since the end of the Great War. Since Versailles so many of the iron laws of economics have been, for better or for worse, hammered out of their classical shape. In a generation which saw England abandon free trade, America leave the gold standard, the Third Reich embrace autarchy, and the Dominions adopt a severer régime of protection, South Africa's insistence that its economic life must be organized to secure the dominant position of the white race is not seriously out of place.

A

Average monthly native wage (including cost of housing and food) £4·10·0

♀ ♀ ♀ ♀ ♀

Average monthly European wage £32·10·0

♀ ♀ ♀ ♀ ♀ ♀ ♀ ♀ ♀ ♀ ♀ ♀ ♀ ♀ ♀ ♀
♀ ♀ ♀ ♀ ♀ ♀ ♀ ♀ ♀ ♀ ♀ ♀ ♀ ♀ ♀ ♀

Number of People Employed in South African Mines
Each figure represents 10,000

Non-European
394,000

European
47,000

Comparative Dominion Populations
Each figure represents 500,000

Union of S. Africa
(1936- 9,589,898)

Canada
(1936-11,028,000)

Australia
(1936-6,806,752)

New Zealand
(1,568,220)

The black figures indicate non-Europeans.

B

Population of Largest Dominion Towns in 1936
Each figure represents 100,000

Johannesburg
519,384

Cape Town
344,223,

Montreal
818,577

Toronto
631,207

Sidney
1,267,350

Melbourne
1,018,200

Auckland
211,380

Wellington
149,812

Urban and Rural Population of South Africa
Each figure represents 1,000,000

Rural

Urban

The black figures indicate non-Europeans.

X

THE REGULATION OF INDUSTRY

'In all societies consisting of various descriptions of citizens, some descriptions must be uppermost.' BURKE, *Reflections on the French Revolution*.

ON the commissions which studied the economic and social problems of South Africa there were politicians and there were economists. The economists did not always agree with the politicians, and the politicians did not always agree with the economists. But on one conclusion their voice was unanimous. The economic and racial problems of the country were made more intractable by its poverty. The chief obstacle to the civilized labour policy, for example, was the meagre wealth which came from the soil, the grass, and the forests. It was the declared policy of the dominion to secure for its white citizens a standard of living comparable with that of other dominions. Yet the annual production of wealth per head of its population was far lower than in any other dominion. Upon the expansion of its production and the development of new sources of wealth depended the country's social structure. South Africa had won its high place amongst the other parts of the British Empire through its mineral wealth. But crises in the gold markets of the world contained the threat that the world might lose its appetite for gold. The endless struggle of the gold-mines to wring a profit out of their reluctant ores showed how close they always were to the brink of crisis. After all, gold was a waning asset. Sooner or later the time must come when South Africa would no longer be able to nurse at the generous wealth of the mines. It was surely the sign of wisdom to uncover new sources of wealth against the day when the production of the gold-mines would seriously lessen. Through the years these observations gathered force until they assumed the dimensions of a national policy. After the Great War, therefore, South Africa grew ever more resolute in her effort to make poor land richer, to cause wealth to grow faster than population, to become more self-sufficient. South Africa had elected to plan her social order. A planned social order led directly to a planned economy.

In the nineteenth century the world of trade had been divided into older industrial and new agricultural countries. Money and manufactures flowed from the older to the new, stimulating in return the flow of foodstuffs and raw materials. After the Great War this distinction grew ever less exact. Manufacturing countries encouraged agriculture; agricultural countries encouraged manufacture. Everywhere the trend towards national self-sufficiency grew stronger. The greater the uncertainty of international equilibrium, the more resolute grew the effort to settle economic problems on a national scale. The slackening of emigration and the restriction of the exchange of credit and goods throughout the world were the result of the tariffs, quotas, and embargoes which the nations used to strengthen their domestic industries, and to lessen their dependence on the outside world. It was the end of the world of British free trade, of the interdependent world envisaged by Richard Cobden, in which each part would contribute to the world those products and services which it was most fitted to contribute by its climate, its natural resources, its geography, and its technical equipment.

It seemed reasonable to suppose that South Africa must look to the land to assume the burden of the country's future prosperity. Since the greater part of the population, black and white, continued to live on the land in spite of the great drift to the towns, it seemed plain that the country knew no greater need than the increase of agricultural prosperity. Had it not been for the mines South Africa would certainly have had to face a generation earlier the problem of the great inefficiency of the agricultural and pastoral industries. The great development of diamond and gold mining had deferred an inevitable land crisis. After the Great War the Government gave battle to the deficiencies and the handicaps of rural industry.

The life of the Boers was the story of their relations with the climate and the soil of the country which they had made their own. In the slow movement of their lives in the eighteenth century and in the career of their nineteenth-century republics may be discerned the obstacles which a twentieth-century government must experience in an effort to increase the wealth of the country-side. The Trekker of the eighteenth century had been a searcher after water. What could engineering and science in the twentieth century do to overcome the drought and aridity which forced the sheep and cattle in some parts of the country to go thirsty every other day, and which made the universal windmill as familiar a symbol of the farm as the ox-wagon? Irrigation and water-conservation schemes were a primary need of agriculture if it was to grow in prosperity. With these it would be possible to use occupied land more fruitfully, and perhaps to bring into production areas which even the land-hungry Boer had so far scorned.[1]

Agriculture could not reach prosperity in an ox-wagon or upon wretched roads. Even after the Boer War the system of communication in large areas of the country was little more efficient than it had been during the Great Trek. Before the Great War housewives still frequently bought fruit for jam and preserves from ox-wagons in the streets of Johannesburg. Though teams of oxen were already out of place in Johannesburg's bustle, they were a sign that the frontiers of the nineteenth century were still very close. Yet until railways and motor transport replaced the ox-wagon there could, for example, be no dairying on a large scale in South Africa, for the slowness and the dust of ox-wagon transport were the enemies of the speed and cleanliness which are essential to an efficient dairy industry. In other words, as long as a span of powerful Afrikander oxen was considered a valuable possession, there was less room for select dairy cattle.

Between the rural population and the more efficient use of modern devices and modern ideas stood also the barrier of their own lack of education. The greater part of the generation of farmers after the Boer War were wanting in

[1] At the end of the Great War there was virtually no fresh land available for settlement. The unoccupied land was hardly fit for either black man or white man.

a knowledge of even the most elementary facts of practical economics or science. Until they themselves had gained some knowledge of science, the benefits of science could not easily be extended to their cattle, their seeds, their fields, or their methods of marketing. Till 1891 in the Cape Colony and 1897 in Natal no provision was made for veterinary research, although cattle diseases had plagued the land for a century. The system of education which Lord Milner vigorously developed after the Boer War was English in character, and its most remarkable achievements were in the towns. The predominantly English temper of the principal towns and the dependence on imported teachers produced a form of education indifferently adapted to the daily needs of the great rural population. While keen and valuable men from the old English universities taught urban schoolboys Latin, history, and mathematics, cricket, soccer, and the long jump, neither the language nor the interests of the rural population were given a place that corresponded to their importance or numbers.

The great triumphs of agriculture in the contemporary world were won by an alliance with science and modern technology. It was through science and organization that New Zealand won for itself a place in the market for dairy products and meat. The dairy and meat industries in New Zealand, like the wheat industry in Canada, discovered that the punishment for inefficient labour and backward methods was a poor yield and inferior quality. The construction of scrupulously up-to-date dairies, and the application of motor power to tractors and combines gave New Zealand and Canadian farmers a great advantage over the unskilled labour and the poor organization of South African farming. Of all the dominions none seemed to have more climatic difficulties to overcome, or more antiquated methods to combat. In the same way that the rural population was accustomed to fat-dripping tallow candles and harsh home-made soap, so did it accept scrub cattle. Poor wine unattractive to foreign palates, bad brandy, good only for the Kafir trade, Boer tobacco or the notorious 'Pondo' leaf which caused experienced smokers to blanch, red scrub cattle of which no more than the hide was marketable—these were obstacles which could not be overcome by ordinary means.

It was not until Union pooled the resources of South Africa that a resolute beginning could be made with the task of modernization. At the time of Union in 1910 South Africa had reached the limit of her sheep-carrying capacity under prevailing conditions and methods. The result was that the droughts of 1914 and 1918 wrought havoc amongst the overcrowded flocks. It was stated by the Drought Commission in 1923 that the practice of confining sheep to a *kraal*, or confined inclosure, at night, and driving them to the grazing grounds in the morning and back again at night, was exhausting to the sheep and harmful to their condition. The introduction of fenced paddocks would enable the animals to lead a more natural life, improve the quality of their wool, and increase the sheep-carrying capacity of the Union by over 50 per cent. Efficient and modern methods were thus the gateway to a bigger production at home and better sales abroad.

As early as 1858 Sir George Grey had seen that only a well-organized centralized government could prevail against isolation and inertia, against disease and drought, against ignorance and inefficiency. The burden of modernization and the task of combating the defects of man and nature became the special responsibility of Government, rather than of private enterprise. South Africa in 1910 was not a young colonial community, vigorous and adaptable, and sensitive as had been Australian sheep-raisers and New Zealand dairymen to modern needs and modern means. The condition of the rural population was more like the condition of backward European communities whose history, too, had closed them against the science and enterprise of the nineteenth century. In such communities the responsibility of the Government for initiative is unusually great. Yet in Australia and New Zealand, which did not experience a Great Trek or the isolation of the Republics, the dependence upon Government was strong, too. In colonial communities as in backward communities many enterprises cannot be left to private initiative, for only the Government has the credit and power to undertake the projects necessary to modernize an undeveloped area. At the end of the nineteenth century New Zealand and Australia were famous the world over for the initiative which Government had taken in regulating the economic life of these communities.

South Africa came therefore increasingly to be farmed from the two capitals, Cape Town and Pretoria. Between 1910 and 1935 eighty-seven Acts were passed by the Union Parliament rendering permanent assistance to the farmers. The first six Acts indicated by their titles some of the most refractory problems of South African agriculture. The Agricultural Pests Act, the Diseases of Stock Act, the Dipping Tanks (Advances) Act, the Irrigation and Conservation of Waters Act, the Land Settlement Act, and the Land Bank Act show that the Union Government advanced along a very broad front.[1] These Acts and the scores of similar Acts which followed them made agriculture the favourite and special charge of the State. There were Acts to place men upon the land and to make credit available for schemes of water conservation and for fencing. There were Acts which imposed standards of quality upon wool, tobacco, raisins, butter, and other farm products. There were Acts to promote co-operation amongst farmers, to improve and regulate the marketing of their products at home and abroad.

From the gold-mines of the Witwatersrand came the bulk of the money which was required for schemes of agricultural planning. The revenue from the mines, for example, provided the funds for a strenuous battle against the many diseases of animals and crops—east coast fever and gallsickness, redwater and scab disease, rinderpest and horsesickness. The land, it was reasoned, was a permanent asset. To devote a share of the wealth of the mines to the land would, it was hoped, substitute the enduring prosperity of fertile seed and fat sheep, of laden trees and lush wheat, for the transitory wealth of low-grade ores and roaring stamps, of cyanide vats and phthisis hospitals. The 11,335,092 fine ounces of gold which were produced in 1936, for example, and the revenue of £14,299,932 which they yielded to the

[1] Nos. 11, 14, 20 of 1911; Nos. 8, 12, 18 of 1912.

Government were the financial backbone of agricultural legislation. The indirect aid of the mining industry was important as well. Because the mines contributed heavily through freight rates to the revenue of the State-owned railways, it was possible to reduce the level of railway rates for agricultural machinery and products. The policy of differentiating in railway rates according to the capacity of the various classes of traffic made it possible to extend rebates on the transport of agricultural machinery and farm produce, or to give exceptionally low rates of transport for cattle that were moved from drought areas to better grazing land.[1]

The Land Bank was established in 1912 to make first mortgage loans to farmers, to advance money for the construction of fences and dipping tanks, for bore-holes and dams, to relieve distress caused by drought, and to promote co-operation amongst the farming population. Between 1932–3 and 1935–6, for example, the Land Bank advanced £8,855,510 to 10,322 individuals and £12,067,032 to co-operative societies. The operations of the Land Bank and the direct expenditure of the Union Government on behalf of the farming population, amounting to £20,428,092 for 'Lands and Agriculture' and assistance to farmers between 1932 and 1936, went far to correct the chronic and discouraging scarcity of capital which had for generations been a leading drawback of agriculture.

Before the Irrigation and Conservation of Waters Act of 1912 irrigation had been almost totally ignored throughout South Africa. By 1936 altogether 32 Acts dealing with irrigation had been passed, and 126 irrigation districts under irrigation boards were constituted. In 1936 these boards controlled irrigation schemes of benefit to approximately 194,000 morgen, nearly 410,000 acres, of land. In addition several more ambitious irrigation schemes were undertaken, of which the twelve most important, with the exception of the Vaal-Hartz Irrigation scheme, begun in 1934, were able to irrigate some 266,000 acres. Nature imposed the severest

[1] In 1933–4 the South African Railways had a surplus of £1,813,506, in 1934–5 the surplus was £3,888,725, and in 1935–6 it was £5,623,158.

restrictions upon the development of irrigation. By the side
of the great marvels of the Bonneville and Boulder Dams in
the United States, South African irrigation schemes were
puny indeed. The poor rainfall and the unreliable flow of
the country's few rivers restricted the scope and success of
irrigation schemes which were undertaken, and made other
schemes economically impossible. The most optimistic estimates placed the irrigable area of the Union at less than
1 per cent. This was a severe limitation on both production
and more intensive settlement.

Since the Land Settlement Act of 1912 the list of further
Land Settlement Acts grew steadily. The Minister of Lands
was empowered to allot Crown lands, to purchase private
land for settlement, and to make loans for the purchase by
settlers of stock and equipment. But against the efforts of
the Minister of Lands was opposed the long history of land
settlement and the inertness of millions of acres which no
subsidy or science could rescue from sterility. During a
period of twenty-six years, following Union, the average
number of settlers placed upon the land each year was less
than 700. By the side of those that left the land each year
the number of settlers was pitifully small.

South Africa's first railways were not built for the farms.
They chose the shortest route between the commercial ports
of the coast and the diamond and gold-mining centres of the
interior. But gradually the railway map began to assume a
more normal appearance. Branch lines left the main trunk
lines to find their way into the veld. By 1937, with some
13,000 miles of railway, South Africa had more miles of
railway per 1,000 of European population than any other of
the dominions. Including the natives the figures dropped
from 6·80 to 1·52 per 1,000 of population. The assault of
the railways upon the ox-wagon and the mule team was
reinforced by an extensive network of road motor services
with a mileage in 1936 actually greater than that of the
railways. The rural motor-roads especially wrought a revolution. It was a revolution that could be measured in
millions of passengers or gallons of cream carried each year.
It could even more familiarly be measured by the letters and

newspapers that came more quickly, by the more vital contact of men with their neighbours, or by the goods and services which enriched the existence of lonely housewives.

As distances shrank and men rubbed shoulders more easily the ground was prepared for co-operation. The dispersed and individualistic nature of rural life had made co-operation difficult. In republican days men did gather together in common effort in times of crisis. But the capacity for co-operation was not sustained. It was at its best in the occasional military commandos. In economic affairs it hardly existed at all. Not even the common front against the natives or the British Government could produce a spontaneous development of co-operation in economic and social affairs. In Canada the Grange movement which began in 1872 educated the rural population in social and economic co-operation and prepared the way for the highly organized and systematic co-operative movement of the next generation. The economic history of New Zealand is in large measure the story of the benefits won by co-operation and combination. In the struggle against foreign competitors and against its geographic isolation New Zealand found that individual effort and courage were not enough. To gain a place in world economy New Zealand had not merely to breed better sheep and manufacture finer butter, but had also to create the loyalty, the spirit, and the habits of mind necessary to collective enterprise.

Agricultural co-operation was not introduced into South Africa until after the Boer War. In 1904 Natal passed the Agricultural Development Act which promised financial aid to co-operative organizations. Similar legislation in the Cape Colony and the Transvaal and the Orange Free State encouraged the movement. The sparse population, the expense of travelling long distances to a meeting, and the lack of a co-operative spirit amongst the farming population, permitted the movement to make only a hesitant and grudging advance. After the Great War the need was urgently felt for an increase in co-operation. The Co-operative Societies Act, passed by the Union Parliament in

1922, placed the influence of the Government more resolutely behind the co-operative movement. Co-operation in South Africa, it was clear, could not be spontaneous. To be brought effectively into being it had to be fostered and cherished by the Government. If the farmers were to sow better seed and breed better cattle, if their minds were to be more fully opened to new methods, and if their produce was to be successfully graded and profitably marketed, they must be made more clearly conscious of their common interests. The formlessness of rural life, it was contended, compelled an aggressive and expansive activity by Government in agricultural affairs. But once again it was learned how obdurate were the consequences of South African history. In 1934, thirty years after the beginning of the co-operative movement, a commission reported that agricultural cooperation had achieved only a limited success. In that year there were 388 registered co-operative societies and companies with a membership of 86,715.

After the formation of the Pact Government in 1924 agricultural policies were spurred on by an even keener feeling of urgency. The time to modernize farming was while the mines provided the means. The time for the transfusion of the new blood into farming was therefore short. A series of Acts struck even more vigorously at the shapelessness of agriculture. Because agriculture itself was laggard, government initiative became more peremptory. The Perishable Products Export Control Act of 1926, the Dairy Industry Control Act of 1930, the Flour and Meal Importation Restriction Act of 1931, the Mealie Control Act of 1931, the Meat Trade Control Act of 1932, the Tobacco Control Act of 1932, the Live Stock and Meat Industries Act of 1934, the Wheat Industry Control Act of 1935, and the important Marketing Act[1] of 1937, all reveal by their very titles the ambitious structure of government regulation which was imposed on agriculture. Through the establishment of a number of boards, such as the Dairy Industry Control Board, the Tobacco Industry Control Board, and the Perishable

---

[1] This ambitious Act established a National Marketing Council to advise the Minister on marketing schemes.

Products Export Control Board, and the National Marketing Council, agriculture was given the co-ordination which it had failed to achieve through its own spontaneous effort. The common purpose of the boards was to take steps for the better organization of each separate industry. The Wool Council was empowered in 1930 to levy a shilling on each bale of exported wool to assist in research work, in the organization of wool growers, and the improvement of the wool market at home and abroad. The Live Stock and Meat Industries Control Board was empowered to impose a levy on animals slaughtered at *abattoirs* for the purpose of encouraging meat export through the payment of bounties, to improve the quality of cattle, to build and supervise cold storages. The Dairy Industry Control Board in similar manner was empowered to impose a levy on butter and cheese manufactured in the Union, as well as on dairy products imported into the Union in order to pay a bounty on exports from the Union of butter and cheese. It was given the power to determine the amounts of butter and cheese to be exported by the dairy industry and to fix minimum prices to be paid by creameries or cheese factories for cream and milk. Thus a growing number of bureaucratic bodies were armed with the power to determine export quotas, to impose levies, and to fix prices in order to strengthen the position of South African agriculture.

After the Great War South Africa was still unable to satisfy her own wheat requirements. As a result of restrictions on wheat imports and the encouragement of domestic production the area sown to wheat increased greatly after 1930, and wheat imports practically ceased. In 1928–9 South Africa still had to import large quantities of butter. Six years later, in 1934–5, she exported nearly 9,000,000 pounds of butter. In 1910 the value of fresh fruit exported from the Union was £46,595. Twenty-seven years later, in 1937, the value of fresh fruit exports had risen to £3,321,251. Exports of wine increased twentyfold in the same period. Yet such figures were no indication of a great agricultural renaissance. Agricultural exports remained a small fraction of total exports. During the six years that the Export Subsidies Act of 1931 was in force a sum of nearly £11,000,000 was expended on export subsidies.[1]

Agriculture in South Africa is poor and precarious. Much of it is beyond the reach of modern science and technical progress. The expenditure and effort required to overcome many of its handicaps are too great to be profitable. Indeed, South Africa is not an agricultural country. It has no natural advantages which, by the help of science and organization, could win for its agricultural products a truly commanding position in the markets of the world. Of its pastoral products wool alone was able to compete successfully in the open market.[2] Without subsidy and under conditions of free competition much of the land could not be economically cultivated, and many of the agricultural and pastoral products could make no headway against the products of New Zealand, Canada, the Argentine, or the United States. During the very years that South Africa sought a wider place for her products the capacity of the world markets to absorb agricultural commodities began to shrink. It was an unpropitious age. Even American and Canadian farmers, who had bought efficient labour-saving machinery with their war-time profits, found their markets increasingly blocked by rising tariffs. In spite of an aggressive régime of bounties the average value of South African agricultural and pastoral exports between 1933 and 1937 was £20,000,000. Of the great depression which began in 1929 a disastrous conjuncture of increased production and decreased demand was a principal cause.

It was the complaint of economists that an aggressive policy of bounties and protection favoured an uneconomic agricultural industry too greatly. Too great a part of the revenue obtained from more efficient industries was transferred to rural industry. Resources invested in mining, for example, yielded a better profit than the same resources invested in agriculture. In 1937 the gold output of the mines was twice as great as in 1914. The taxation paid by the mines was twelve times as great. Each uneconomic benefit

[1] The payment of export subsidies was discontinued in 1937.
[2] Even wool received a subsidy of £5,345,934 between 1931 and 1937.

given to the farming community was a burden upon the rest of the country. High domestic prices for foodstuffs placed still more weight upon the straining shoulders of the mining industry. High prices for butter, sugar, and meal made the problems of poor whites and poor blacks still more intractable by decreasing the purchasing power of their scanty incomes. Capital and labour were diverted into less efficient and less remunerative fields. The increase in the protection given to sugar from £7 a ton in 1926 to £12. 10*s*. in 1930, and to £16 in 1932 did indeed cause an increase in the production of sugar. But the increase was won by bringing under cultivation marginal land. The profits of the sugar growers were illusory; they did not come from the land but from the pockets of domestic consumers who paid artificially high prices for sugar. One undesirable result of protection was, therefore, the subsidization of inefficiency, the inflation of land values, and the creation of vested mendicant interests which could not continue to exist without support. As early as 1908 the Transvaal Director of Agriculture declared that during the past twenty years more money had been spent per head of South Africa's farming population than in any other country of the world. Much of the resources which were transferred to rural industry was a waste of capital and not an investment for the future.[1] The State supplied the farmers with money with which they gambled against the hazards of the climate. By placing inefficient men upon inefficient land South Africa hindered the redistribution of population and the adjustment of industry and production on an economic basis in accordance with her real wealth, which was not agriculture.

In no dominion were the aims of protection purely economic. They were social and political as well. In South Africa one intention of tariffs and bounties was to give a greater prosperity to agriculture. But their intention was also to soften the rude shocks that were detaching the rural population from the land. Tariffs and bounties were akin to the employment of European labourers on the railways.

Between 1910 and 1936 the State spent £112,000,000 from revenue and loan funds for agriculture.

They were a means of strengthening the white farming population. The ideal result of such help would be the creation
of a more wealthy and firmly established rural population.
Yet much would be won by preventing the disintegration
of white rural society. The maintenance of as vigorous
a rural population as possible was a 'reason of State' that
could not be adequately measured by profit and loss. By the
side of its economic value should also be placed its social
value. The land was the home of the Boer, of his language,
and the source of his excellence. It was upon the land that
were bred the men who had made the Republics. It was
from the land that the towns must expect to recruit their
population. Farming was a way of life. The poverty of
nations was not always in money. There was also the poverty
of a wasting country-side. Economists frowned upon aids
and subsidies, upon the remission of debts and the heavy
expenditure on irrigation and branch railway lines. Were
there not social reasons, outweighing all others, for saving
a large community from the disintegrating effects of free
competition? Though tariffs and bounties might exact a
price in money, they gave a return which was greater than
material wealth.

Intimately connected with the effort of each dominion
towards the self-consciousness and self-assurance, which is
sometimes called Australian or South African or Canadian
nationalism, was the desire to achieve a fuller and more
complex social existence. Through a greater diversification
of their industries these parts of the Empire lost the purely
colonial status which they had when their economic life depended upon the export of a few primary products like wool
or furs or lumber or fish. The growth of industries, like the
development of their political institutions, was a sign of
greater maturity. Political self-direction carried with it the
plain obligation of greater economic self-sufficiency. Patriotism and self-government went farther than political life.
Economic independence made political independence more
real. Settlers became more than colonials working in field
and forest for a distant metropolis; they became citizens
of a modern State, marked by a diversity of economic

undertakings and a wide variety of opportunities for engineers, fitters, electricians, and pattern-makers as well as lumbermen, sheep-farmers, and trappers. The tariff as a whole, declared an Australian committee on the tariff in 1929, was 'a potent instrument in maintaining at a given standard of living a larger population than would have otherwise been obtained'.

Until 1925 South African tariffs were imposed mainly for purposes of revenue. Although there is, strictly speaking, no revenue tariff which is not at the same time a protective tariff, yet the principal goal of the tariffs of Cape Colony and Natal before they entered the Union was to obtain revenue from import dues. In young colonial communities such dues have always proved to be the easiest way of obtaining an income for the Government. One of the first laws to be passed by the Cape Parliament after the grant of representative institutions in 1854 was the Customs Tariff Act of 1855. Four years later the essentially similar and even more famous Cayley-Galt tariff was adopted in Canada. It is a commonplace that the movement of all colonial tariffs, once they have been adopted, is rarely downward. Whether they can be defined as revenue tariffs or protective tariffs they tend to take an ascending course. The Cape tariffs of 1864 and 1884 imposed increasingly higher duties. The tariff of 1889, introduced at the time of the customs union with the Orange Free State, was even assailed by some as a protective tariff. It is true that it made an important concession to local manufacturing interests by reducing the duties on imported raw materials like leather and timber. But it also reduced the duties on machinery and mining tools and was therefore not a genuine protective tariff. The economic life of the Cape Colony after 1870 was based on diamond mining and stock farming, which were not in need of protection. The customs barriers erected on the borders of the two Boer Republics in the nineties were in no sense protective. They were simply a natural attempt by two impecunious communities to increase their revenues. They were the direct outcome of the selfish refusal of the two British coastal colonies to share the duties collected at the ports with their landlocked neighbours. As the Transvaal's gold-mines attracted more men and goods to the Transvaal, the tariff also became a powerful political weapon against the pressure of British interests. This political and economic rivalry between the four communities prevented a truly protective tariff policy. As long as Natal, for example, fought with the Cape Colony for control of the interior trade by maintaining a low level of import dues, a true protective policy was not possible.

During the first fifteen years of its existence the Union depended on customs dues for a large part of its revenue. In the Customs Tariff Act of 1914 there was indeed a definite measure of protection, but protection was as much the indirect result as it was the deliberate purpose of the Act. In 1925 South Africa adopted a frankly protective tariff. It was a truly historic year, for it was in 1925 that Germany, too, adopted a vigorous protective tariff which, in its direct and indirect consequences, was of world-shaking importance. The Customs Tariff and Excise Duties Amendment Act of 1925 was an integral part of the entire complex of laws by means of which the Government endeavoured to regulate and promote the economic and social life of the Union. The Act, for example, did more than impose protective and dumping duties in order to protect local industries. It also became an instrument in favour of the civilized labour policy, for the Government was given discretionary power to apply a minimum instead of a maximum duty, and so reduce the protection afforded by the Act to any industry which maintained 'unsatisfactory labour relations'.

The original stimulus to manufacture in South Africa was not given by tariff protection. It was the discovery of diamonds and gold that first created markets in which local producers had a natural advantage. Yet diamonds and gold did much to restrict industrial development. They absorbed skilled and unskilled labour alike. They paid such high wages that other employers could hardly compete with them for the services of skilled labour. They brought such an increase in prosperity to the land that the protection of local industries did not become an imperative issue. It was the Great War which gave the greatest stimulus to manufacture.

264 *The Regulation of Industry*

Prices were high and cargo space was limited. High freight and insurance rates on imported goods had the practical effect of a protective tariff. Between 1911 and 1920–1 the value of factory production, calculated at 1910 prices, was trebled. Once the special conditions of the War had brought industries into existence they became vested interests, which demanded protection after the War. It was the familiar story of each dominion. The demands of the young industries fell upon willing ears. In all of the dominions there was a keen sense that the War had increased their stature and affirmed their self-reliance. In the development of the dominions political and economic nationalism were closely connected.

The arguments which were used to justify policies of protection are very familiar. Infant industries, it was claimed, needed a period of nurture and protection before they could meet the competition of old and established industries in other countries. To arguments such as these South Africa added another which was peculiarly her own. The diverse and skilled operations of manufacturing industries were exceptionally favourable to the employment of white labour. It was the great defect of the mines that they could not dispense with cheap native labour. In manufacture the ratio of white to black workers could be much higher. In 1916–17 the number of whites engaged in manufacturing production was 46,100 and the number of non-Europeans was 77,742, giving a ratio of 1 : 1·65. In 1934–5 the numbers were 115,971 white workers, who received 74 per cent. of the wages and salaries paid, and 149,877 non-Europeans, giving a ratio of 1 : 1·3. This should be compared with the ratio of approximately 1 : 9 in the mining industry. The protection of industry was, therefore, the protection of white leadership in the sub-continent.

'Protection in Australia', wrote a brilliant Australian historian,[1] 'has been more than a policy: it has been a faith and a dogma. In young democracies patriotism and sentiment are powerful allies of protectionism. The belief was easily held by uncritical electorates that there was something vicious and undermining about foreign imports, so that

[1] W. K. Hancock, *Australia*, p. 89.

tariffs were a proper and natural defence of domestic interests. The temptations of self-sufficiency were great and difficult to resist. The use of electricity or steam trains easily led to the temptation to manufacture electric equipment or railway materials instead of importing them. The export of raw materials appeared to be the undue concession of opportunities to foreign industries and workmen. The difference between the price of exported raw wool and the higher price of imported woollen cloth often seemed to the untrained voter as a subsidy to foreign producers. In all of the dominions sentimental and patriotic motives were an important part of the history of protection. Although industries have grown up to greatness behind tariff walls, the opportunities are not the same for all parts of the world. The colossal expansion of American industry was not caused by protection alone. Its great natural resources, the rapid growth of a numerous and resourceful population, the size and the purchasing power of the domestic market, the efficiency of industrial organization—these are important explanations of the growth of American industrialization. South Africa does not possess these advantages in any comparable degree. The poverty of agriculture is a restraint upon manufacture. The low standard of living of much of the white population, and the still lower standard of living of the entire native population, create a negligible domestic market. As a source of labour the population is expensive where it is efficient, and inefficient where it is inexpensive. Greater efficiency and cheapness in Europe, Asia, and America make it unlikely that South Africa can develop for some considerable time to come any manufacturing industries which can compete in the open world market. Practically all manufacturing industry, as well as most agricultural enterprise, is dependent on protected or sheltered markets. There is no want of certain raw materials. The iron ores and coal measures of the Transvaal are close to each other and repeat a condition which was very favourable to the English Industrial Revolution of the eighteenth century. The coal is plentiful and of good quality. The reserves of iron ore are vast enough to compare with those of the United States or France. Few other South African industries enjoy such natural advantages as the industry which was established in 1929 by the Iron and Steel Industry Act.

In countries with diversified resources and products the costs of protection are distributed. In countries with limited resources and with few staple products the costs of protection cannot be easily distributed. The position of the Union in the markets of the world is based upon three products, gold, diamonds, and wool. Since Union in 1910 these three products have consistently accounted for 80 per cent. or more of the total export trade. Upon the export of these products South African economic life depends in an unusual degree. With the possible exception of New Zealand there is no other dominion which is so dependent for its well-being upon its export trade. Gold, diamonds, and wool are primary products which cannot obtain any benefit from tariff protection. By raising the cost of materials and increasing the cost of living protection places added costs upon the primary export industries. The sponsorship of less economical industries weakens the position of industries which possess better natural advantages. In the steel industry there are many competitors; in gold production, from which came one-half to two-thirds of her exports, South Africa has few competitors. In an appendix to a famous Australian report of 1929 on tariff protection there appeared a statement which immediately attracted the attention of South African economists and historians.

'A country with very rich gold mines,' declared the Brigden Commonwealth Committee, 'which provided all the exports, and no lower grade ore, could gain a very considerable population by using the profits of the mines to subsidize manufacturing industry, unless its disadvantages in manufacturing were very exceptional. But if the country depended for its exports on low grade ore, mostly near the margin of production, no appreciable increase of population could be achieved by protection in any form.'

Even the argument that tariff protection would enlarge the scope of white employment is qualified by the truth that industries which need subsidy and support cannot increase the wealth of a country, and yet divert labour and capital from more self-reliant industries. By increasing the cost of living, tariffs actually lessen the ability of the whites to compete with native labour. Since a tariff also depresses the standard of living of the natives it lessens their value as consumers of domestic products, and makes their competition even more deadly.

Having called manufacturing industries into being, South Africa had to provide them with rules and regulations. It is within the British Empire that some of the most noteworthy experiments have been made to bring the problems of industry and labour within the orderly province of law. The Australian Commonwealth and States each developed, for example, legislation in order to minimize industrial disputes, to eliminate sweated labour, and reduce insecurity in industry. At the beginning of the century students of social and industrial reforms like André Siegfried paid no attention at all to South Africa. Until the decade after the Great War there was little to study. The focus of attention in the British Empire was upon New Zealand and Australia. In South Africa both industry and industrial legislation were a generation later. Even though diamonds and gold had caused two industrial centres to spring up in the middle of the veld, each bristling with the characteristic problems of labour, there were still other and more compelling problems that called for attention. Until the political relations of the Dutch Republics with the British Government and the British colonies in South Africa were settled, the regulation of industry was nothing more than a patchwork of temporary expedients. In the wayward and changeful atmosphere of the Witwatersrand before 1914 regulation of industry was difficult. Conditions of employment were unstable. Men moved readily from one mine to another, or came to snatch the high rates of pay for work under ground and depart again before the fell miners' disease had wrecked their bodies. At least one of the reasons why the rents of the houses in which they lived were so appallingly high was that they were unsatisfactory tenants, moving from house to house, even as they moved from job to job. The 'moonlight flit' was the despair of many Johannesburg landlords. Miners lived

obviously in an atmosphere of dust under ground and impermanence above the ground. *Esprit de corps* amongst the
working population was weak. The strikes of 1907, 1913,
and 1914 were evidence of the poor relations between workers
and the mine managements. During such strikes men spat
at the name of the Chamber of Mines, and spoke of its
building, the Corner House, as if it were a seat of the worst
capitalistic tyranny and financial greed. Schoolboys who
heard the language of their fathers learned to look up at its
unfashionable exterior as if it might be a South African
Kremlin or Bastille. True, the population of miners and
workers who depended on the mines did not have the feverish
qualities of the earlier diamond-digging days, when each man
felt that fortune depended upon the turn of a spade, and
when the reports and rumours of successful finds swayed the
mob like the wind swept the dust from the heaps of drying
blue ground. But there was upon the Witwatersrand very
largely the same crowd of metropolitan miners. 'Cousin
Jacks' from Cornwall, Hollanders, Germans, Americans, and
Australians sweated and blasted in the depths of the mines,
desperately and often fatally hurrying after the earnings
which they hoped would bring ease to themselves and their
wives and children over the sea. They were never a majority.
Their numbers decreased as their places were taken more
and more by the landless sons of 'backveld' farmers. But
they were a ferment of unrest. They disturbed labour conditions, for they were quick to resent restrictions imposed
in the interest of health, and to resist regulations aimed at
efficiency if the regulators impaired their earning power.
Because skilled labour was not yet plentiful it was too often
true that the mining companies had to employ poorly skilled
workers, or even men with no experience at all, who were
rushed through an imperfect period of training damaging to
health and efficiency. Small wonder that the calling of the
miner was not always attractive to conservative men who
resisted the attraction of high rates of pay, and shrank back
before the dangers and the turbulence of mining.

In 1880 there was not a trade union in the whole of South
Africa. In 1881 there was formed at Cape Town the first

South African branch of the Amalgamated Society of Carpenters and Joiners. Even at the end of the Boer War trade unionism was undeveloped and all but powerless. The strike upon the Witwatersrand in 1907 gave some strength to the trade-union movement. Yet the slow development of labour organization was indicated by the fact that it was not till 1911 in the Transvaal and 1913 in the Cape Colony that Federations of Trades were established, and even then their constituency by no means comprised the entire working population. The truth was, it has already been observed, that skilled labour in the large centres was in a privileged position, and did not feel itself compelled to seek protection and strength in compact organization. Organization was still further impeded by the absence of any uniform conditions of labour throughout the Union. Workmen in Cape Town had coloured helpers, in Durban they had Indian 'coolies', in Johannesburg they had Kafirs. Rates of pay in Johannesburg were higher than in Bloemfontein, and in Bloemfontein they were higher than in Cape Town. A worker in a small rural town, whatever his skill, could not expect the wages of a worker, for example, upon Johannesburg's fine new town hall. At the outbreak of the Great War, therefore, wages and conditions of labour were singularly lacking in uniformity and co-ordination. They were established irregularly, sometimes through the activity of trade unions, sometimes through the uncontrolled decisions of employers, often through the force of local tradition and custom. In certain occupations a disjointed series of parliamentary Acts and provincial laws laid down rules concerning health, hours of labour, and other conditions of work, such as the Transvaal Workmen's Compensation Act of 1907, the Transvaal Industrial Disputes Prevention Act of 1909, the Mines and Works Act of 1911, the Workmen's Wages Protection Act of 1914. But the strikes of 1913 and 1914 revealed the great diversity of practice amongst employers of labour even on the favoured Witwatersrand, and the sense of instability and insecurity about the future which pervaded the world of labour. There was a notable absence of the means of effective deliberation. There were too few institutions possessed of experienced men, competent to allay unrest or to steer grievances into channels of discussion. There was no effective government agency entrusted with the responsibility of surveying industrial problems in the interest of the community as a whole. Above all, there was no machinery of conciliation. At the back, therefore, of the labour disputes up to the year 1922 lie the imperfect unionization and the divided ranks of the workers, and the want of principles established by legislation for the regulation and settlement of industrial disputes.

The first serious attempt to bring South Africa abreast of other dominions in her industrial legislation was made in 1918. The Factories Act made provision for the registration of factories, and for their more effective supervision in the interest of the safety and welfare of their employees. Although the conditions of 1889 no longer prevailed, when employees of Johannesburg engineering shops went on strike against a fifty-four hour week, the limitations in the Factory Act on hours of work, and the provision for the payment of overtime, were important sections of the Act. The Regulation of Wages, Apprentices and Improvers Act of 1918 provided for the establishment of wage boards, the regulation of the wages of women and young persons and of the conditions of employment of apprentices and improvers in certain specified trades and occupations. That this Act achieved little success was hardly surprising. It stepped into that confused and controversial field that lay outside the boundaries of skilled labour. It was the field of unskilled and semi-skilled labour, the field in which Cape coloured folk, Natal Indians, Kafirs, white women and youths, and poor whites struggled for employment and preferment. The Act succeeded in focusing attention upon the great complexity of these problems; otherwise its history was a record of neglect, hostility, and indifference. The Juveniles Act of 1921 provided for the establishment of boards to deal with the employment, the training, and welfare of white juveniles. Once more this Act directed attention to the predicament of young boys who tried to find a place on the ladder of employment. For youths in other lands the road to skilled employment and the better positions lay through unskilled and semi-skilled work. Yet that road in South Africa was made narrow and exceedingly difficult by the habit of using native and coloured labour. A further Act, the Apprenticeship Act of 1922, came to the support of the Juveniles Act. Its clear purpose was to enlarge the place of white youths in skilled industry. Apprenticeship was considered a necessary form of education which the State was entitled to supervise and control. In a number of industries Apprenticeship Committees were established with power to recommend for the approval of the Minister conditions of apprenticeship, wages, and the number of apprentices in any designated trade.

After the great strike on the Witwatersrand in March 1922, the Mining Industry Board recommended the creation of permanent machinery of conciliation for the gold and coal-mines. In the Industrial Conciliation Act of 1924 the principle of conciliation was extended to all industrial undertakings with the exception of farming and government employment. The purpose of the Act and of later amending Acts[1] was to facilitate the settlement of disputes by voluntary discussion and conciliation within each industry. The Act encouraged the creation of both employers' organizations and trade unions and required their official registration. Under the Act the associations of employers and the trade unions in each industry were permitted to set up industrial councils to maintain the best possible understanding between both sides. If for reasons peculiar to any industry it was impossible to establish industrial councils, conciliation boards might be established. In accordance with the principle of the greatest possible measure of self-government in each industry, a majority of the representatives of the employers and a majority of the representatives of the employees on an industrial council could agree to accept the result of arbitration; or if the arbitrators themselves were unable to agree, to accept the award of an umpire.

Acts of Parliament, however useful, rarely work miracles. Even the Industrial Conciliation Acts made slow headway

[1] Act No. 24 of 1930, Act No. 7 of 1933, and Act No. 36 of 1937, which repealed former Acts.

against the shapeless and disjointed character of much South African industry. Implicit in the Acts was the desire that, wherever possible, industries should be organized on a national rather than a local basis. Yet after the system had been in operation for twelve years only three industrial councils had been set up on a national basis. On the other hand, strikes grew less frequent and less costly after 1925. Between 1916 and 1925 there were some 214 strikes, involving a loss of over 2,890,000 working days and an estimated loss in wages of £2,383,456. Between 1925 and 1936 there were some 137 strikes, involving a loss of only 196,000 working days and an estimated loss in wages of £98,000. The comparative freedom from expensive industrial disturbances co-operated with protection to encourage the development of industries. Considering the economic importance and the inflammable properties of the mining industry, it was of the greatest significance that after ten years of industrial conciliation twenty-eight out of eighty-nine conciliation boards had sat upon disputes in the mining industry.

The Industrial Conciliation Act devoted its attention principally to the province of skilled labour. A partner Act, the Wage Act of 1925,[1] undertook to regulate the field of unskilled and poorly organized labour. The Act established a wage board for the Union. The board, which could be set in motion either by the Minister or by a request from an employers' organization or trade union, was given the power of investigating wage and labour conditions. Together the two Acts made possible the regulation of the entire wage system of the Union. The power given by the two Acts to the Minister of Labour to give the force of law to recommendations of the Wage Board and to agreements of industrial councils provided the opportunity for harmonizing and integrating wage rates throughout the country. Against industrial legislation was, however, ranged all the complexity of the country's social order, and all the inertia of its poverty. Industrial legislation could not proceed on the assumption, which was possible in New Zealand or even in Australia, that

[1] Amended by Acts No. 23 of 1930, No. 16 of 1935, and repealed by Act No. 44 of 1937.

its province was industrially and socially homogeneous. Because the Industrial Conciliation Act tended to enhance the solidarity and to confirm the high wages of skilled labour, it became much more difficult for awards to be made increasing the wages of unskilled labour. South Africa remained, after all, a land of low general productivity. The high level of wages for one group in industry led necessarily to a low level of wages outside that group. Some of the problems which confronted the Wage Act seemed to be as intractable as the infertility of the Kalahari Desert, for wealth cannot be called into being by laws alone. Although the Wage Board was instrumental in maintaining the standard of living of many industrial employees, and of raising the standard of living of others, it was nevertheless possible for an Industrial Legislation Commission which sat in 1935 to complain of the 'failure to make reasonable provision for semi-skilled labour'.

The preceding pages have widely traversed South Africa's historical and economic landscape. Yet wherever the observer may stand, wherever he may direct his gaze, one phenomenon is never absent from his attention. It is the native population, compelling to the view like a great mountain set in a plain, ever present and inescapable. All the other problems with which industrial laws must contend—the evasions, technical objections, and the delays of men and courts—are as nothing by the side of the fact that the great bulk of workers in industry are not white men but natives. The Industrial Conciliation Acts and Wage Acts worked in the shadow of the Union's Colour Bar and its white labour policy. Was the Union's industrial legislation devised for all workers, or did it accept the distinction between civilized and uncivilized labour? Neither Australian nor New Zealand industrial legislation made or accepted any such distinction. The basic wage, the living wage, or the 'fair and reasonable' wage of Australian courts have been consistently determined by 'the normal needs of an average employé regarded as a human being in a civilised country'. In practice the margin between the wages of unskilled and skilled workers remained narrow, and gross inequalities between different groups of workers were removed. In the Industrial Conciliation Act the word 'employee' was defined so as to exclude all natives who were required by law to carry passes. The Act was therefore not applicable to the great mass of native labour. All native areas were excluded from the operation of any agreement or award. When it was found that certain employers began to replace white workers by natives in order to escape regulations, the Act was amended in 1930. Henceforth agreements by industrial councils could be made applicable to native employees as well. Though theoretically it was made possible for natives to benefit from the same rates of pay and hours of work as white workers, the clear intention of the amendment was to prevent the substitution of natives at low wages for more highly paid white workers. Because the Act applied to workers organized in registered trade unions, its facilities were made still more inaccessible to the natives. Native labour was notoriously disorganized, and the greatest obstacles stood between them and effective organization. Acts such as the Native Labour Regulation Act of 1911 made it a criminal offence for a native employee to break his contract of service. To strike became accordingly a breach of the peace to be opposed by the power of the police and punished by imprisonment. The history of native labour organization was mainly a sorry record of impermanence, internal weakness, and external hostility. Although the entry of natives into a number of white trade unions was theoretically possible, the organized trade-union movement was predominantly white.

In the Wage Act no distinction was drawn between native and white workers. The Wage Board, in other words, had no power to fix wages according to race or colour. In the first decision which it was called upon to make, the Wage Board decided that it could no more single out native or white workers for special attention than it could single out 'red-haired or blue-eyed employees'. Yet the differences between rural and town workers, between skilled and unskilled Europeans, between Asiatics, coloured folk, and natives, confronted the Wage Board with problems of the greatest complexity. It had of necessity to steer a cautious and experimental course between the opposite extremes of fixing a high minimum wage or a low minimum wage. A high wage for all workers would have the double effect of excluding most natives from industry and of greatly increasing the costs of industrial production. A low wage would sharply lessen the demand for European workers. In consequence the pattern of wage decisions was empirical and irregular. A natural 'basic' wage or a 'fair and reasonable' wage for all workers in industry could not be imposed. Both economic realities and social and racial aspirations exerted their differing influences on the levels and arrangements of wages. That the more profitable economic activities had been set aside for Europeans by tradition and legislation gave to industrial and wage regulation a narrow and less flexible field in which to work. There were in consequence decisions beyond their power, arrangements which they could not alter, and areas into which they were forbidden to trespass. Conscious of the wide disparity in the earnings of skilled and unskilled workers, it was the effort of the Wage Board to establish intermediate levels of wages, so that South African industry, too, might have the healthier and more gradual transition of wage levels and spheres of opportunity between the top and bottom rungs of industry. But it was beyond the power of the Board to recommend wage scales upon which men could not maintain themselves 'in accordance with civilized habits of life'. Since a very high proportion of unskilled labour was performed by natives who were not possessed of civilised habits of life, the Board was compelled in all industries in which its reference applied to native workers to inform the Minister that it could not recommend a civilized wage. This distinction, which very greatly influenced the problem of wage regulation, was officially given in Circular 5, 31 October 1924. Civilized labour was defined as

'the labour rendered by persons whose standard of living conforms to the standard of living generally recognised as tolerable from the usual European viewpoint. Uncivilised labour is to be regarded as the labour rendered by persons whose aim is restricted to the bare requirements of the necessities of life as understood amongst barbarous and undeveloped peoples.'

This meant in effect that wage regulation could not be entire or uniform. It cannot be gainsaid that the effect of the total body of industrial legislation was to increase white solidarity, enhance its bargaining power, and consider the range of its opportunities, without granting the native workers the same protection against the vagaries and inequalities of the economic system of which they were an intimate part. Taken as a whole, industrial legislation was a protective barrier against the competition of men in a lower social and economic position, and against their encroachment upon spheres of employment and standards of living dedicated to white labour. The native paid at the rate of a pound a week and the skilled European paid at the rate of a pound a day were inexorable realities of industrial life. They were the complex effects of climate and soil, of history and race. They were the living evidence that the language of the other dominions cannot altogether be applied to South Africa, and similarities between them are matched by the widest differences.

APPENDIX OF PRINCIPAL OFFICIALS

British Commanders:

Admiral Sir G. K. Elphinstone, Majors-General A. Clarke and J. H. Craig, Sept. 16–Nov. 15, 1795.

British Commandant:

Major-General J. H. Craig, Nov. 1795–May 5, 1797.

British Governors (first British occupation):

Earl Macartney, May 5, 1797–Nov. 20, 1798.
Major-General Francis Dundas, acting Nov. 1798–Dec. 9, 1799.
Sir George Yonge, Dec. 1799–Apr. 20, 1801.
Major-General Francis Dundas, acting Apr. 1801–Feb. 20, 1803.

Commissioner-General (under Batavian Republic):

J. H. de Mist, Feb. 21, 1803–Sept. 25, 1804.

Governor (under Batavian Republic):

Lieut.-General J. W. Janssens, Mar. 1, 1803–Jan. 18, 1806.

British Governors (second British occupation):

Major-General David Baird, acting Jan. 10, 1806–Jan. 17, 1807.
Lieut.-General H. G. Grey, acting Jan.–May 1807.
Earl of Caledon, May 22, 1807–July 4, 1811.
Lieut.-General H. G. Grey, acting July–Sept. 1811.
Lieut.-General Sir John Francis Cradock, Sept. 6, 1811–Apr. 6, 1814.
Lieut.-General Lord Charles Somerset, Apr. 6, 1814–Mar. 5, 1826.
(Major-General Sir Rufane Shaw Donkin, acting Jan. 1820–Dec. 1, 1821.
Lord Charles Somerset left on leave Mar. 5, 1826, and resigned April, 1827.)
Major-General Richard Bourke, acting Mar. 1826–Sept. 9, 1828.
Lieut.-General Sir Galbraith Lowry Cole, 1828–Aug. 10, 1833.
Lieut.-Colonel Thomas Wade, acting 1833–Jan. 16, 1834.
Major-General Sir Benjamin D'Urban, 1834–Jan. 20, 1838.

Major-General Sir George Thomas Napier, Jan. 22, 1838–Mar. 18, 1844.

Lieut.-General Sir Peregrine Maitland, Mar. 18, 1844–Jan. 27, 1847.

High Commissioners and Governors of Cape Colony:

Sir Henry Eldred Pottinger, Jan. 27–Dec. 1, 1847.

Major-General Sir Harry George Wakelyn Smith, Dec. 1, 1847–Mar. 31, 1852.

Lieut.-General Sir George Cathcart, Mar. 31, 1852–May 26, 1854.

Charles Henry Darling, acting May–Dec. 1854.

Sir George Grey, Dec. 5, 1854–Aug. 15, 1861.

Lieut.-General Robert Henry Wynyard, acting Aug. 20, 1859–July 4, 1860; acting Aug. 15, 1861–Jan. 15, 1862.

Sir Philip E. Wodehouse, Jan. 15, 1862–May 20, 1870.

Lieut.-General C. C. Hay, acting May 20–Dec. 31, 1870.

Sir Henry Barkly, Dec. 31, 1870–March 31, 1877.

Sir Bartle Frere, Mar. 31, 1877–Sept. 15, 1880.

Major-General Henry Hugh Clifford, acting Sept. 15–Sept. 27, 1880.

Sir G. C. Strahan, acting Sept. 27, 1880–Jan. 22, 1881.

Sir Hercules Robinson, Jan. 22, 1881–May 1, 1889.

> (Lieut.-General Sir Leicester Smyth, acting 1883.
> Lieut.-General H. D. Torrens, acting 1886.
> Lieut.-General H. A. Smyth, acting May 1–Dec. 1889.)

Sir Henry B. Loch, Dec. 1889–Mar. 1895.

> (Lieut.-General W. G. Cameron, acting 1891–2 and 1894.)

Sir Hercules Robinson (Lord Rosmead, 1896), May 30, 1895–Apr. 1897.

Sir Alfred Milner, May 5, 1897–Mar. 6, 1901.

> (Sir William Butler, acting Nov. 1898–Feb. 1899.)

Sir Walter Hely-Hutchinson, Mar. 6, 1901–May 1910.

ADMINISTRATIVE OFFICERS FOR NATAL:

Commandants-General:

Andries Willem Jacobus Pretorius, Nov. 1838–July 1842.

G. Rudolph, 1842–3.

Special Commissioner:

Henry Cloete, May 10, 1843–May 1844.

Lieutenant-Governors:

M. West, Dec. 4, 1845–Aug. 1, 1849.
Benjamin Chilley Pine, Apr. 19, 1850–Mar. 3, 1855.
John Scott, Nov. 1856–Dec. 31, 1864.
Lieut.-Colonel John Maclean, Dec. 1864–July 26, 1865.
Robert William Keate, May 1867–July 19, 1872.
Anthony Musgrave, July 1872–Apr. 30, 1873.
Sir Benjamin Chilley Pine, July 1873–Apr. 1, 1875.

Administrator:

Sir Garnet Wolseley, Apr.–Sept. 3, 1875.

Lieut.-Governors:

Sir Henry E. Bulwer, Sept. 1875–Apr. 20, 1880.
Sir George Pomeroy Colley, July 1880–Feb. 27, 1881.

Governors of Natal:

Sir Henry Bulwer, Mar. 6, 1882–Oct. 23, 1885.
Sir A. E. Havelock, Feb. 1886–June 5, 1889.
Sir C. B. H. Mitchell, Oct. 1889–Aug. 1893.
Sir Matthew Nathan, Sept. 2, 1907–Dec. 23, 1909.
Lord Methuen, Jan. 17–May 1910.

PREMIERS OF THE UNION OF SOUTH AFRICA:

General Louis Botha, May 31, 1910–Aug. 28, 1919.
General J. C. Smuts, Sept. 3, 1919–June 1924.
General J. B. M. Hertzog, June 20, 1924–Sept. 5, 1939.
General J. C. Smuts, Sept 5, 1939– .

HIGH COMMISSIONERS AND GOVERNORS-GENERAL OF THE UNION OF
SOUTH AFRICA:

Viscount Gladstone, May 31, 1910–July 1914.
Baron de Villiers, (acting) July–Nov. 1912 and July–Sept. 1914.
Viscount Buxton, Sept. 8, 1914–June 1920.
Prince Arthur of Connaught, Nov. 20, 1920–Nov. 1923.
Earl of Athlone, Jan. 21, 1924–Nov. 21, 1930.

GOVERNORS-GENERAL OF THE UNION OF SOUTH AFRICA:

Earl of Clarendon, Jan. 26, 1931–Mar. 1937.
Sir Patrick Duncan, Apr. 5, 1937– .

SECRETARIES OF STATE FOR WAR AND COLONIES:

Henry Dundas, July 1794–Mar. 1801.
Lord Hobart, 1801–May, 1804.
(Batavian Council for the Asiatic Possessions, Feb. 1803–Jan. 1806.)
Viscount Castlereagh, July 1805–Feb. 1806.
William Windham, 1806–Mar. 1807.
Viscount Castlereagh, 1807–Oct. 1809.
Earl of Liverpool, 1809–June 1812.
Earl Bathurst, 1812–Apr. 1827.
Viscount Goderich, Apr.–Sept. 1827.
William Huskisson, 1827–May 1828.
Sir George Murray, 1828–Nov. 1830.
Viscount Goderich, 1830–Mar. 1833.
Edward George Stanley, 1833–June 1834.
Thomas Spring-Rice, June–Nov. 1834.
Duke of Wellington, Nov. 1834.
Earl of Aberdeen, Dec. 1834–Apr. 1835.
Charles Grant (Lord Glenelg, May 1835), 1835–Feb. 1839.
Marquis of Normanby, Feb.–Sept. 1839.
Lord John Russell, 1839–Sept. 1841.
Lord Stanley (Earl of Derby), 1841–Dec. 1845.
William Ewart Gladstone, 1845–July 1846.
Earl Grey, 1846–Feb. 1852.
Sir John Pakington, Feb.–Dec. 1852.
Duke of Newcastle, 1852–June 1854.

SECRETARIES OF STATE FOR THE COLONIES:

Sir George Grey, 1854–Jan. 1855.
Sidney Herbert, Feb. 1855.
Lord John Russell, Feb.–July 1855.
Sir William Molesworth, July–Oct. 1855.
Henry Labouchere, 1855–Feb. 1858.
Lord Stanley, Feb.–June 1858.
Sir Edward Bulwer-Lytton, June 1858–June 1859.
Duke of Newcastle, June 1859–Apr. 1861.
Edward Cardwell, Apr. 1861–June 1866.
Earl of Carnarvon, June 1866–Mar. 1867.
Duke of Buckingham, Mar. 1867–Dec. 1868.
Earl Granville, Dec. 1868–July 1870.
Earl of Kimberley, July 1870–Feb. 1874.
Earl of Carnarvon, Feb. 1874–Jan. 1878.

Sir Michael Hicks Beach, Jan. 1878–Apr. 1880.
Earl of Kimberley, Apr. 1880–Dec. 1882.
Earl of Derby, Dec. 1882–June 1885.
F. A. Stanley, June 1885–Feb. 1886.
Earl Granville, Feb.–Aug. 1886.
Earl Stanhope, Aug. 1886–Jan. 1887.
Sir Henry Holland (Lord Knutsford, 1888), Jan. 1887–Aug.
  1892.
Marquis of Ripon, Aug. 1892–June 1895.
Joseph Chamberlain, June 1895–Oct. 1903.
Alfred Lyttelton, Oct. 1903–Dec. 1905.
Earl of Elgin, Dec. 1905–Apr. 1908.
Earl (Marquis) of Crewe, Apr. 1908–Nov. 1910.
Lewis Harcourt, Nov. 1910–May 1915.
Arthur Bonar Law, May 1915–Dec. 1916.
W. H. Long, Dec. 1916–Jan. 1919.
Viscount Milner, Jan. 1919–Feb. 1921.
Winston S. Churchill, Feb. 1921–Oct. 1922.
Duke of Devonshire, Oct. 1922–Jan. 1924.
J. H. Thomas, Jan.–Nov. 1924.
L. C. M. S. Amery, Nov. 1924–June 1929.
Lord Passfield, June 1929–Aug. 1931.
J. H. Thomas, Aug.–Nov. 1931.
Sir Philip Cunliffe-Lister, Nov. 1931–June 1935.
Malcolm MacDonald, June–Nov. 1935.
J. H. Thomas, Nov. 1935–May 1936.
W. G. A. Ormsby-Gore, May 1936–May 1938.
Malcolm MacDonald, May 1938–May 1940.
Lord Lloyd of Dolobran, May 1940–Feb. 1941.
Lord Moyne, Feb. 1941–

SECRETARIES OF STATE FOR DOMINION AFFAIRS:

L. C. M. S. Amery, 1925–9.
Lord Passfield, 1929–30.
J. H. Thomas, 1930–5.
Malcolm MacDonald, 1935–8 (May).
Lord Stanley, May–Nov. 1938.
Malcolm MacDonald, Nov. 1938–Feb. 1939.
Sir Thomas Inskip (Visc. Caldecote), Feb. 1939–

SOME NOTABLE EVENTS IN SOUTH AFRICAN HISTORY

1652 First settlement under van Riebeeck.
1657 First free Burghers.
1658 First introduction of West African slaves.
1688 Landing of French Huguenot settlers.
1706 Agitation of colonists against the governor.
1760 First crossing of the Orange River by white hunters.
1779 First Kaffir War.
1789 Second Kaffir War.
1795 First British occupation.
1799 Third Kaffir War, and rebellion on eastern frontier.
1800 First printing press at Capetown.
1803 Cape handed over to the Batavian Republic.
1806 Second British occupation.
1811 First circuit court established.
1812 Fourth Kaffir War.
1814 Great Britain acquires sovereignty over the Cape.
1818 Fifth Kaffir War.
1820 Arrival of five thousand British immigrants at Port Elizabeth.
1824 Publication of first regular newspaper, the *Commercial Advertiser.*
1825 Conversion of depreciated rixdollars into British currency.
1828 Passage of Ordinance No. 50. Recognition of the freedom of the Press.
1834 Establishment of Executive and Legislative Councils. Sixth Kaffir War.
1836 Great Boer Trek from the Cape Colony.
1838 Republic of Natal founded by emigrant Boers.
1843 Natal annexed by British Government.
1846 Seventh Kaffir War.
1848 British sovereignty proclaimed between the Orange and Vaal Rivers.
1850 Rebellion and war on the eastern frontier.
1852 Beginning of copper mining. Sand River Convention, which recognizes independence of the Transvaal.
1854 Bloemfontein Convention which recognizes independence of Orange Free State. First Cape Parliament (representative government).

1859 First railway in South Africa begun in Cape Colony. Failure of Sir George Grey's proposals for South African confederation.

1860 Introduction of Indian labourers into Natal.

1865 War between Orange Free State and Basuto.

1867 Discovery of diamonds.

1868 British annex Basutoland.

1871 British annexation of diamond fields.

1872 Grant of responsible government to the Cape Colony.

1875 Proposal by Lord Carnarvon of a scheme of South African confederation.

1877 British annexation of the Transvaal. Ninth Kaffir War.

1879 Zulu rebellion.

1880 Basuto War. Formation of Afrikaner Bond. Outbreak of the first Anglo-Boer War.

1881 Independence of Transvaal recognized by convention of Pretoria.

1884 First important goldfield at Barberton.

1885 Railway communication opened between Capetown and Kimberley. Creation of British Bechuanaland.

1886 Witwatersrand goldfields opened. Foundation of Johnnesburg.

1888 Foundation of British South Africa Company.

1889 Customs union between Cape Colony and Orange Free State

1890 Railway communication between Capetown and Bloemfontein. British troops occupy Mashonaland.

1892 Johannesburg connected with Cape railway system.

1893 Grant of responsible government to Natal.

1894 Johannesburg connected with Delagoa Bay by rail.

1895 Johannesburg connected with Durban by rail. Jameson raid.

1897 Railway opened from Capetown to Bulawayo. Natal joins customs union. Establishment of South African Postal Union.

1898 Kruger elected President of South African Republic for fourth time.

1899 Beginning of Boer War.

1900 British occupation of Bloemfontein, Johannesburg, and Pretoria.

1902 Peace of Vereeniging.

1904 Chinese labour introduced on the gold-mines.

1906 Responsible government granted to Transvaal and Orange Free State.

1908 National convention to consider South African Union.

1910 Constitution of the Union of South Africa.

1912 Establishment of Union Land and Agricultural Bank.

1913 Labour unrest on the Witwatersrand.

1914 Serious industrial disturbances on the Witwatersrand. Outbreak of European War.

1915 Capture of German South-West Africa.

1919 Union mandate over South-West Africa Protectorate.

1921 Amalgamation of South African Unionist Political Parties. South African Reserve Bank. Serious post-war depression.

1922 Bloody strikes and revolutionary movement in South African industry, especially on Witwatersrand. Rhodesia refuses to enter Union.

1923 Grant of responsible government to Southern Rhodesia.

1924 Formation of ministry by General the Hon J. B. M. Hertzog.

1925 Union reverts to gold standard. Afrikaans declared an official language.

1926 Colour Bar Bill passed.

1930 Enfranchisement of European women.

1931 Statute of Westminster passed by Imperial Parliament.

1932 Abandonment by Union government of gold standard.

1933 Political coalition of South African and Nationalist Parties. Beginning of South African iron and steel industry at Pretoria.

1935 Pan-African Postal Conference held at Pretoria.

1936 Passage of *Representation of Natives Act*.

1939 War with Germany.

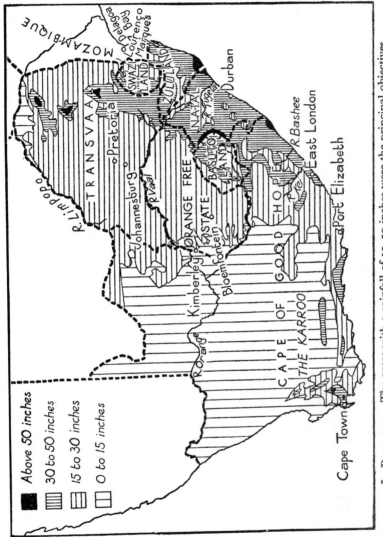

I. RAINFALL. The areas with a rainfall of 15–50 inches were the principal objectives of white and black colonizing movements.

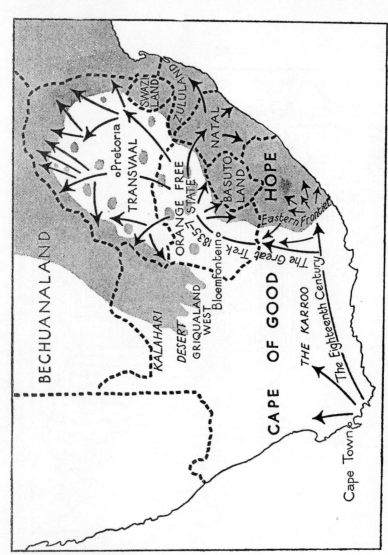

The shaded area represents the general distribution of the main bodies of Bantu population between approximately 1835 and 1850. The smaller patches represent scattered settlement. The arrows indicate the dynamics of the trek movement and the relationship between the forces of white and black settlement. The boundaries are modern.

II. WHITE AND BLACK SETTLEMENT IN THE EIGHTEENTH CENTURY

INDEX